Life history and the Irish migrant
experience in post-war England

Copyright © Barry Hazley 2020

The right of Barry Hazley to be identified as the author of this work has been asserted by him in accordance with the Copyright, Designs and Patents Act 1988.

Published by Manchester University Press
Oxford Road, Manchester M13 9PL
www.manchesteruniversitypress.co.uk

British Library Cataloguing-in-Publication Data
A catalogue record for this book is available from the British Library

ISBN 978 1 5261 2800 3 hardback
ISBN 978 1 5261 6375 2 paperback

First published 2020
Paperback published 2022

The publisher has no responsibility for the persistence or accuracy of URLs for any external or third-party internet websites referred to in this book, and does not guarantee that any content on such websites is, or will remain, accurate or appropriate.

Typeset by Newgen Publishing UK

Life history and the Irish migrant experience in post-war England

Myth, memory and emotional adaption

Barry Hazley

Manchester University Press

This book is dedicated to the memory of Tom Jordan, David and Rachel Hazley, and Sarah Ford

Contents

List of figures	page ix
Preface	x
Acknowledgements	xiii
List of abbreviations	xvi
Introduction: Myth, memory and emotional adaption: the Irish in post-war England and the 'composure' of migrant subjectivities	1
1 Narratives of exit: the public meanings of emigration and the shaping of emigrant selves in post-war Ireland, 1945–1969	35
2 In-between places: liminality and the dis/composure of migrant femininities in the post-war English city	76
3 Lives in re/construction: myth, memory and masculinity in Irish men's narratives of work in the British construction industry	105
4 Falling away from the Church? Negotiating religious selfhoods in post-1945 England	149
5 Nothing but the same old story? Otherness, belonging and the processes of migrant memory	188
Conclusion: Myth, memory and minority history	220

Appendix: Interviews 226
Select bibliography 230
Index 245

Figures

1. Till, 'Wisha, Michilin Pat, you're not the same at all since you emigrated to London', *Dublin Opinion*, December 1954 (Dublin City Archives). © Business and Finance. Image courtesy of Dublin City Library & Archive — page 51
2. Joseph Lee, 'Sure an' it's himself miscalling the dacent Oirish-American President o' the U.S.A. an American-Oirishman that'll be starting the throubles all over again ... lemme admonish him!', *Evening News*, 26 June 1963, BCA/03673. © Solo Syndication — 115
3. Michael Cummings, 'Begorrah – can't have you fearful English living with us ... and mind you do nothing to prevent us from living with you fearful English', *Sunday Express*, 16 November 1961, BCA/MC1019. © Express Syndication — 191
4. Les Gibbard, 'When Irish eyes are smiling', *Guardian*, 9 March 1973, BCA/03673. © Estate of Les Gibbard — 194

Preface

> Founded on the rupture between a past that is its object, and a present that is the place of its practice, history endlessly finds the present in its object and the past in its practice.[1]

In Northern Ireland, the 1980s and 1990s were years in which discussion about questions of identity, religion and political allegiance was intense. As well as some of the worst atrocities of the Troubles, these years saw the emergence of all-party peace talks, leading eventually to the signing of the Good Friday Agreement in 1998. Growing up in a small town in Tyrone during this period, as I reached adolescence I remember becoming increasingly aware of this political saturation, both at home and in school, and of course within the wider media. I also remember, however, coming to view this saturation in terms of limitation and constraint. This, I think, had something to do with where I lived and the religious composition of the peer group I became part of around the age of 13. The largely Protestant housing estate that I lived on backed on to and adjoined another, largely Catholic, housing estate. Up until around the time I went to secondary school this spatial arrangement tended to foster a social segregation in playtime: we played football on our streets, and the Catholic boys did likewise on theirs, and there was little or no interaction between the two groups. This changed as a result of shared adolescent experiments with cigarettes and alcohol, and later, recreational drugs and music-making.

Around about the same time members of both groups discovered that the cut-through path linking the two estates, known to us as 'dump hill', was a strategically good place to smoke and drink because the bend in the path meant that parents and neighbours could not observe what was going on, yet we could see investigators approach from both ends of the path well in advance of them reaching us. During the summer holidays the hill became a shared rendezvous point, and by the beginning of term the two groups had effectively merged. Over the next five years the group came to take priority over school friends as a focus of socialising, and what had initially been an unspoken agreement not to talk about religion and politics eventually gave way to a more rebellious attitude of denigration towards political leaders on both sides of the political divide, men who became for some of us objects of ridicule and satire. Although shaped by the wider sectarian culture in which it was embedded, the group constituted an in-between space in which we could contest some of its most divisive effects, while fashioning ourselves through shared adolescent practices whose structuring ideals and logics had little, or seemed to have little, to do with being Irish or British.

Looking back at this period, it occurs to me that the construction of this space, at least from my standpoint, may have involved a process of splitting whereby confusing and difficult questions about identity, nationality and politics were denigrated and devalued, while other aspects of the self untainted by association with these themes were idealised. My choices of London or Glasgow, rather than Belfast or Coleraine, as prospective university cities when filling out my UCAS forms may also have been conditioned by this, in that, at an unconscious level, I understood my migration out of Northern Ireland as a further moving away from those divisive questions about identity and towards some kind of urban cosmopolitanism where such things were not relevant.

If this was the plan, it didn't work out too well. Going to the University of Glasgow in 2002 certainly supplied access to new social worlds, but it involved too the new phenomenon of being constantly identified as 'Irish' by others who did not themselves identify as 'Irish'. This was unsettling, not only because my Protestant background had furnished me with few ideas about just what kind of 'Irish' I might be, but because my experiences growing up in Cookstown contradicted and conflicted with the sharp, politicised divisions brought into play by such designations, so that terms like Irish/British, unionist/nationalist or Catholic/Protestant could be experienced as an external imposition and a simplification. When taxi drivers, frequently the boldest of specialists on Anglo-Irish relations, would ask whether I was a Catholic or a Protestant, it was difficult to satisfy the expectations implicit in the question without a loss of authenticity.

The effect of such questions was not so much to bring me to a realisation about my 'true' identity, as to alert me to the fact that migration to Britain involved one, or me at any rate, in complex negotiations with issues of meaning and identity, negotiations which I had given little thought to when choosing where to go to university. As well as becoming conscious of unresolved aspects to my own identity, and perhaps because of this, I became increasingly aware of the fact that complex sets of meanings attached to the term 'Irish' in Britain, meanings that could condition how I was interpreted when I spoke and that could create walk-on roles within particular situations and conversations. Sometimes, these meanings related to the legacies of the Troubles in Britain, which in Glasgow, a city with its own sectarian tensions, meant something quite specific. As I would gradually learn, however, such meanings were difficult to disentangle from a much longer history of Irish migration to Britain, a history that, despite having studied Irish history at A-level, I knew little about.

If I had stayed in Ireland and gone to university there when I was eighteen, would I have embarked on doctoral research into the experiences of the Irish in Britain five years later? Almost certainly the answer to this question is no. This book grew out of the points of cultural contact established when I arrived in Glasgow from Cookstown to take up a place at university in 2002. More precisely, it grew out of feelings of unsettlement connected with issues of cultural positioning and belonging, and so can be seen as part of a broader quest to make sense of myself within a new environment where ways of framing 'Irishness' preceded me. Back in 2002 this quest would lead me in a variety of directions, into a range of conversations with differently situated others. This book continues this ongoing process, in dialogue this time with the otherness of the past.

Note

1 M. Certeau, *The Writing of History* (New York, 1988), 36–37.

of her important archival work on the county associations in London. For similar reasons I owe thanks to the staff at Liverpool University Library, who spent the best part of three days patiently photocopying articles from *The Bell*, and to Niall Carson for directing me towards this source material in the first place. Fr David Lannon helped me make sense of the holdings at Salford Diocese Archives on more than one occasion, and Elsbeth Millar, archivist at the British Cartoon Archive, helped me track down elusive copyright holders.

Many people have helped me develop the ideas on which this book is based. My deepest debt of gratitude is to Charlotte Wildman, Till Geiger and Penny Summerfield. Over the course of the project they were patient, supportive and wise, encouraging me to explore, yet reining me in when I strayed beyond the bounds. Their sharp, incisive comments have contributed to the shaping of this book in innumerable ways, and for the time, effort and imagination they have invested I am eternally grateful.

Thanks are due to Maria Luddy, who provided useful comments on the manuscript, and to Liam Harte and Lynn Abrams, both of whom encouraged the development of the project, reading chapters and offering excellent advice. Similarly, I am grateful to the book's three reviewers and Tom Dark at Manchester University Press, all of whom contributed insightful recommendations, the implementation of which has undoubtedly strengthened the final text. Of course, responsibility for the finished product is solely my own.

The Institute of Irish Studies offered the ideal environment in which to complete the research for the book between 2017 and 2018. As well as the excellent resources available in the Mac Lua Archive, Pete Shirlow, Diane Urquhart, Frank Shovlin, Sean Bean, Ailbhe McDaid, Dorothy Lynch, Viola Segeroth and the wider research community within the Institute all contributed in different ways to creating a stimulating atmosphere in which to think through the core ideas of the book.

Bernard Canavan granted me permission to use his exceptional artwork on the cover, but he also spoke to me about his own experiences of moving to England and the deeper emotional questions English urban life raised for many post-war settlers. I am grateful for his generosity, and I only hope the book gets at even a small portion of the emotional complexity he captures so evocatively in his paintings.

At Manchester, lively, lubricated conversations with Jim Greenhalgh, Paddy Doyle, Kat Fennelly, David Woodbridge, Mark Crosher and James Hopkins were consistently enlightening and entertaining. Likewise, during my postdoctoral stint in Glasgow wide-ranging after-hours debates with DJ kept me awake at night, pushing me to the edge of sanity, but stimulating rich journeys of reflexivity in the process.

Catherine's family, my family over here, have been generous, encouraging and kind, consistently offering support and succour. A special

Acknowledgements

The research for this book would not have been possible without the financial support of the Economic and Social Research Council, which funded the doctoral project via a 1+3 award between 2008 and 2012. Nor would it have been completed without the extraordinary generosity of Mervyn and Helen Busteed, who financed a postdoctoral research fellowship at the Institute of Irish Studies, University of Liverpool, allowing me the necessary time to redraft and extend the final manuscript.

The book would not exist without the participation of the interviewees who agreed to tell me about their lives as migrants in England. To these people, who took time out of their lives to answer my questions, and who provided me with source material of incomparable richness, I offer my deepest thanks.

Parts of the book have previously been published elsewhere as journal articles. Chapter 2 draws on 'Ambivalent Horizons: Competing Narratives of Self in Irish Women's Memories of Pre-Marriage Years in the Post-War English City', *Twentieth Century British History* 25:2 (2014), 276–304; and Chapter 5 is based on 'Re/Negotiating "Suspicion": Exploring the Construction of Self in Irish Migrants' Memories of the 1996 Manchester Bomb', *Irish Studies Review* 21:3 (2013), 326–341.

In helping me locate respondents, I owe a debt of thanks to Carmel at Manchester Community Care, and to Patrick Doyle, friend and fellow historian. In helping me with archival sources, I owe thanks to the staff at London Metropolitan University, who allowed me to rummage freely through the materials housed in the Archive of the Irish in Britain, and who graciously accepted my constant stream of requests for photocopies. A special thanks to Dr Nicole McLennan, who not only helped me track down sources on the Catholic Church, but supplied me with a transcript thanks to Sarah, who, at the same time as being a wife, mother and attending to her own job, found time to read and check parts of the original thesis. I wish I could manage time as efficiently.

While further away geographically, my own family, Mummy, Daddy, Granny and Denise, have supplied unstinting emotional, and frequently financial, support over the years. Academia is a precarious, frustrating and often demoralising profession in which to pursue some form of career, and I doubt I would have survived this long without the confidence they have shown in me.

Above all, Catherine has watched the evolution of this project at close quarters over many years, and knows more than anyone what it has cost and what its completion means. No one means more.

Abbreviations

AIB	Archive of the Irish in Britain
BAA	Birmingham Archdiocesan Archives
BCA	British Cartoon Archive
BCC	Birmingham City Council
CTS	Catholic Truth Society
DCA	Dublin City Archives
GMCRO	Greater Manchester County Record Office
HHC	Hull History Centre
IBRG	Irish in Britain Representation Group
NAI	National Archives of Ireland
PIRA	Provisional Irish Republican Army
PTA	Prevention of Terrorism Act

Introduction: Myth, memory and emotional adaption: the Irish in post-war England and the 'composure' of migrant subjectivities

Centring the migrant experience

The history of British–Irish relations is often told through the prism of political events. When such an approach is adopted, the plot is woven around moments of high political drama and the legacies of episodic conflict. Yet this relationship, so important in the development of both countries, has always had a less conspicuous human dimension: the traffic of ordinary people who cross the Irish Sea to fashion new lives amidst unfamiliar settings. These journeys are more than a lens through which to read the hidden societal effects and experiential realities of a fraught political relationship; migration between the two islands is a vector through which the British–Irish connection is lived and defined. Migrants are participants in, as well as artefacts of, an evolving dialogue, and their life histories enact, as well as register, its diverse reciprocities, unresolved contradictions and unconsidered possibilities.

This chapter outlines one approach to analysing such life histories and the light they shed on the Irish migrant experience in England. Two critical arguments are developed, namely that existing approaches to migrant 'identity' within the historiography of the Irish in Britain have underplayed the complexity of Irish subjectivities in England; and that, where it has been employed as a 'record' of migrant experience, oral historical research has been complicit in this, due largely to the 'recovery' approach which scholars have employed to reconstruct the Irish migrant experience in the twentieth century. To address these concerns, this Introduction outlines an alternative, dialogic approach to the migrant experience based on Popular Memory Theory, the central framework employed in this book.

2   Life history and the Irish migrant experience

From 'segregation' to 'assimilation'

In the first chapter of his celebrated account of working-class life in Edwardian Salford, *The Classic Slum*, the teacher and writer Robert Roberts described the strict social hierarchies governing everyday life in the neighbourhood he knew as a boy. As Roberts recalled, forming 'the base of the social pyramid' were 'bookies' runners, idlers, part-time beggars and petty thieves, together with those known to have been in prison'. Below even that, however, were Irish Catholic immigrants, who, until the arrival of newcomers after 1945, inhabited a milieu all of their own:

> Still another family would be scorned loudly in a drunken tiff for marrying off its daughter to some 'low Mick from the Bog'. With us, of course, as with many cities in the North, until the coming of the coloured people Irish Roman Catholic immigrants, mostly illiterate, formed the lowest socio-economic stratum. A slum Protestant marrying into the milieu suffered a severe loss of face. Such unions seldom occurred.[1]

Roberts's depiction of the lowly status of the Irish, published in 1971, portrays one of the most pervasive stories of Irish settlement circulating within post-war English culture. According to this view, while the Irish formed an 'outcast' population within Victorian society, when Irish migration to Britain peaked, the 'coming of the coloured people' after 1945 effected a major transition in their position, marking their integration into English working-class life.[2] As a more recent tradition of representation contends, however, the sharpness of this arc of transformation is open to serious question. While prominent Victorian reformers certainly mobilised the Irish as a scapegoat for contemporary urban problems, the imagery of otherness they bequeathed to popular memory exaggerated the extent of Irish communal segregation.[3] As a revisionist counter-historiography here suggests, Irish settlement experiences in nineteenth-century Britain were characterised by variation and change over time: although the Irish often inhabited the worst sections of the labour and housing markets, and were subject to overlapping forms of racial, religious and class-based hostility, rarely did they form a cohesive community impermeably divided from local populations; indeed, having occupied a 'curious middle place' for most of the century, by 1914 'successive generations' appeared to have 'merged into the anonymous background of English and Scottish urban life'.[4] Declining numbers, the arrival of migrants from Eastern Europe, increased upward mobility and the growing incorporation of the Irish into the patterns of mainstream politics all played a part in facilitating the long-run integration of the Irish, well before the seminal transformations of the post-war decades.[5]

As such, according to this revisionist perspective, the 'arrival of the coloured people' after 1945 confirmed, rather than initiated, a transformation in the position of the Irish within British society. If the Irish continued to come to Britain in large numbers in the twentieth century, the historiography of their experiences peters out at the end of the nineteenth, a fact explained by some historians in terms of the increasing ease with which the Irish have been able to melt into British society. In the decades after 1945 in particular, when the numbers of Irish migrants to Britain rose to levels comparable with the mid-nineteenth century, few, it seemed, would encounter the sorts of problems experienced by settlers in that earlier period. Where the 'arrival of the coloured people' generated serious social and political tensions in post-war society, contemporary policy makers and social experts appeared to regard the Irish as members of the same racially homogenous British 'family': despite Eire's withdrawal from the Commonwealth in 1949, Irish migrants retained dual citizenship rights in Britain at a time when other, less numerous migrants were made subject to new immigration controls.[6] When these benign official responses are added to Irish migrants' relatively high rates of occupational and social mobility, relatively high rates of intermarriage and exogamy and relatively low rates of reported discrimination, 'Irish assimilation into British society' appears 'among the fastest that occurs among immigrant groups anywhere in the world':

> Assimilation is practically complete in a single generation. The children of Irish immigrants, sometimes to the distress of their parents, grow up seeing themselves as English or Scots; they may acknowledge their Irish ancestry and exhibit a few inherited traits, but for all practical purposes they are indistinguishable from their British peers whether in respect of dress or in social, cultural or religious behaviour.[7]

If the experiences of Irish migrants, presented as a set of discrete statistical averages, are set in comparison with those of migrants from beyond the 'British Isles', and if they are measured over the long term, this assimilation perspective appears plausible from a *relative* standpoint. A major problem for such an approach, however, concerns just what can be inferred about the *meaning* of migrant experience from the calculation of group averages. It is not just that the aggregation of data at group level tends to obscure important variations at the level of the family or individual, or that assimilationists underplay the significance of important continuities in the experiences of Irish migrants in the twentieth century, but that criteria such as intermarriage, occupation and mobility are automatically assumed to provide objective evidence of *identification*, the dual possibilities for which have already been set by the native/immigrant opposition underlying the framework.

A given migrant may attain levels of occupational and social mobility similar to that of the 'average' English person, but it does not follow that this migrant *experiences* mobility in the same way. The migrant's experience, rather, is mediated by a range of factors, from the nature of their pre-departure socialisation to the persistence of anti-Irish stereotypes, all of which differentiate how mobility is interpreted and a sense of settled selfhood established. Assimilation and ethnic belonging are not mutually exclusive processes; *integration* may encompass both, engendering adaptions and continuities simultaneously, yielding plural and mutative attachments.

Green, white and invisible: Irish identity and the 'ethnic turn'

In light of its various problems, and in keeping with wider intellectual trends in the 1990s, the assimilation paradigm has come under heavy attack, most powerfully in the work of Mary J. Hickman. According to Hickman, whose formulations have had a major influence on recent academic production within the historiography, the Irish in Britain have not 'assimilated' per se; rather, their experiences have been rendered 'invisible' due to the masking effects of a state-sponsored 'myth of white homogeneity that implicitly includes a myth of assimilation'.[8] This thesis rests on a number of premises. In opposition to revisionist accounts of the 'outcast' status of the Irish in modern British history, Hickman stresses the role of the Irish Catholic as a constitutive other in the formation of a coherent British national identity. The Irish Catholic was not only a colonial and religious other in Victorian society, but embodied a serious political threat to national elites: 'a particular fear was that political unity might be forged between the Irish peasantry and the English working-class'.[9] In response, the British state sought to 'incorporate' the Irish as part of its project of producing British national identity. At the conceptual level, this involved constructing the different peoples of the 'British Isles' as 'one race'. At the institutional level, 'state-assisted Catholic elementary schools came to be viewed as the principal long-term means of resolving the "problem" posed by the Irish Catholic working-class'. At the state's behest, the Catholic Church would thus secure the 'incorporation' of the Irish through an education-based programme of 'denationalisation', 'strengthening their Catholic identity at the expense of weakening their national identity'.[10]

Post-war discourses on race and immigration reinforced the masking effects of these strategies. In this period, in the context of debates concerning who legitimately belonged to the nation, social scientists and the state cooperated in the construction of a 'race relations industry'. Underpinned by the assumption that contemporary problems of 'immigration' and racism were of recent origin, 'race relations' institutionalised skin colour as the key criterion in relation to which questions of belonging and discrimination were analysed. In so doing, the paradigm reinforced the idea that British culture had been 'racially' homogenous prior to post-war immigration from the New Commonwealth and Pakistan. Consequently, the position of the Irish as an internal other of British national culture in both the nineteenth and twentieth centuries was rendered 'invisible' in contemporary discussions of discrimination and minority status.[11] In a context where a steady flow of mobile Irish labour was indispensable for British economic reconstruction, this omission enabled politicians to publicly justify Irish migrants' exclusion from immigration controls in terms of a shared 'British' racial heritage that distinguished them from 'coloured' migrants.[12]

For Hickman, two important implications follow from these points. Insofar as we can talk about Irish 'assimilation' in Britain, this should not be seen as a voluntary or unmediated process, but as the effect of state-led projects of 'incorporation' and 'denationalisation'.[13] Secondly, while the state's project of producing the peoples of the 'British Isles' as 'one race' may have rendered the distinctiveness of Irish experiences 'invisible', it does not automatically follow that the Irish 'assimilate' in the way described by scholars such as Akenson or Hornsby-Smith. The state's attempts to neutralise the threat posed by 'the Irish' did not, according to Hickman, necessarily lead to a 'loss' of identity. Religiously segregated education, the principal means by which denationalisation was to be achieved, reinforced the segregation of the Catholic Irish within the British working class, such that 'the assiduous training of the young in the primacy of Catholic identity ensured that ... the differentiation of Irish Catholics and their descendants, from their neighbours and often from their workmates, was regenerated across many decades'.[14] On the other hand, many Irish Catholics would also maintain 'spheres which were protected from the interference of the Church ... in which a variety of forms of belonging were possible'.[15] Thus, 'the quiescence of Irish Catholics lay in the acceptance of a public mask of Catholicism as its communal identity',[16] a fact which does not disturb 'the twentieth-century legacy' of a coherent Irish 'community' existing beneath the veneer of 'invisibility':

> The Irish had formed a community. One which is characterised by heterogeneity; its differentiation from the indigenous working class: having been historically segregated in its own social space; and by an ethnicity formed by the articulation of religion, class and national identity in a context of anti-Irish and anti-Catholic discourses and practices.[17]

Having redefined 'assimilation' as 'invisibility', the intellectual goal thus becomes 'visibility'. Working off the assumption that 'the Irish' constitute a hidden 'ethnic minority' in Britain, from the 1990s scholars across a range of disciplines have undertaken investigations into the experiences of Irish migrants that implicitly or explicitly sought to 'make visible' the object of their analysis. As well as demonstrating the continued salience of Irish ethnic identifications in twentieth-century Britain, such as in the work of Sharon Lambert, Louise Ryan and Sean Sorohan,[18] this has involved uncovering experiences of marginalisation and discrimination.[19] At the heart of the 'invisibility' paradigm, and stemming from the idea that 'invisibility' is an effect of the British state's efforts to manage the social and political threat Irish people are perceived to pose in Britain, is the claim that the Irish, like immigrant groups from Africa, the Caribbean and Asia, suffer forms of exclusion and racial oppression in Britain. More than any others, such themes have informed academic production in the last three decades, prompting and taking centre stage in enquiries into Irish experiences in relation to work, physical and mental health and the effects of the Troubles in Britain.

Deconstructing the optical metaphor: the politics and paradoxes of 'invisibility'

In the 1990s, such studies helped reopen debate on questions of Irish identity in Britain, stimulating much-needed discussion on the experiences of the Irish in the twentieth century. In the pivotal work of Mary Hickman, this was achieved through unmasking the unexamined but inherently political assumptions underlying monoculturalist claims about the inevitability of 'assimilation', and through reintroducing the fraught history of British–Irish political relations and British colonialism in Ireland as structuring variables of the experiences of Irish migrants in Britain. In this respect, the 'invisibility' paradigm poses a critical challenge to the cultural and historiographical forgetting of a much longer pre-Windrush history of 'multicultural racism' in Britain,[20] and in the process makes an important contribution to the emerging literature on 'whiteness' in the British context.[21]

More critically, however, a number of problems attach to various emphases central to the 'invisibility' framework, not least of which concerns the way British–Irish relations, defined in terms of conflict and opposition, have been mobilised as a principle of continuity in the determination of Irish identities. So although it is the incorporating impulses of the British state and 'British national identity' more generally which are held responsible for Irish 'invisibility', it is only through narrating the story of the Irish in Britain as a struggle for identity, in which 'the Irish' and

'British' are figured as protagonist/antagonist, that opposing Irish/British collectivities are established. Through treating British–Irish relations as a constant principle of binary division, in other words, overlapping oppositions between Irish/British, Catholic/Protestant and immigrant/native labour may be mapped onto the ethnic minority/majority opposition in order to secure the boundaries and internal coherence of an Irish ethnic identity at the level of theoretical discussion.

One obvious concern with such a framing is the lack of room it leaves for difference *within* the Irish migrant experience in modern Britain: not all Irish migrants were Catholic; nor were they all working class. More fundamentally, however, the binary structure of this formulation unduly limits the possibilities of identity formation: relations between Britain and Ireland, and the forms of ascription Irish migrants have been subject to in Britain, have been marked as much by change, ambivalence and plurality as they have by continuity. British culture registers a powerful tendency to forget Britain's problematic historical involvement in Ireland, and this has important implications, not only for the representation of the Irish within British memory, but for the counter-formation of Irish communal mythology. It does not follow from this, however, that the relationship between Britishness and Irishness is intrinsically antagonistic: 'the dichotomy of self and other' does not adequately capture the ways in which British–Irish conflict and the constant presence of the Irish were negotiated within modern English society. As Steven Fielding has argued, if interwar English culture continued to display an ingrained 'cultural bias', migrants neither assimilated under duress nor lived lives apart from their English neighbours, isolated by 'impermeable boundaries'. Settlement, rather, involved 'adaption of both immigrant and indigenous peoples': 'the experience of Irish Catholics was partly structured by the culture in which they found a place and that culture was, in turn, transformed by their presence'.[22]

As Mo Moulton has convincingly argued, this exchange was powerfully impacted by the domestic cultural legacies of the Anglo-Irish war, shaping how Irishness could be imagined in interwar England and the 'middle place' Irish migrants could inhabit. While the Anglo-Irish Treaty achieved a political settlement of the Irish Question, the creation of a parliament in Dublin left unaddressed the fact that Irish people and cultures would remain an integral part of British society. To navigate this contradiction, Irishness was rendered simultaneously foreign and familiar; the production of domestic British stability after 1922 was here partially predicated on a form of disavowal which enabled the accommodation of Irish identities within the British state while containing their subversive implications.

On the one hand, the political connotations of Irishness continued to pose a symbolic threat in the aftermath of war and had to be rendered 'foreign' to secure the boundaries of Englishness – an institutionalised ethnic politics could not be accommodated within the English party system, and the arrival of large numbers of Irish labour migrants in the 1930s 'sparked a set of anxieties about immigration and racial purity that foreshadowed the discourses around post-colonial immigrants after 1945'.[23] On the other hand, however, 'Irishness remained embedded in the very fabric of English life' in ways that reflected the influence of wider modernising trends within English popular culture. While the English population continued to engage with Irishness enthusiastically, through literature, travel and public spectacle, the Irish in England adopted a 'strategy of partial assimilation, in which leisure, nostalgic commemoration, and religious community mostly displaced the active political mobilisation of 1919–21'. In this way, Irishness was 'removed from the volatile realm of politics and reassigned to the rich interwar landscape of domestic and associational life' where it became an integral but distinctive identity within English culture:[24]

> Its salience varied widely and its meanings were often deeply personal and idiosyncratic, but it remained, after 1921, a bright green thread woven into the lives of people of many backgrounds and perspectives. Its presence was not merely decorative but indicative of important mechanisms of social accommodation in the face of ethnic diversity at the beginning of decolonisation.[25]

The arrival of black and Asian migrants in the decades after 1945 both extended and reconditioned this process of accommodation. From one perspective, since the domestication of Irishness was necessarily unstable, so the foregrounding of colour as a key criterion of cultural difference could mask how the reverberating effects of Anglo-Irish conflict continued to articulate in the period after 1945. In turn, the 'whitewashing' of Britishness can be seen as implicated in the production of the Irish as an 'invisible ethnic minority', first in the sense that the assumption of white homogeneity masks variation and hierarchy within experiences of whiteness, but also, paradoxically, in the sense that designation as an 'ethnic minority' itself depends upon the formulation of a racialised ontology of a multicultural society. Recognition as an 'ethnic minority' was not possible during the Victorian or interwar periods, but it became an option once an official 'race relations' paradigm was constructed and elaborated from the 1960s.

At the same time, however, the 'whitewashing' of Britishness after 1945 might also be seen to have reinforced the production of Irishness as a domesticated form of ethnic identity, identified, by community leaders as well as external observers, with conservative Catholic values, the performance and consumption of Irish cultural traditions and a limited social welfare function. This held true, for example, for many of the Irish clubs, centres and associations established in the larger post-war settlement destinations, a process initiated in the 1950s, and powerfully influenced and financially aided by the Church.[26] Thus, while the disorderly behaviour of young male and female migrants did attract attention from contemporary observers in this period, particularly from within the networks of Catholic welfare in England, institutions such as the county associations conceived themselves as non-political social bodies, their itineraries and records reflecting a combined interest in respectable sociability and social networking, socio-economic advancement and the celebration of national origins.[27] According to the journal of the largest such body, the London Irish Counties Association:

> Being a member of a County Association has its advantages in so far as one meets many old friends of former years, and makes new friends and one need never feel lonely in this great City when, for the asking, one can enjoy a pleasant conversation, a dance, a quiet drink, or a social evening amongst your own people and see them at their best. One becomes conversant with all aspects of Irish life in London, which opens up a new vista in the social sphere. Ladies are not alone welcome, but indeed encouraged to join their Association and to play their part as members of various committees. It has been said that the County Associations are one of the greatest organised bodies of Irish people in London and, being non-sectarian and non-political, we enforce no code in politics and no creed in religion, but we expect all our members to be national in outlook, promoting at all times the image of Ireland and things Irish so that our Homeland may benefit from our connection.[28]

Similarly, while popular stereotypes of the Irish continued to betray latent anxieties around the unresolved political relationship between Britain and Ireland, in general Irish migrants were not publicly defined 'in terms of an incapacity for domestic and familial life'[29] in the manner which positioned other migrants beyond the boundaries of white Englishness. The relationship between internal and external designations was thus complex in the Irish case: if the academic discourse on 'invisibility' has sought to define the boundaries of Irish ethnicity in terms of a series of vertically aligned oppositions (Irish/British, Catholic/Protestant, invisible/visible), in practice Irish migrants were confronted with a shifting and contradictory scheme of external designations (immigrant/white/ethnic) by which to locate themselves.

This flattening of the history of categorical designations is in turn symptomatic of a more general problem in approaches stressing 'invisibility', namely the way the rhetorical nature of the concept habitually retreats to transparency in discussions of Irish identity, disguising how the context of its production conditioned its formulation and deployment. For 'invisibility' never merely described an objective historical reality, but was fashioned through a politically active form of ethnic mobilisation in the 1980s. Initiated during a period in which the political representation of post-war immigrant groups emerged as a major theme of public debate in Britain, this process embodied a coordinated attempt by a network of Irish activist groups, academics and social welfare organisations to campaign for the inclusion of Irish migrants within the framework of multicultural politics in Britain, and as such marked an important shift in how bodies identified with 'the Irish in Britain' addressed themselves to governmental institutions and the public sphere.[30] Focused initially on securing access to local policy networks, from the mid-1980s activists turned increasingly to building a case for ethnic recognition at the national level, combining demands for identity recognition and socio-economic redistribution, and coming to centre on the inclusion of an 'Irish' ethnic category on British census forms. At the heart of the discourse generated around ethnic mobilisation thus lay a dynamic of application and refusal whereby activist-researchers attempted, unsuccessfully until 1997, to persuade the Commission for Racial Equality of 'the need to make Irish issues more visible so that their existence and legitimacy is acknowledged'.[31]

Ethnic mobilisation thus stimulated a proliferation of discursive practices on Irish experience that, drawing heavily on the language of contemporary anti-racism movements, sought to make 'visible' a history of anti-Irish racism. As well as the surveys and reports of local welfare organisations, these dynamics informed practices of letter-writing to influential figures in the media and government, the literature of newly formed activist groups such as the Irish in Britain Representation Group and the London Irish Women's Centre and even the journalism of the *Irish Post*, whose founder Brendan Mac Lau frequently used his editorial to popularise the notion of an 'Irish ethnic community' among the paper's readership. So long as recognition was refused at an official level, however, a story of 'invisibility' was also necessary in order to explain why the evidence for anti-Irish discrimination seemed so elusive and, implicitly, to explain why no post-war history of Irish mobilisation was apparent, when Irish migration was at its peak.[32] The notion of Irish 'invisibility' was thus not only produced in relation to that of 'assimilation', but drew its meaning from the construct of the 'ethnic minority', specifically black ethnic minorities. 'The Irish' were thus not 'invisible' per se, but *relative* to black and Asian minorities, and activists and researchers sought to convince sceptical authorities that black and Irish migrants shared common histories and experiences. In November 1992 Angie Birtill, a housing and welfare rights officer at London Irish Women's Centre, wrote to Jim Smellie, senior manager of Homeless in London, to complain about the organisation's failure to distinguish the Irish as a separate group in a recent report on homelessness in the City. Birtill felt that:

> The fact that the 'Health and Homeless in Hackney' report fails to acknowledge the ethnic minority status of the Irish is deeply insulting. Your omission not only ignores the scale of disadvantage and discrimination facing Irish people in this country. It also represents a very narrow application of the race relations legislation to the concerns of the Irish community. The disadvantage and discrimination facing Irish people is rooted in the historical and continuing colonial relationship between Britain and Ireland in a way that effectively mirrors the colonial relationship between Britain and non-white communities ... We do not accept your justification for putting all the European 'white' groups together.[33]

As Birtill's reference to the 'continuing colonial relationship between Britain and Ireland' here indicates, portraying the Northern Ireland Troubles as a 'colonial war' offered one means by which activists attempted to elide differences between the Irish and other non-white minorities. As Paul Gilroy has noted, the intensification of political mobilisation among black activists in the 1980s took place amidst vocal public debates about the national belonging of the British-born offspring of post-war immigrants then 'coming of age' within Thatcherite Britain.[34] Irish ethnic mobilisation too may be read as a response to these developments: collective biography of the actors involved suggests that participants were not by and large migrants of the post-war decades, but drawn from a more self-consciously political second generation, many of whom were beneficiaries of expanding opportunities in British higher education in the post-war period. But in the Irish case mobilisation was also triggered and shaped by the effects of the Troubles in Britain, which, particularly in the wake of Provisional Irish Republican Army (PIRA) attacks in England, incited a resurgence of popular anti-Irish racism. According to *Discrimination and the Irish Community in Britain*, 'attitudes which had been expressed openly in the 1950s and 1960s in the advertisements in newsagents windows as "No Blacks, No Irish" and "No Irish need apply"' were now 'raised to a new level of intensity', while there was 'very little attempt to understand the political situation out of which the bombings came'. In turn, 'Irish responses to this hostility invariability took the form of avoidance of contact with British people and attempts to remain invisible by staying silent.'[35] Yet, for many second-generation activists the Troubles formed the context in which they became politically conscious of their Irishness. At a time when 'relations between the neighbouring islands are at the most serious for perhaps sixty years', observed Ivan Gibbons in 1981, 'more and more Irish people in this country are becoming aware of what is loosely called their "heritage" and "culture".[36] Angie Birtill herself, whose mother had migrated to England from Meath in the post-war years, recalled that:

> The civil rights movement and Bloody Sunday focused my Irishness and I think it did for a lot of other people as well. Suddenly there were images being flashed up on the television of Irish Catholics like ourselves being batoned by the RUC and B-Specials and later being shot by British paratroopers. I remember big arguments breaking out in my classroom at school amongst daughters of service people who attempted to justify what the troops had done and those of us who were absolutely mad about it. I remember falling out with some of my friends over Bloody Sunday and being aware of other girls who were second-generation Irish, suddenly forming a connection with them, and not realising or ever having been conscious that they had been Irish until that point and suddenly I saw their anger that I felt too. For a lot of second-generation Irish people, not just from Liverpool but throughout this country, Bloody Sunday forced those who had not been conscious of their identity or who had brushed it to one side to take stock of who they were.[37]

A similar motif of ethnic awakening, centring on the effects of the Troubles, was also hinted at in the recollections of Mary Hickman, whose parents migrated to England before the Second World War:

> Now my Irishness is to the forefront as director of an Irish Studies centre. I'd say my sense of Irishness went through a process of dormancy in my late teens when I was at university, but, inevitably, like a lot of people, Northern Ireland made one have to think about it.[38]

Representing the Troubles as a 'colonial war' was part and parcel of the discourse around ethnic mobilisation because it helped erode the categorical distinction between black and Irish experience through projecting a shared history of British colonisation. But the Troubles was also a trigger for mobilisation because the discriminatory practices it generated in England could be read as an effect of conflict in the 'homeland', a conflict through which the difference between 'British' and 'Irish' could be clarified. The Troubles thus provided the stimulus for a diasporic politics through which some members of the second generation, their sense of difference hitherto hidden or 'dormant', could secure recognition for a felt sense of difference outwardly 'invisible' within British culture.

Crucially, however, this diasporic politics could only function as a means of becoming 'visible' to the extent that it sharpened the distinction between 'Irish' and 'British', that is, to the extent the conflict in

Northern Ireland could be seen as a 'war' between the British state and 'Irish Catholics like ourselves' in which second-generation activists could recognise their own struggles. As well as predisposing activist groups involved in ethnic mobilisation towards an anti-colonial Republican interpretation of Irish history, this kind of investment motivated the discovery of analogies between the situation in Northern Ireland and the experiences of the Irish in Britain. Where the community bodies established by post-war settlers viewed the Troubles apprehensively, as endangering the myth of Irish respectability they worked hard to promote, second-generation activists recast the history of the Irish in Britain within the context of a nationalist mythology of dispossession and struggle between 'these islands'.

Perhaps most significant in this respect were the 1981 Republican hunger strikes in the Maze Prison, the emotive outcome of which stimulated the replenishment of a powerful myth of Irish suffering at British hands within the columns and letters pages of the *Irish Post*. Where the founders of the paper had singularly failed to mobilise the 'Irish community' as cohesive voting bloc since its establishment in 1971, from 1981 onwards the publication became a focus for the organisation of new activist groups who, critical of what they perceived as the docility of the pre-existing Federation of Irish Societies, advanced a militant perspective on the Troubles' implications for the Irish in Britain.[39] According to the newly established Irish in Britain Representation Group (IBRG), the discriminatory operation of the 1974 Prevention of Terrorism Act, as well as the wider hostility displayed towards Irish people, merely reflected a longer history of British oppression, rooted ultimately in colonial domination.[40] According to a 1986 policy statement:

> [T]he lives of Irish people living in Britain are underscored and structured by Britain's relationship to Ireland and … this relationship has historically been one of intervention on the part of Britain. It is this intervention which has resulted in the situation in Ireland and the disadvantaged position of the Irish community in Britain. The IBRG recognises that the statelet of 'Northern Ireland' was deliberately created by the 1920 Government of Ireland Act and maintained against the wishes of the majority of Irish people. The IBRG also recognises that the war in 'Northern Ireland' is a direct result of British colonial policy and we therefore maintain that any just and lasting solution must include a recognition of the island of Ireland as a single, independent, sovereign political unit. The IBRG recognises that this continuing war has led to attacks on the civil liberties and political rights of Irish people living in Britain.[41]

The discourse on Irish experience generated around ethnic mobilisation in the 1980s thus syncretised the schemas of British multiculturalism and a nationalist mythology with much deeper roots in British–Irish history. Multiculturalism supplied the concept of an 'ethnic minority' entitled to recognition on the grounds of cultural difference and discrimination, and Irish nationalism supplied an adversarial interpretation of Anglo-Irish history that helped legitimate the insertion of Irish migrants within that framework, that could naturalise the basis of difference and discrimination and that could even explain its 'invisibility' in terms of the incorporating strategies of the coloniser.

The importance of these observations is not that the history of ethnic mobilisation invalidates the use of 'invisibility' as an analytic category, but that any attempt to understand the production of Irish identities in England needs to think reflexively about how the discursive practices and circuits of knowledge transmission engendered through this process have played into the shaping of Irish subjectivities after 1945. The point is not that the findings of activist-researchers associated with mobilisation struggle to meet standards of evidential reliability, but that ethnic mobilisation subjected Irish experiences in Britain to a state-sponsored 'multicultural gaze', rendering them 'visible' in ways consonant with the criteria for ethnic recognition. In so doing, ethnic mobilisation constructed, generalised and disseminated a powerful version of Irish experience, incorporating a repertoire of stock images and categories of self-ascription, while actively submerging and reediting others. These meanings shaped and were transmitted through the practices of community bodies, academics, writers and journalists, but they also competed with other narratives of experience within the communal memory of post-war settlement, and as such had to be negotiated by ordinary migrants, who might incorporate, rework or contest them as part of personal strategies of memory. To date, however, the relationship between these memory processes and the racialised categories of identity generated through ethnic mobilisation has not registered as an important dynamic in research on Irish subjectivities in Britain.[42]

It follows from this that the deployment of 'invisibility' as a transparent concept in relation to post-war migration has also involved a kind of historical projection, by which an institutional discourse generated in the 1980s and 1990s has been imaged back on to processes of settlement and identification that have their own historical specificity. A problematic consequence of this is that post-war migrant experiences tend to be figured in terms of negation and lack. Where the community histories of other minority groups have been criticised for portraying sanitised accounts of harmonious integration, Irish community activism during this period has utilised a form of 'oppression history' where themes of suffering, discrimination and disadvantage are amplified.[43] Whether they are figured as 'invisible', 'unrecognised' or 'incorporated', or nostalgicised as the last traces of a disappearing communal authenticity, post-war

Irish subjectivities are routinely treated as something absent or lost, diminished or repressed.

Undoubtedly, this tendency is associated with the ephemerality and dispersal of the post-war migrant community, but it is also an effect of conceiving the British–Irish relationship solely in terms of domination. Not only does this framing assign post-war migrants the position of victim; it implicitly equates 'agency' and personhood with the realisation of a particular normative definition of ethnic empowerment inscribed within the debates around official multiculturalism in the 1980s. The point, however, is that migrants were never merely *effects* of a static political relationship; they *made themselves* through active negotiation of the discourses of identity they encountered in both sending and receiving societies, and through this shaped the post-war development of the British–Irish relationship and its reciprocal impacts on both cultures. The subjectivities constituted through this process thus have a validity of their own as a research object, and require to be treated on their own terms, within the lived contexts in which they were generated.

This last point leads into a third general problem, namely that approaches which deploy 'invisibility' unflexively, positing British–Irish antagonism as the underlying determinant of Irish subjectivities, tend to obscure the ways wider processes of cultural production and social interaction play into the dynamics of migrant self-fashioning. Although Ireland left the Commonwealth in this period, in reality mass migration enhanced the socio-cultural interconnections between England and Ireland after 1945, fostering diverse forms of exchange within a wider context of societal transformation. Irish people left Ireland, not only because the Irish economy was stagnant, but because British social and economic reconstruction offered expanding opportunities for employment and leisure, consumption and sociability. One implication of this was that emigrants, via the extensive transnational networks they created, formed a powerful vector of cultural change within post-war Irish society: returning home at regular intervals, flush with money and stories about the excitements of urban life, emigrants helped disseminate alternative models of individuated selfhood within rural culture, disturbing the hegemony of Catholic-nationalist ideals in the process. A second implication, however, was that these investments in English urban identity also shaped migrants' negotiation of difference within the settlement process: migrants were subject to a shifting repertoire of racial categories, in both sending and receiving societies, but how they responded to these discourses and fashioned new forms of belonging was unavoidably mediated through the advent of 'affluence' and the idealisation of domesticity, social liberalisation and religious decline.

So while the Irish in post-war England could be 'immigrant', 'white' and later 'ethnic', their experience of these designations was mediated through, and inseparable from, the broader economic, social and cultural transformations affecting the lived experience of everyday life in both sending and receiving societies. Thinking about the production of difference within the Irish migrant experience does not, therefore, only involve acknowledging how the boundaries of Irish ethnicity have been contested and redrawn over time; it involves too consideration of how individuals negotiate the particularities of migrant 'journeys', fashioning and refashioning competing versions of self at different moments in the life cycle, through articulation with a variegated and constantly changing discursive environment.[44]

Taken collectively, these various points suggest a more fundamental concern with the academic discourse that has emerged out of ethnic mobilisation. For although much of this discourse has consistently employed the vocabulary of 'construction' and 'difference' when talking about Irish 'identity', the habitual omission of the dynamics outlined above suggests that interest in how Irish subjectivities have been constructed and remade historically is in practice limited. As Stuart Hall has emphasised:

> Cultural identities come from somewhere, have histories. But, like everything which is historical, they undergo constant transformation. Far from being eternally fixed in some essentialized past, they are subject to the continuous 'play' of history, culture, power.[45]

In the Irish case, however, the imperative of ethnic 'visibility' appears to have encouraged representations of 'identity' as 'an already accomplished fact'.[46] Just as the assimilationists tacitly assumed their 'whiteness' made the Irish suitable candidates for the assimilation paradigm, such that certain behavioural trends were automatically read as expressions of a pre-given 'white' identity, so claims about the 'invisibility' of the Irish take for granted that a coherent, unproblematic Irish 'identity' is always already *there*, primed to become outwardly 'visible'. Instead of treating 'identity' as a category to be historicised, interrogated and deconstructed, it is implicitly conceived as a property which individuals 'have', whose ontological *existence* precedes its expression in speech and behaviour. The point is not that Irish experiences are indistinct from those of the 'native' population, or that these experiences have not been subject to ideological exclusion; it is, rather, that the optical rhetoric of 'invisibility' tends to naturalise 'identity', discouraging its problematisation as an unstable, incomplete and internally riven historical *production*. Ultimately, the tendency to treat 'identity' as a normative ideal within official ontologies of the multicultural society contributes to its reification, impeding understanding of how the 'I' is formed dynamically in and through the migration process. As anthropologist Richard Jenkins has stressed, however, ethnic selfhood is intrinsically processual and performative:

> Although we talk about them in these terms endlessly, neither culture nor ethnicity is 'something' that people 'have', or, indeed, to which they 'belong'. They are, rather, complex repertoires which people experience, use, learn and 'do' in their daily lives, with which they construct an ongoing sense of themselves and an understanding of their fellows.[47]

It is these repertoires, as sites where migrant subjectivities are formed through the reciprocal workings of emotion and social narrative, which this book seeks to investigate. Such an investigation presupposes access to the lives of Irish migrants who settled in England during the post-war period, and to a methodology suited to exploring the dialogic constitution of subjectivities. To that end, we turn to a discussion of oral history, the chief methodology deployed in this book.

Oral history, migration and the 'turn to memory'

> It is the task of those who deal with history rather than chronicles to study, not only the mechanics of the material event, but the events of the remembering and the telling – the patterns of the remembering and the forms of the telling – through which we are able to perceive the 'event' in the first place.[48]

In the second half of the twentieth century oral history became a key methodology for scholars researching social groups whose experiences have been neglected within traditional archival sources. Along with scholars of the experiences of women, the working classes and colonised peoples, historians of migration have been to the fore in this trend.[49] As the oral historian Alistair Thomson has observed, 'a central and abiding claim of oral historians of migration has been that the migrant's own story is likely to be unrecorded or ill-documented, and that oral evidence provides an essential record of the hidden history of migration.'[50] In the case of Irish migrants in twentieth-century Britain, oral history has thus provided an important means of contesting Irish 'invisibility' and authenticating claims about identity. The process of ethnic mobilisation described above stimulated and utilised the products of a rash of oral history projects conducted by community activists and academics in the 1980s and 1990s, and funded by charities, local government and, in one important instance, the Commission for Racial Equality.[51]

Frequently based on group reminiscence, many of these community-based projects produced histories whose function was both commemorative and therapeutic, a tendency which became increasingly pronounced following the election of 'New' Labour in 1997 and the signing of the Good Friday Agreement the following year. Others have tended to produce histories in the mode of what Ann Laura Stoler, writing about the study of colonialisms, has termed 'subaltern memory'. Memory in this mode is

> the medium, not the message, the access point to untold stories of the colonised. In efforts to restore a more complete memory of the colonial and struggles against it, oral histories are often invoked to counter official versions and the sovereign status they implicitly give to European epistemologies. Subaltern acts of remembering have not been in question, because it is the official memory that is on the line; the process of remembering and the fashioning of personal memories are often beside the political points being made – and may in fact be seen to work against them.[52]

Virtually all book-length oral histories of the Irish in Britain published in the last 35 years have used oral narrative to gain access to 'untold stories' about the experiences of the Irish in twentieth-century Britain.[53] Against an official myth of white homogeneity and historiographical assumptions about 'assimilation', these stories often recover experiences of disadvantage and discrimination, as well as evidence of the persistence of an authentic Irish identity. Within this mode of memory, oral narrative thus functions as the medium via which an Irish voice muted through incorporation becomes audible, and which makes visible an Irish ethnic community within Britain's multicultural landscape.

As Thomson notes, the distinctive contribution of oral history in this mode concerns the agency it makes possible for individuals and groups previously written out of history. Through 'recovery' history, 'working-class men and women, indigenous peoples or members of cultural minorities ... have inscribed their experiences on the historical record and offered their own interpretations of history'.[54] Yet as Stoler suggests, such histories also tend to neglect 'the process of remembering and the fashioning of personal memories'. In the case of the Irish in Britain, while interviews with Irish migrants have allowed for the accumulation of rich personal data on the lives of Irish people in modern Britain, most oral history projects neglect their status as sites of memory, productive of narratives of experience whose form is shaped by the wider cultural and political context of the 1980s and 1990s and the goals of the activist-researchers involved. More generally, as a result of the way 'recovery' approaches have been allied to collective notions of ethnicity, the specificity of individual migrant journeys has usually been subordinated to narratives of collective experience, such that memory has not registered as a source of historical evidence in its own right. Absent from studies of the Irish in modern Britain are investigations of how processes of autobiographical and collective remembering interact over the migrant life course, leaving unaddressed the issues of conflict, plurality and long-term psychic adaption seen as inherent in recent theorisations of memory production.[55]

These absences have in part been underwritten by a particular reading of the relation between the subject and social context: if memory here functions as a medium through which a muted Irish voice becomes audible, this medium is conceived as transparent. The 'recovery' of 'invisible' experience implicitly assigns personal narrative the status of an unmediated reflection of an objective realm, or the direct expression of a pre-given 'identity' held apart from the 'distortions' of discourse and the 'rewritings' of personal and cultural memory. Such a model of social experience, however, has been one of the main casualties of the epistemological rethinking initiated as part of debates about the status of historical knowledge in the 1980s and 1990s. Post-structuralist problematisation of empiricist methodology has yielded the claim that the 'evidence of experience' is never direct in a simple, unmediated way. As Joan Scott has argued, it is not individuals who have access to an objective external reality through some looking-glass of 'experience'; rather, it is individuals who are constituted through 'experience', where 'experience' is a 'linguistic event'.[56] Margaret Somers frames this 'event' in terms of narrative: 'it is through narrativity that we come to know, understand, and make sense of the social world, and it is through narratives and narrativity that we constitute our social identities'.[57] In short, narrative is constitutive of our experience of reality; it thus cannot be separated from it.

These points concerning discursive mediation render oral history in the 'recovery' mode inherently 'unreliable' within the frame of a correspondence theory of knowledge. If form and content are effectively inseparable, the idea of oral narrative as a repository of 'facts' about the world and self becomes untenable. On the other hand, they also point to new possibilities for the study of migrant subjectivity. If migrants make sense of their experiences through locating themselves as the subjects of narratives drawn and adapted from collective repertoires, so study of the processes of narrative self-location can yield insight into how subjectivity is shaped through culture. By focusing on how narrative subjects draw on 'the generalised subject available in discourse to construct the particular personal subject', oral narrative becomes evidence for the inter-subjective constitution of subjectivities.[58] Approached thus, personal narratives of migration potentially supply access to a dynamic often neglected within migration histories: migrants' constitutive dialogues with the different discursive environments they inhabit as part of the migration process.

In order to exploit fully the possibilities opened by this notion of narrative inter-subjectivity, theorists of oral history have brought it into relation with a view of memory as psychically active, subject to reworking and shaped constantly by wider processes of collective and public myth.

A key concept here, developed by the Popular Memory Group, is that of 'composure':

> Composure is an aptly ambiguous term to describe the process of memory making. In one sense we compose or construct memories using the public languages and meanings of our culture. In another sense we compose memories that help us to feel relatively comfortable with our lives and identities, that give us a feeling of composure.[59]

If 'experience' does not occur outside of language, neither then does 'memory'. Autobiographical remembering is not a passive process of retrieval, whereby copies of prior experience are brought before the mind, but a creative and interpretative act through which experiences are selectively reconstructed through the process of recall. Crucially, this process of interpretative reconstruction is informed by the emotional needs and desires of the subject engaged in the act of telling. The act of composing a story about one's life is shaped by a desire to form a unified and integrated whole from the different and potentially conflicting parts of the self, to achieve a sense of 'psychic integration'. Integration here encompasses a crucial temporal dimension: the act of narrating a history of the self's experiences over time involves an attempt to synthesise past and present, to make the experiences of the past acceptable to the self situated in the present, in order to promote a sense of subjective continuity, security and well-being. Simultaneously, however, this integration of past and present also occurs in relation to a need for social recognition focused on various real and imagined audiences. Composing past and present is never a private act, governed solely by a personal need for subjective continuity; it is also conditioned by subjects' need to belong and feel understood within a range of external publics, local and particular, national and general. In this sense, memory composure is an inherently social process, shaped (and limited) by the norms, ideals and prohibitions embedded within wider narratives of collective self-understanding.[60]

In turn, since social collectivities change over time, so too do the possibilities for self-understanding available within them. A third useful concept for understanding the production of cultural myth is that of the 'cultural circuit'. According to this formulation, the relationship between consumers and producers of culture forms is not one-way, but is better approached in terms of reciprocity, via circuits of discursive production. Within such circuits, stories and images constructed by groups and individuals at one location, situated at the local and private, may be appropriated for particular purposes by groups or institutions situated at the national and public levels. Over time, and under the influence of diverse social forces, the 'original' stories are reworked and generalised for distribution to a wider, typically mass, audience, at which point they become available once more for personal consumption in reshaped form. What memory theorists have emphasised about this process is its adaptive and power-laden character, not only in the sense that a politics necessarily underpins the question of whose stories gain access to a public audience and in what form, but in the sense that widely distributed generalised forms powerfully shape and reshape the possibilities for private memory production.

The circuit gives groups and institutions with particular interests and agendas a powerful role in forming collective memory and public norms, a process which inevitably affects how individuals reconstruct and understand their own pasts, even as they engage actively in interpreting and reworking those pasts. Sometimes, the subject-positions the circuit makes available for self-understanding and expression are not universally accessible: personal experience often conflicts with the interpretation of the past projected through public memory.[61] In such instances, if personal experiences cannot be made to fit with dominant meanings and an alternative mode of expression cannot be located or formulated, the voice of personal experience becomes 'muted'.[62]

On the other hand, it is important not to see public memory merely as something imposed upon ordinary people 'from above', but as a process individuals and communities contribute to and take from. If ordinary people have been excluded from the means of cultural representation in the past, the twentieth century has witnessed an explosion of discursive activity around the personal and the everyday, as part of which the voice of personal experience has been fetishised as a sign of authenticity within Western culture. While this process necessarily enacts its own exclusions, distortions and appropriations, the development of a 'public culture of self-divulgence' has nevertheless fostered intense societal interest in the elicitation, recording and consumption of personal experiences and histories across a range of fields and media.[63] Arguably, the contemporary landscape of popular memory has become more storied and differentiated, marking the development of an increasingly complex 'narrative ecology' within post-war English society: official and public narratives must increasingly contend with, and adapt themselves to, self-representational practices generated 'from below', signalling an epochal tightening of the circuit between personal experience and public re-presentation.[64]

With respect to the wider historiography on British migration, these points caution against framing questions about migrant memory in dichotomous terms. It is certainly true that the inclusion of migrant histories within dominant myths of the British nation has been a fraught and selective process. Where some groups have been feted as 'model minorities', others have been subject to racism and xenophobia, the extent and effects of which have been actively erased from British cultural memory. In such instances, where there is active resistance to acknowledging histories of persecution, memory may take the form of a struggle against national forgetting and disavowal, locking minority and dominant memory into a relation of contest and opposition.

At the same time, however, memory production may also be related to other aspects of the migration process and the possibilities contemporary practices of self-representation offer for their negotiation. Collective self-narration may be motivated, for example, by a need to preserve emotional connections to a homeland, but in a way that simultaneously enables adaption to the demands and possibilities of the 'here and now'. Via diverse forms of transnational communication, and in particular diaspora newspapers, circuits of transmission articulate *between* places and *across* national borders, as well as 'vertically' between personal and public levels of representation within national space. In turn, these transnational processes intersect with circuits of production operative *within* the 'particular public' of settled migrant communities.[65] In particular, representations of communal identity may reflect the cultural hegemony of particular interests and value alignments within the community, expressing, naturalising and preserving the personal experiences of some migrants at the expense of others.

Perhaps most significantly, memory production may reflect a need to record and commemorate the personal and collective achievements of the migration journey in a rapidly changing world where spatial dispersal, increasing individualisation and inter-generational forgetting militate against the reproduction of embodied communities. Under the conditions of 'liquid modernity', memory practices are triggered, not so much by a sense of injustice or desire to contest the silences of national memory, as by a sense of loss and communal withering attendant upon cultural change and generational ageing.[66] In this mode, the generalising processes inherent to the cultural circuit evolve towards a retrospective recycling of aspects of the past from which an affirmative image of settlement can be fashioned and a sense of belonging to an 'imagined community' extended.

These various points have a particular salience for the development of Irish communal memory in post-1945 England. If the Troubles formed one important context for the incitement of collective memory practices, the conflict occurred against the backdrop of wider debates over multiculturalism and national identity in Britain, as part of which the 'contribution' of immigration to 'rebuilding Britain' after the war surfaced as a focus of popular memory. More so than for many other post-war groups, this context has supplied considerable opportunities for Irish bodies across England to foster commemorative activities. Where the network of centres, clubs and associations established by post-war migrants has long served as a context for the performance of a semi-official code of Irish respectability, in recent times these spaces have also become focal points for community history projects and exhibitions, reminiscence groups and book launches, dedicated to the preservation and display of the achievements of the post-war generation.⁶⁷ Instead of a story of discrimination and disadvantage, these histories portray a heroic narrative of hardship, endurance and success, reflecting the emotional needs of an ageing and spatially dispersed post-war generation, as well as the continuing hegemony of post-war migrant values in defining the usability of the past.

In theorising remembering as an act of interpretative reconstruction, underpinned by a need for subjective coherence, these concepts of 'composure' and the 'cultural circuit' thus address squarely earlier criticisms of oral history centring on the 'unreliability' of memory. By suggesting that we read the integration of narrative forms as a kind of metaphor for an interior process of subjective integration, where this process is conditioned by sets of overlapping dialogues playing out against broader cycles of cultural production, composure transforms the subject's tendency to rewrite past experience into a resource. Inaccuracies, tendencies towards forgetting and occlusion, exaggeration and fictionalisation, become evidence of the reworking of subjectivities over time through dynamic interaction with a social environment in which the forms of public memory are themselves being recycled and reworked in particular ways.

As this suggests, change is not solely explainable in terms of culture. By stressing the importance of the subject's need for internal coherence as a structuring dynamic of narrative production, composure draws our attention to a crucial psychic dimension in social life, alongside the stress on discourse. As Michael Roper suggests:

> What emerges from this kind of approach is a sense of subjectivity, not as wholly composed by ideological formations – competing, contradictory or otherwise – but as a matter of personality formed through lived experience and the emotional responses to those experiences. A biographical perspective allows us to see the assimilation of cultural codes as a matter of negotiation involving an active subject ... [and] ... as a selective and partial process, never complete, and always partly dependent on earlier experience.⁶⁸

Experience is not only a 'linguistic event'; it is a psychic one too. Discourse supplies the terms within which thought and action are formulated, but formulation is also an active negotiation whereby subjects, apprehending the world through the 'screen' of their own emotions, invest differently in the forms available. It is thus necessary to conceive of the subject, not only as discursively constituted, but as a subject of desire.

Informed by the framework developed by the cultural historian Graham Dawson, this book makes use of Kleinian formulations to further delineate the role of desire within the theory of memory outlined above. Where this discussion has made reference to the subject's need for 'integration' as a structuring principle of memory, Kleinian thought further emphasises the particularity of lived relationships as the context in which an integrated sense of self evolves dynamically in relation to the external world. In particular, the emotions and desires which constitute the subject's internal psychic landscape are powerfully shaped by the ways in which basic psychic needs and impulses are accommodated or denied by significant others (especially parental figures), and by how subjects handle and assimilate these responses in turn. The external world here supplies the 'external objects' from which 'internal phantasy objects' are developed, while forming a site on to which desires and anxieties associated with these internal objects are projected in turn.[69] Subject-formation within a Kleinian framework is thus an ongoing process of exchange between internal and external worlds, whereby internal phantasy objects ('imagos') are constituted, broken apart and split off through alternating processes of introjection (by which the self incorporates external objects into its internal phantasy world) and projection (by which it expels or projects internal feelings or impulses into the social world).[70]

As this suggests, Kleinian thought places emphasis on the reciprocity of emotion and culture in subject-formation. If the external objects from which the subject's internal phantasy world is developed are embedded within the concrete practices of everyday life, so the codes and values which regulate social relations are centrally implicated in the shaping of personal emotions and desires. In turn, these personal subjectivities condition how individuals adapt and adapt to the constraints and possibilities of social life. In terms of the positioning effects of discourse, to say that the 'assimilation of cultural codes' is 'a matter of negotiation involving an active subject' is to say that how subjects invest in their discursive environments (the forms they select and how they interpret and make use of them) is conditioned by desires, impulses and beliefs formed through previous interactions between the psychic and the social. The subject-in-formation is thus 'always partial, never complete' in that it is constantly being added to and split, reordered and subdivided in a ceaseless bid to form a coherent whole through interaction with its environment.

It thus follows that subject-formation is a necessarily *ambivalent* process, where different parts of the self exist in conflict, and where unsettling emotions pose an ongoing threat to psychic stability. While, for Klein, this ambivalence originates in the early splitting of the subject in response to its own inborn self-destructive urges, the internal division of the self becomes more complex as the relationship between the developing ego and its internal objects evolves.[71] As Dawson explains, the diverse and fragmentary quality of the identifications established via these relations engenders 'incompatibility', leading to 'psychic conflict'. In the Kleinian account psychic life is thus conceived as a 'continual struggle, unconscious in the first instance, for a narrative phantasy capable of reconciling conflict and subsuming difference'. Narrative reconciliation, however, constantly negotiates a countervailing tendency towards defensive 'splitting':

> Chief among the factors that provoke splitting of the self and its imagos are the disintegrating effects of anxiety and the defences developed in self-protection against it. These 'ego defences' work to prevent anxiety from undermining the self by containing it within a limited zone of the psyche. 'Resistances' are established between anxiety-producing and anxiety-free imagos (and thus, also, between parts of the psyche) resulting in the 'different identifications becoming cut off from one another'. The self's defences against anxiety therefore produce narrative phantasies that exacerbate the existing fragmentation of the internal world: splitting interferes with more inclusive processes of integration, and ensures further psychic conflict will occur.[72]

Oral narratives of experience do not just register 'the self'; they register the self as a *divided* formation, where unconscious desires constantly suffuse and condition conscious self-presentations. As well as the desire for coherence and integration, this also includes the work of psychic defences engaged in the management of fears and anxieties. The importance of this here is that the 'identities' which migrants articulate need to be seen as the unstable outcome of psychic conflicts which both originate in past experience and, under the conditions of the present, exercise an influence over how that past can be represented to the self. The implication is that, as well as reading for coherence, it is necessary also to read for conflict and the events which occasion it. This underscores the point that the self is an accretion of past experience, the unresolved conflicts of which influence memory production; the prism of the present cannot be easily separated from the enduring significance of people and places in one's past. But it also opens a window onto the phenomenon of subjective change over the life course: the psychic conflicts present within migrants' narratives are not only records of the subjective impact of difficult aspects of the migration journey; they are records too of adaption to these pressures, of the reworking of the self and formation of new identifications in pursuance of the goals of settlement.

Lastly, one final kind of dialogue affecting the production of memory within the interview concerns the interview relation itself. As Summerfield states:

> The process of the production of memory stories is always dialogic or inter-subjective in the sense that it is the product of a relationship between a narrator and a recipient subject, an audience.[73]

As noted above, this 'audience' may be constituted in the abstract, as a particular public shaping the interview from outside, but 'audience' also refers to the dynamics obtaining within the interview itself. The narrative produced is always shaped by a relation between how the interviewer attempts to structure the interview, and how the interviewee interprets the interview situation, including the overarching goals of the interaction and the identities of the interviewer. In terms of the research on which this book is based, a number of aspects of my own autobiography are important here. My own migration to Glasgow in 2002 not only sparked my initial interest in the Irish in Britain, but stimulated too a theoretical interest in issues relating to 'identity', an interest subsequently developed through my chosen undergraduate programmes of study in philosophy and social history. In terms of the current project, this was to translate into a preference for frameworks and methodologies orientated towards the study of 'interiorities'. Interviews were 'semi-structured' in that they were based on a schedule of questions informed by the research goals of the project and my reading of the historiography, yet were approached in such a way as to encourage respondents to talk about what most interested them, even if this did not appear at the time to correspond to pre-defined themes. Interview strategy was based on trying to elicit memories rich in emotion rather than external 'fact', using both negative and positive techniques. As well as trying to appear non-threatening and deferential, so as to put subjects at their ease, I tried to ask questions that encouraged story-telling by focusing on contextual details and personal feelings rather than the abstract issues that lay behind the questions. In this way, I sought to prompt respondents to talk about what was most meaningful to them about their lives as migrants.

Finally, how subjects constructed themselves within the interview was also conditioned by how they perceived and identified me. In this respect, the production of memory was affected by the various visual and aural markers of social identity I carried into the interview situation. At the time the interviews were carried out I was a student researcher, aged between 25 and 27, based at the University of Manchester. In addition, I was male, white and, significantly, spoke with a Northern Irish accent. Thus, while some respondents identified me with the institution of the university, others focused on my accent, prompting questions and discussion about Northern Ireland and Ireland more generally. As we shall see, in some instances the influence of this dynamic was particularly marked, inciting and shaping memory production in relation to themes connected with Northern Irish politics.

Myth, memory and migrant life stories: key themes and dynamics

At stake in debates over the development of Irish identities in Britain is the characterisation of the British–Irish relationship itself. As such, the migrant experience forms a lens through which to read the changing significance of this relationship and its overlooked social and cultural effects. Additionally, however, migrants also participated in the making of this relationship, shaping the everyday contexts and discourses in which British–Irish difference became meaningful. This book shifts attention from 'Irish identity' as a reified collectivity to what Paul Gilroy terms 'the always unpredictable mechanisms of identification'; it foregrounds how migrants encountered, internalised and transformed the various subject-positions they were assigned within post-war English and Irish societies.[74] In so doing, it shows how the post-war Irish experience resists simple incorporation within an assimilation/collective identity dichotomy. The Irish did not 'assimilate' effortlessly into the background of English cultural life, but nor were migrants 'members' of a bounded ethnic group, the boundaries of which were sharply defined against an oppositional discourse of Englishness. Examined from the perspective of individual lives, the liminal position which migrants negotiated in post-war England was dynamic: migrants located themselves as the subjects of a diverse and historically evolving repertoire of narratives, signalling adaption, difference and integration as co-articulating features of the post-war migrant experience.

This broad agenda is developed via a focus on the dynamics of memory production, concerning three principal aspects. Firstly, focusing on key 'episodic' moments in individual and collective memory of the migration journey, chapters identify important *lieux de mémoire* in the formation of a distinctive post-war Irish communal memory, centring on the lived contexts of migration. Focused on the context of departure, Chapter 1 addresses experiences of leaving home after 1945. Chapter 2, addressing the 'liminal' phase between arrival and 'settlement', examines women's negotiation of femininities in the post-war English city. Chapter 3, focused on experiences of work, explores the construction of Irish masculinities in the post-war construction industry. Chapter 4 investigates migrants' changing attitudes to religion, marriage and the Catholic Church. And Chapter 5 addresses experiences of difference and otherness through the lens of the Troubles in England. Employing the notion of the 'cultural circuit', each chapter explores how lived experiences of these everyday contexts have been generalised within diverse forms of representation, and in turn, how these representations become 'useable pasts' for both individuals and groups. The book is thus concerned with how the lived experiences of migration have been condensed into a set of popular myths of Irish settlement in post-war England, and with interrogating the relationship between these myths and the versions of Irish experience projected within academic historiography; more particularly, it is concerned with how personal reconstructions of migrant experience are mediated through such myths, such that the historical reworking of dominant settlement myths necessarily redefines the possibilities for personal remembering at different moments in the life course.

Secondly, as this focus on the routing of popular memory back into autobiographical remembering here implies, chapters pay special theoretical attention to the functions of collective myth at the level of personal memory production: to the differentiated and psychically active ways individual migrants interact with communal and public myths as they endeavour to 'compose' 'settled' versions of self. While the production of an Irish communal memory in post-war England was organised around common sites of memory, these were sites of plurality and contest as much as they were repositories of shared meaning. There was never only one collective memory of post-war settlement, but a mosaic of competing narratives of experience, each of which interpreted the meaning of Irish settlement and identity in different, often contradictory, ways. At the core of the book are the 'expressive possibilities' this complex and shifting memory formation makes available for self-understanding and the distinctive ways individual migrants manipulate and exploit these possibilities, in response to the specific circumstances structuring their experiences and the psychic desires these engender. Rather than the 'fit' between personal reconstructions and a definite scheme of migrant 'scripts', the book thus foregrounds how migrants negotiate the tensions between multiple subject-positions inscribed within a diverse repertoire of available narratives, selecting and adapting available formulas in an effort to 'compose' a version of past experience which validates the migration journey.

Finally, this concern with the 'composure' of migrant memories is also mobilised to explore the dynamics of subjective change over the course of the migration journey, at both individual and collective levels. Where existing approaches to the use of oral history tend to abstract segments of migrants' narratives from the overall story of migration in which they are embedded, each chapter is based on in-depth analysis and comparison of a small number of migrant life histories, wherein particular themes are explored within the context of the individual life narrative as a whole.[75] In this way, subjects' representation of significant features of the migration journey are understood in terms of the subjective legacies of prior events and experience, as well as in terms of the narrator's standpoint and emotional needs in the present. As such, this focus on the interaction between part and whole affords a means of analysing the dynamic relationship between past and present, 'there' and 'here', within migrants' narratives of settlement. Through investigation of how versions of past experience have been 'rewritten' at different points in the migration journey, and by analysing the dynamic relationship between these 'rewritings' and wider shifts in popular myth, chapters trace how understandings of self have been renegotiated through psychic adaption to the pressures and

Introduction   29

possibilities of settlement, whilst simultaneously illuminating the changing contours of Irish collective memory since 1945.

As these points imply, the approach taken here does not offer a quantitative solution to the problem of representivity. Chapters examine ten case histories in depth, drawn from and supported by a wider sample of 45 oral histories, migrant diaries, autobiographies and memoirs.[76] However, while the lives of these migrants share some basic features in common (they all left the south of Ireland for England between 1945 and 1969) they are different in countless other respects.[77] Individual narratives have been selected, not because they reflect some notion of 'the average' Irish migrant experience, but because of what their comparison reveals about the underlying dynamics of migrant subjectivity, dynamics not graspable through the compilation of a collective profile. In this regard, while a focus on individual migrant trajectories points up the specificity of individual experiences, by holding the interrelation between self and society in constant play it becomes possible to analyse how difference is shaped through shared 'horizons of possibility', as well as to illustrate the processes by which such horizons are reinterpreted and transformed in the course of individual life experiences. Within this conception, generalisability does not depend upon the weighting of samples or enumerating the characteristics of a pre-defined group, but upon generating critical insight into the shifting relations between the self and the social under particular historical conditions. Oral history in this mode is thus concerned with a different kind of representivity. As Alessandro Portelli puts it:

> Oral history ... offers less a grid of standard experiences than a horizon of shared possibilities, real or imagined. The fact that these possibilities are hardly ever organised in tight, coherent patterns indicates that each person entertains, in each moment, multiple possible destinies, perceives different possibilities, and makes different choices from others in the same situation. These myriad individual differences, however, only serve to remind us that, beyond the necessary abstraction of the social science grid, the actual world is more like a mosaic or patchwork of countless different shapes, touching, and overlapping, and sharing, but also cherishing their irreducible individuality. As sciences of the individual, oral history and literature deal with the portions of the mosaic that cannot be subsumed under the grid. They give us unwieldy representations, often harder to handle and work with, but perhaps more consistent not only with the presence of subjectivity but also with the objective reality of things.[78]

The interviewees in this sample came from different places in Ireland; they moved at different times between 1945 and 1969; they settled (and resettled) in different places, at different times; they did different jobs, married different people and lived different individual lives in multiple ways. However, what they share is a relation to the broad experience of Irish migration to post-war England and the societal discourses and historical forces which shaped this experience; their lives, in different and specific ways, are representative of this experience, and of the realities of difference within it. We turn now to the empirical analysis of such issues, beginning in post-war Ireland.

Notes

1 R. Roberts, *The Classic Slum: Salford Life in the First Quarter of the Century* (London, 1971), 22–23.
2 The locus classicus of the 'outcast' thesis is J. M. Werly, 'The Irish in Manchester, 1832–49', *Irish Historical Studies* 18:71 (1973), 345–358. More generally, see the contributions to R. Swift and S. Gilley (eds), *The Irish in the Victorian City* (London, 1985), and esp. M. A. G. Ó Tuathaigh, 'The Irish in Nineteenth-Century Britain: Problems of Integration', *Transactions of the Royal Historical Society* 31 (1981), 149–173; and F. Finnegan, *Poverty and Prejudice: A Study of Irish Immigrants in York, 1840–1875* (Cork, 1982).
3 On the origins and popularisation of Victorian images of the Irish ghetto see D. MacRaild, 'Irish Immigration and the "Condition of England" Question: The Roots of an Historiographical Tradition', *Immigrants and Minorities* 14:1 (1995), 67–85.
4 D. Fitzpatrick, 'A Curious Middle Place: The Irish in Britain, 1871–1921', in R. Swift and S. Gilley (eds), *The Irish in Britain, 1815–1939* (London, 1989), 10–59; J. Walvin, *Passage to Britain: Immigration in British History and Politics* (Harmondsworth, 1984), 59.
5 For revisionist accounts emphasising variation, change gradual assimilation see the contributions to Swift and Gilley, *The Irish in Britain, 1815–1939*, in particular Fitzpatrick, 'A Curious Middle Place'. See also J. Hutchinson and A. O'Day, 'The Gaelic Revival in London, 1900–22: Limits of Ethnic Identity', in R. Swift and S. Gilley (eds), *The Irish in Victorian Britain: The Local Dimension* (Dublin, 1999), 254–276; and P. O'Leary, 'From the Cradle to the Grave: Popular Catholicism among the Irish in Wales', in P. O'Sullivan (ed.), *The Irish World Wide*, vol. 5: *Religion and Identity* (Leicester, 1996), 183–195. For revisionist accounts which give more weight to the notion of an enduring Irish communal identity see M. Busteed, *The Irish in Manchester c. 1750–1921. Resistance, Adaption and Identity* (Manchester, 2016) and J. Belchem, *Irish, Catholic and Scouse* (Liverpool, 2007).
6 R. Weight, *Patriots: National Identity in Britain 1940–2000* (London, 2002), 145.
7 D. H. Akenson, *The Irish Diaspora: A Primer* (Belfast, 1993), 211. British scholars, both quantitative sociologists and social historians, have likewise stressed the easy assimilability of the Irish during the post-1945 period. See M. P. Hornsby-Smith, *Roman Catholics in England: Studies in Social Structure since the Second World War* (Cambridge, 1987); M. P. Hornsby-Smith and A. Dale, 'The Assimilation of Irish Immigrants in England', *British Journal of Sociology* 39:4 (1988), 519–544; J. Rex, 'Immigrants and British Labour: The

Sociological Context', in K. Lunn (ed.), *Hosts, Immigrants and Minorities* (London, 1980), 122–142; E. Royle, *Modern Britain: A Social History 1750–1985* (London, 1989), 69–73.
8 M. J. Hickman and B. Walter, 'Deconstructing Whiteness: Irish Women in Britain', *Feminist Review* 50 (1995), 7.
9 M. Hickman, *Religion, Class and Identity* (Aldershot, 1995), 17 and ch. 2
10 Ibid., 12–13, 17.
11 Ibid., 2–7.
12 M. Hickman, 'Reconstructing and Deconstructing "Race": British Political Discourses about the Irish in Britain', *Ethnic and Racial Studies* 21:2 (1998), 296–299.
13 Hickman, *Religion, Class and Identity*, 13.
14 M. J. Hickman, 'Alternative Historiographies of the Irish in Britain: A Critique of the Segregation/Assimilation Model', in Swift and Gilley, *The Irish in Victorian Britain*, 250.
15 Ibid.
16 Ibid., 252.
17 Hickman, *Religion, Class and Identity*, 248–249.
18 S. Lambert, *Irish Women in Lancashire, 1922–1960: Their Story* (Lancaster, 2001); L. Ryan, 'Migrant Women, Social Networks and Motherhood: The Experiences of Irish Nurses in Britain', *Sociology* 41:2 (2007), 295–312; S. Sorohan, *Irish London during the Troubles* (Dublin, 2012).
19 Studies which explicitly take 'invisibility' as a premise include P. J. Bracken and P. O'Sullivan, 'The Invisibility of Irish Migrants in British Health Research', *Irish Studies Review* 9:1 (2001), 41–51; M. Buckley, 'Sitting on Your Politics: The Irish among the British and the Women among the Irish', in J. MacLaughlin (ed.), *Location and Dislocation in Contemporary Irish Society: Emigration and Irish Identities* (Cork, 1997), 94–133; T. P. Coogan, *Wherever Green is Worn: The Story of the Irish Diaspora* (London, 2000); L. Curtis, *Nothing but the Same Old Story: The Roots of Anti-Irish Racism* (London, 1984); L. Greenslade, M. Pearson and M. Madden, *Generations of an Invisible Minority: The Health and Well-Being of the Irish in Britain* (Liverpool, 1991); C. Lloyd, *The Irish Community in Britain: Discrimination, Disadvantage and Racism* (London, 1995); M. Mac an Ghaill, 'The Irish in Britain: The Invisibility of Ethnicity and Anti-Irish Racism', *Journal of Ethnic and Migration Studies* 26:1 (2000), 137–147.
20 P. Panayi, *An Immigration History of Britain: Multicultural Racism since 1800* (Harlow, 2010).
21 On the utility of the Irish case for histories of whiteness in the British context see G. Schaffer and S. Nasar, 'The White Essential Subject: Race, Ethnicity, and the Irish in Post-War Britain', *Contemporary British History* 32:2 (2018), 209–230.
22 S. Fielding, *Class and Ethnicity: Irish Catholics in England, 1880–1939* (Buckingham, 1993), 11
23 M. Moulton, *Ireland and the Irish in Interwar England* (Cambridge, 2014), 7, 240.
24 Ibid., 3, 241, 4.
25 Ibid., 7.

26 On the role of the Church in establishing the London and Birmingham Irish centres see H. Ewart, *Caring for Migrants: Policy Responses to Irish Migration to England, 1940–1972* (Liverpool, 2017). See also D. M. MacRaild, *The Irish Diaspora in Britain, 1750–1939* (London, 2011), 80–88.
27 Minutes of the Executive Council of the Irish County Associations, London, 1969–75, Archive of the Irish in Britain, London (hereafter AIB), ICA/Z/1/1.
28 *Irish Counties Journal*, December 1970, 5–6, AIB/ICA/Z/5/1.
29 W. Webster, *Imagining Home: Gender, 'Race' and National Identity, 1945–64* (London, 1998), xii.
30 'Homelessness, Racism and Jobs Top Priorities', *BIAS Bulletin: The Newsletter of Brent Irish Advisory Service*, October 1984, AIB/BIAS/1/10.
31 M. J. Hickman and B. Walter, *Discrimination and the Irish Community in Britain: A Report of Research Undertaken for the Commission for Racial Equality* (London, 1997), 235.
32 J. Inglis, 'The Irish in Britain: A Question of Identity', *Irish Studies in Britain* 3 (Spring/Summer 1982), 13, AIB/ISIB/2/2.
33 Correspondence from Angie Birtell, Housing and Welfare Rights Officer at the London Irish Women's Centre, to Jim Smellie, Homeless Senior Manager for City and East London (16 November 1992), AIB/LIWC/3.
34 P. Gilroy, *There Ain't no Black in the Union Jack: The Cultural Politics of Race and Nation* (London, 1987), 69–70.
35 Hickman and Walter, *Discrimination and the Irish Community in Britain*, 203.
36 'Editorial', *Irish Studies in Britain* 2 (Autumn 1981), 3, AIB/ISIB/Z/1.
37 Interview with Angie Birtell, carried out by Anne Holohan and taken from her book *Working Lives: The Irish in Britain* (Hayes, Middlesex, 1995), 60–61.
38 Interview with Mary Hickman, carried out by Anne Holohan and taken from *Working Lives*, 131.
39 'An Excuse for Postponing Effective Action', *Irish Post*, 1 August 1981; 'Now's the Time for Action', *Irish Post*, 5 September 1981; 'In Search of a Political Voice', *Irish Post*, 14 November 1981; 'Irish Must Look to Themselves for Help', *Irish Post*, 14 November 1981.
40 IBRG, 'Justice for the Irish' (Manchester, 1989), Ahmed Iqbal Ullah Race Relations Resource Centre, Manchester, AIURRRC/GB3228.29/1/23.
41 IBRG, 'Policy Statement on Northern Ireland' (Birmingham, 20 September 1986), Birmingham City Council (hereafter BCC), Acc/MS 1611/F/3.
42 An important exception here is a handful of articles by Marc Scully. See in particular, 'Emigrants in the Traditional Sense'? Irishness in England, Contemporary Migration and Collective Memory of the 1950s', *Irish Journal of Sociology* 23:2 (2015), 133–148.
43 For criticism of community history approaches see K. Myers, 'Historical Practice in the Age of Pluralism: Educating and Celebrating Identities', in K. Burrell and P. Panayi (eds), *Histories and Memories: Migrants and their History in Britain* (London, 2006), 35–53; C. Hoffman, 'Community History', in J. Craig-Norton, C. Hoffman and T. Kushner (eds), *Migrant Britain: Histories and Historiographies. Essays in Honour of Colin Holmes* (London, 2018), 103–105.
44 'Journey' here refers not only to the physical means of mobility, but the development of the self through migration, involving the crossing of social and cultural boundaries and its 'wider symbolism and refraction through memory

work'. See T. Kushner, *The Battle of Britishness: Migrant Journeys, 1685 to the Present* (Manchester, 2012), 72–73, 213.
45 S. Hall, 'Cultural Identity and Diaspora', in J. Rutherford (ed.), *Identity, Community, Culture, Difference* (London, 1990), 225.
46 Ibid., 222.
47 R. Jenkins, *Rethinking Ethnicity: Arguments and Explorations* (London, 1997), 14.
48 A. Portelli, *The Death of Luigi Trastulli and Other Stories: Form and Meaning in Oral History* (New York, 1991), 73.
49 The most influential use of oral history as a source for 'history from below' is P. Thompson, *The Voice of the Past: Oral History* (Oxford, 1978). See also E. Roberts, *A Woman's Place: An Oral History of Working-Class Women 1890–1940* (Oxford, 1984).
50 A. Thomson, 'Moving Stories: Oral History and Migration Studies', *Oral History* 27:1 (1999), 26.
51 For example, Caoin na Gael: The Hammersmith Irish Reminiscence Group, *Ethnic Communities Oral History Project* (London, 2000); M. Lennon, M. McAdam and J. O'Brien, *Across the Water: Irish Women's Lives in Britain* (London, 1988); A. Lynch (ed.), *The Irish in Exile: Stories of Emigration* (London, 1988); A. O'Grady, *Irish Migration to London in the 1940s and 1950s* (London, 1988); L. O'Hare (ed.), *Thousands are Sailing: A Collection of Memories* (London, 2000); P. Schweitzer (ed.), *Across the Sea* (London, 1991).
52 A. L. Stoler and K. Strassler, 'Memory Work in Java: A Cautionary Tale', in R. Perks and A. Thomson (eds), *The Oral History Reader*, 2nd edn (London, 2006), 287.
53 See, for example, Lennon et al., *Across the Water*; O'Grady, *Irish Migration to London*; Lambert, *Irish Women in Lancashire*.
54 A. Thomson, '"Unreliable Memories?" The Use and Abuse of Oral History', in W. Lamont (ed.), *Historical Controversies and Historians* (London, 1998), 25.
55 A. Green, 'Individual Remembering and "Collective Memory": Theoretical Presuppositions and Contemporary Debates', *Oral History* 32: 2 (2004), 35–44; G. Smith, 'Beyond Individual/Collective Memory: Women's Transactive Memories of Food, Family and Conflict', *Oral History* 22:1 (2007), 77–90.
56 J. Scott, 'The Evidence of Experience', *Critical Inquiry* 17 (1991), 793.
57 M. Somers, 'The Narrative Constitution of Identity: A Relational and Network Approach', *Theory and Society* 23:5 (1994), 606.
58 P. Summerfield, *Reconstructing Women's Wartime Lives* (Manchester, 1998), 15.
59 A. Thomson, *Anzac Memories: Living with the Legend* (Oxford, 1994), 8. For the classic statement of the Popular Memory framework see Popular Memory Group, 'Popular Memory: Theory, Politics, Method', in R. Johnson (ed.), *Making Histories: Studies in History-Writing and Politics* (London, 1982), 205–252.
60 My discussion of 'composure' here is indebted to Summerfield, *Reconstructing Women's Wartime Lives*, 16–23; Thomson, *Anzac Memories*, 7–13; and G. Dawson, *Soldier Heroes: British Adventure, Empire and the Imagining of Masculinities* (London, 1994), 22–26.

61 Dawson, *Soldier Heroes*, 24–26. See also R. Johnstone, 'What is Cultural Studies Anyway?', *Social Text* 16 (Winter 1986–1987), 38–80.
62 On 'muting' see Summerfield, *Reconstructing Women's Wartime Lives*, 27–30.
63 L. Abrams, *Oral History Theory* (London, 2010), 36–37.
64 Y. Gabriel, 'Narrative Ecologies and the Role of Counter-Narratives: The Case of Nostalgic Stories and Conspiracy', in S. Frandsen, T. Kuhn and M. Lundholt (eds), *Counter-Narratives and Organization* (London, 2016), 208–225.
65 According to Thomson 'the "general public" includes the various media which provide generally available representations and interpretative categories in an indirect, impersonal relationship'. We also, however, 'make sense of experience by using the meanings available within the active relationships of a 'particular public' group, such as a wartime platoon'. See Thomson, *Anzac Memories*, 9.
66 P. Nora, 'Between Memory and History: *Les Lieux de Mémoire*', *Representations* 26 (1989), 12.
67 For a representative sample of these commemorative histories see the Select bibliography.
68 M. Roper, 'Slipping Out of View: Subjectivity and Emotion in Gender History', *History Workshop Journal* 59 (2005), 65–66.
69 An 'object' in psychoanalytic writings is that towards which action or desire is directed by the subject. Objects are nearly always persons, parts of persons or symbols of one or the other. An 'external object' is one recognised as being external by the subject; an 'internal object' by contrast is an *object-representation* which has acquired the significance of an external object but is conceived to be located in internal psychic reality. As Charles Rycroft states, internal objects are phantoms, i.e. they are images occurring in phantasies which are reacted to as 'real'. See C. Rycroft, *Critical Dictionary of Psychoanalysis* (London, 1995), 113–114.
70 Dawson, *Soldier Heroes*, 28–33. 'Imago' is another term for internal phantasy objects – object-representations shaped via the interplay between internal psychic impulses and external objects.
71 H. Segal, *Introduction to the Work of Melanie Klein* (London, 2008), 25 and ch. 3.
72 Dawson, *Soldier Heroes*, 34.
73 Summerfield, *Reconstructing Women's Wartime Lives*, 20.
74 P. Gilroy, *Postcolonial Melancholia* (New York, 2005), xv.
75 The best examples of this intensive approach to oral history analysis are Thomson, *Anza Memories* and D. James, *Dona Maria's Story: Life History, Memory and Political Identity* (Durham, NC, 2000), which analyses the testimony of one interviewee over some 300 pages.
76 See Appendix and Select bibliography for details.
77 Northern experiences are the subject of a current AHRC project, 'Conflict, Memory and Migration: Northern Irish Migrants during the Troubles in Great Britain'.
78 A. Portelli, *The Battle of Valle Giulia: Oral History and the Art of Dialogue* (Madison, WI, 1997), 86–89.

1

Narratives of exit: the public meanings of emigration and the shaping of emigrant selves in post-war Ireland, 1945–1969

> Emigration has been for years and years a severed artery from which this nation is slowly but surely bleeding to death.[1]

Mythologies of exit in modern Ireland

National imaginaries are not only constructed in relation to external rivals and incoming aliens; they are also fashioned through the 'politics of exit', in relation to the outgoing departee.[2] Nowhere was this more apparent than in nineteenth-century Ireland, where, against a backdrop of mass departure unparalleled in modern Europe, the emigrant was mobilised as a metaphor for national dispossession amidst the country's developing politics of independence.[3] Where leave-taking was associated with ambition and aspiration in other European sending societies, observes Kerby Miller, in Ireland the departee was an 'exile'; a displaced refugee, forced from 'his' homeland due to the deleterious effects of British 'misrule'.[4] Consequently, within emergent myths of the nation, and at the inception of the modern Irish state, emigration was coded as an injustice and a pathology, the invidious causes of which would disappear following the acquisition of sovereignty. A 'free Ireland', maintained Patrick Pearse, leader of the Easter Rising, would not have 'hunger in her fertile vales' nor 'squalor in her cities', and no Irish-born man or woman would be forced from their homeland once imperial rule was overthrown.[5]

In the event, emigration did not cease following the achievement of Irish independence in 1921. On the contrary, since the policies pursued by successive Irish governments tended to consolidate the post-famine rural order of which emigration was a structural feature, so high rates of emigration persisted as a controversial aspect of Irish society, resulting in the departure of well over a million men and women between 1921 and 1971.[6] In this context, where the revivalist code of national identity promoted by elites was antipathetic to both the persistence of emigration and the forms of industrial modernisation necessary for its reduction, the fatalistic rhetoric of 'exile' was now redirected against internal aspects of Irish life. Where previously the 'exile' signified the injustice of external misrule, mass emigration to the 'auld enemy' after 1945 provoked agonised self-inspection, engendering a public discourse of emasculation and loss. This was underpinned, not only by concerns over the economic failure of the new state, but by racial fears that emigration was 'draining' the nation of its 'life blood', 'bleeding' the country of 'the very best and ablest' sections of the population.[7] 'Everybody knows', argued Labour TD William Norton, speaking in the Dáil after the war, that

> emigration is probably the most dangerous social evil, the most dangerous cancer, of our national life from which it is possible for a nation to suffer. It has been heart-breaking for the last six years to see the finest of our young men and young women pleading and begging at the labour exchanges throughout the country to get a permit to go to work in Britain ... because they could not get here the employment which ought to be available for them. Of course it must be tackled if there is to be any Irish nation left. Of course it must be tackled if there is to be any virility left in the nation. Of course it must be tackled unless we are to see the end of the Celt and the entire extinction of the Irish people as a race.[8]

This chapter addresses two interrelated questions provoked by this cultural politics of exit, namely: how did migrants who left for England during this period interpret the meaning of their own departure? And to what extent and in what ways were these personal understandings of leaving affected by the wider discourse of national crisis generated around emigration during the period? According to perhaps the dominant view at the time, post-1945 emigrants experienced their departure in the same way as previous generations: as reluctant 'exiles', 'forced' from their homeland with 'black despair in their hearts and tears in their eyes'.[9] However, while Ireland's economic stagnation certainly formed an essential condition of mass emigration after 1945, it did not automatically follow that migrants themselves interpreted their departure through the rhetoric of exile. Popular representations, then and since, which depict migrants' actions as an effect of 'economic necessity' here tend to screen out the diverse mechanisms by which migrants made sense of the social worlds they inhabited. These included the affective relationships and informal personal networks in which intending migrants were enmeshed, but they also included the 'cultural circuit' by which personal understandings of self were fashioned through articulation with wider constructions of emigrant identity circulating within post-war Irish culture.

It is here important to recognise that, although the post-war crisis replenished conventional narratives of exile, it also fuelled a wide-ranging debate over the causes, consequences and remedies of emigration, contributing to a wider contestation of the Catholic-nationalist settlement which had come into being during the first 30 years of independence. Between 1945 and 1965, the 'emigration problem' formed the object of a vast and variegated discourse, articulated through priestly sermons and Lenten pastorals, journalist exposés and editorial letters, government reports and Dáil debates, local theatre productions and National School essay-writing competitions. Across these various forms, the desires of the emigrant functioned as a heated site of ideological struggle, as different commentators sought to enlist the 'plight of the emigrant' in support of their own interpretation of the failures of post-independent Irish society.

While some observers here presented the emigrant as a victim of incompetent governance, others framed the post-war 'crisis' as the crystallisation of a 'modern sensibility' among Ireland's increasingly restless 'youth'. This sensibility was apparent in young people's expanding consumption of modern commercial leisure, but it was most pronounced in relation to emigration itself, which performed the double function of an escape route for those desiring 'adventure or change', and a feedback loop by which the 'enjoyments of modern city life' were recirculated back into rural parishes, enticing others to the city.[10] For cultural nationalists and large sections of the clergy, these processes of cultural transfer were instinctively perceived as a threat to the racial and religious purity of the Gael. Where Irish people had been content to 'work for a living' in the past, claimed Captain Patrick Giles, mass emigration was motivated by an unsavoury desire to 'get things more easily', showing that 'our people have become more or less soft and sloppy'.[11] Emigration was a barometer, not of economic inadequacy, but of cultural degeneration, conferring upon the intending emigrant a moral and patriotic duty to resist the materialistic allure of the city:

> Tell the youth that for seven centuries brave men of every generation fought and died to uphold our God-given right to be masters of our own destiny ... Tell them that the land of Ireland is their sacred trust, and if they want to show their love for their country, if they want to show their appreciation for the sacrifices which former generations have made for the sake of freedom, let them do so by living and working in Ireland.[12]

For other commentators, however, 'the right of citizens' to 'fare forth into the new world' in order to 'better themselves' was itself a necessary condition of 'freedom'.[13] And to the extent the emigrant's decision to exercise this right signalled a new collective desire to 'chose one's own way of life', so mass emigration pointed the way forward, not to racial extinction, but to Ireland's participation in the epochal transformations of the wider post-war world.[14] For the writer and novelist Sean O'Faolain in particular, post-war Ireland was scene to the birth of an ambitious and increasingly self-confident generation no longer prepared to submit to the oppressions foisted upon their parents by a restrictive cultural conservatism:

> We are rearing generations in Ireland that have ten times more pride and ambition than their parents ever had, and good luck to them for it. As one young woman put it to me in two sentences: 'I saw what my mother went through. Not for me, thank you!'[15]

This chapter applies Nancy Green's insight that the 'attitudes and constraints surrounding departure' constitute an 'important framework' within which migrants construct the personal meanings of emigration.[16] Mass departure for England fundamentally undermined Catholic-nationalist cultural hegemony in post-war Ireland, in that public discourse on the emigrant formed a dynamic space where competing understandings of Irish selfhood could be ventilated and defined during the period. But these representations also *fed back into* the practice and experience of emigration, in that these public narratives informed and complicated individual interpretations of personal agency. Precisely because of the tensions between these representations and the emotional demands of the personal relationships implicated in departure, migrant motivations were rarely coherent or straightforward, but characterised by division and ambivalence. Personal stories of leaving thus present more than mere evidence of migrant intentionality; they are also a record of the enduring emotional impact of departure and its ongoing negotiation through remembering.

National ideals and quotidian realities: narratives of obligation and self-determination

Aboard a steamer from Liverpool to Dublin in the mid-1950s, the German writer Heinrich Böll found himself listening to a fraught exchange between a young Irish woman and a priest as he settled down to sleep on the ship's deck just after midnight:

> 'No, Father, no, no … it hurts too much to think of Ireland. Once a year I have to go there to visit my parents and my grandmother is still alive. Do you know County Galway?'

'No,' murmured the priest.
'Connemara?'
'No.'
'You should go there, and don't forget on your way back in the port of Dublin to notice what's exported from Ireland: children and priests, nuns and biscuits, whiskey and horses, beer and dogs ...'

'My child,' said the priest gently, 'you should not mention these things in the same breath.'

A match flared under the green-gray blanket, a sharp profile was visible for a second or two.

'I don't believe in God,' said the light clear voice, 'no, I don't believe in God – so why shouldn't I mention priests and whiskey, nuns and biscuits, in the same breath? I don't believe in *Kathleen ni Houlihan* either, that fairy-tale Ireland ... I was a waitress in London for two years: I've seen how many loose women ...'

'My child,' said the priest in a low voice.

'... how many loose women *Kathleen ni Houlihan* has sent to London, the isle of the saints.'

'My child!'

'That's what the priest back home used to call me too: my child ... but even he couldn't stop *Kathleen ni Houlihan* exporting her most precious possession: her children.'[17]

Observed from the deck of a ferry strewn with bodies, suitcases and 'scraps of whispered conversation', Böll's snapshot captures one of deepest contradictions structuring everyday life in mid-century Ireland. Where the achievement of independence in 1921 was celebrated as a seminal moment in the history of the nation, political sovereignty did not deliver an economic transformation. Instead, self-governance sharpened the discrepancy between an idealised Gaelic Ireland and the unsettling permutations of what Fintan O'Toole has termed the 'demographic Ireland'.[18] In the former mythic place of 'cosy homesteads' and morally pure rural communities, the Irish people were innately 'satisfied with frugal comfort', their leisure time devoted to 'things of the spirit'. In this official version of *Kathleen ni Houlihan*, a chief object of national self-realisation was the defence of an authentic rural 'tradition', secured via expulsion of the secularising impulses of the modern world. In the other 'demographic' Ireland, however, the Irish economy's dependence upon British markets constantly worked to dissolve the fantasy of cultural autonomy. Here, where limited economic horizons governed the realities of everyday life, the illusion of cosy homesteads gave way to a different landscape: the hospitals, factories and building sites of the disavowed English city.

For young Irish women in particular, this contradiction between ideal and reality could be especially acute. If official conceptions of the nation defined Ireland as a 'traditional' rural society, they also valorised the

Catholic family as its central institution. Herein, where Irish masculinity was identified with the control and management of the land, women were sanctified as mothers of the nation and guardians of the domestic sphere.[19] In practice, however, while nationalist ideology elevated the status of women's domestic roles, lived conformity to these prescriptions was always difficult to realise. Although the post-famine family was certainly predicated on a sharp separation of gender roles, social status in rural Ireland was also dependent upon continuity on the land, secured through the practices of patrilineal inheritance and late, dowered marriages for daughters. Emigration, while existing within rural culture in a number of forms, was a function of these imperatives, resolving the contradiction between high fertility rates and the impartible transfer of land.[20] Because it brought only minimal changes to the structure of the Irish economy, political independence did little to alter these practices, particularly in areas, such as the 'congested' west, where the economy of the small farmer proved especially resilient, and where migrant remittances formed an important contribution to material living standards. Particularly for the young undowered daughters of the smallest farmers, emigration thus remained a vital familial strategy in the decades after 1922, mitigating the effects of overcrowding in a context of scarce employment opportunities for women within the Irish countryside.

One kind of emotional response to this disjunction is suggested in Böll's depiction of the young female emigrant's exchange with the priest. For this young woman it 'hurts' to think of Ireland, not only because she sees her family but once a year, but because 'exportation' to England exposes the 'fairy-tale Ireland' as a deception. Thus betrayed, exposure engenders bitterness and the erosion of the moral authority of the architects of the illusion. For other migrants, however, the same disjunction could be interpreted in different ways. Brenda Grady was born in 1927 and grew up on her family's smallholding in Co. Galway, the third-born of six children. Unlike a number of other respondents who grew up in similar rural environments in this period, Brenda recalled her childhood as a particularly 'happy' phase in her life course. Although 'Ireland was poor', Brenda considered herself to be 'one of the lucky ones' because 'we had the farm and we were kind of well looked after by our parents'. Herein, while her father was described as 'more of a loving person', her mother was depicted as the source of domestic authority and the embodiment of housekeeperly prowess:

> I was one of the lucky ones that we had the farm and we were kind of well looked after by our parents but … well, my mother was quite strict, my father was more of a loving person, … good memories, they were very hard-working people, and my mother did a lot of knitting and, she'd go out and buy some material and in the morning there'd be a dress made, that was the kind of life.[21]

Nevertheless, although Brenda enjoyed growing up on her family's smallholding and admired her parents, in 1946 she departed the family home to take up employment as a child carer in Cheshire. Travelling in the immediate aftermath of the war, when wartime travel restrictions were still in operation, Brenda recalls the documentary and administrative procedures she was subject to as she crossed over:

Brenda: I leaved in 1946 and how it come about, one of my school friends had left quite a number of months before me, and she came over to Lymme in Cheshire, not far from Warrington, to a, I think she was housekeeping, and [pause] I came over to her then, and, there again now we were looking after children, coming to it we were paid, our fare was paid by the government or by the people who we were coming to work with ... we had to have passports and identity cards and a visa, and you had to stay on the job 12 months if you liked it or not, if you did leave before the 12 months you had to pay the money back, the fare, and that's how I came about coming, and then, eh, some more of the girls from the village came over, I think there was about six or seven of us, in a group.
Barry: And, did you want to go?
Brenda: Did I want to come to England?
Barry: Yeah.
Brenda: Yes I did.
Barry: You did?
Brenda: Yeah, because my oldest brother and, eh, he was sending home money, and money for himself and I sent money home, every week or every two weeks, there was money sent.[22]

Rather than linking narrative clauses in a direct and purposeful way, so as to steadily move the action forward, Brenda's experience of leave-taking is recounted through non-narrative clauses that incorporate contextual details and the stories of proximate others. Since it works to slow the pace of the narrative, this relational mode of narration supplies a vivid sense of the processual nature of leaving, offering a glimpse into the ways in which the act of departure was necessarily entangled with and contingent upon other circumstances and the actions of other people. Thus, Brenda depicts her leave-taking as part of a process of chain migration, whereby a concatenation of 'girls from the village' followed the same migratory route across to Leigh. And she recalls too how this process was facilitated and regulated by the British state, which, during the immediate post-war years, sought to encourage Irish migration via targeted recruitment schemes which directed migrants into particular occupations.

Additionally, however, as well as capturing a sense of the interdependent nature of leaving, Brenda's relational style also works to background her intentionality. Instead of an account of motivations or aspirations, the memory embodies a description of a process, the formal features of which tend to submerge the personal voice. This is reflected, not only in the repeated slippage to collective and second-person pronouns, but in the tendency to refract explanations of mobility through the intentions and needs of others. As well as the state, the presentation of whose administrative regulations intimate the strangeness and imposed character of Brenda's departure, significant others referenced in Brenda's account also include her family. Having been invited to express her personal feelings about departure directly, Brenda explains her motivations in a markedly ambivalent way: while she affirms that she did 'want to' go to England, she wanted to go so that, like her brother, she could send money home to her parents. Leave-taking is thus equated, not only with strangeness and imposition, but with the servicing of familial needs.

The deeper significance of these features of Brenda's narrative become clearer as her narrative of leaving evolves. Asked why she thought emigration was so common in Ireland at that time, Brenda explained that:

> Well there was big families, and the money, aye, the work and all, and there wasn't the money around because … didn't get wages or anything that they were like here, and if there was five or six in some families there might be 12 or 13, there wasn't room for everybody, one'd come and the others followed 'em.[23]

Instead of suggesting that people themselves desired to go, in Brenda's perspective departure is presented as something beyond the control of the individual, bound up with 'big families' and the routine practices of rural society. Reflecting an understanding of emigration as a 'familial survival strategy' deployed to reduce overcrowding, Brenda explains the causes of emigration by reference to the fact that 'there wasn't room for everybody': sons and daughters, whether they wanted to or not, had in many cases to emigrate in order to ensure continuity on the land. However, as Brenda subsequently points out, leaving was not expected of everyone:

> I think the men, they mostly worked on the farm with their father and the ones who didn't work on the farm came away to England, and the girls, sometimes they might get married off into another farmer, yeah, if the money was in the home to get them to go into the other home.[24]

'Sometimes', as Brenda states, 'if the money was in the home', 'girls' could avoid emigration through becoming the wife of a farmer, thus allowing them to remain within the home. Such an aspiration, 'to get married off into another farmer' and so embody the ideal her mother represented, was in fact harboured by Brenda herself:

> I was courting a person, a lad over there, and ah, if you got married over there, in them days you had to have money to go into another farm house, and this boy was very nice, and we liked each other, but eh, his brothers and sisters are having three hundred pounds.[25]

While Brenda had been 'courting a person' in Galway before her departure to Leigh, her desire 'to go into another farmhouse' could not be fulfilled because 'his brothers and sisters are having three hundred pounds'. Significantly, the issue of Brenda's own dowry, which reflected a daughter's 'worth' and was usually a prerequisite for marriage on the land, is omitted in her account. The reason for this would appear to be that she was not the daughter chosen to receive one:

> The other, my sister, oldest sister, she more or less was mammy's pet and she always helped her in the house and that, and I was the third one and as I said I went out to work.[26]

Being 'the third one' and so further down the sibling hierarchy, Brenda 'went out to work'. By contrast, her oldest sister, who later married on the land and so received the dowry, was afforded the opportunity to remain within the home helping her mother. As the characterisation 'mammy's pet' intimates, however, Brenda viewed her sister's privilege with some jealousy, suggesting her own preference for this role alongside her mother within the family home, a role which would have improved her chances of marrying on the land.

Set against the backdrop of these reflections on family life, Brenda's initial account of departure takes on a deeper complexion. While Brenda confirmed that she 'wanted to go' to England in order to support her family financially, such confirmation can be read as a performance of daughterly obedience. This performance enables Brenda to recall the young self as a 'good' daughter, her intentions in conformity with prescribed ideals of young femininity, but it also screens out the extent to which emigration was an externally imposed process, undertaken because 'there wasn't room for everybody'. In particular, Brenda's emphasis on daughterly obedience exists in tension with the young self's unrealised desire to marry on the land and 'go into a farmhouse', a destiny impeded due to the inequities of rural inheritance practices.

These dynamics of latent tension and retrospective negotiation come into clearer view when Brenda reflects upon the day of her leave-taking:

Barry: What sticks out in your mind about that day?
Brenda: Well erm … there again, I was just 19 and erm … came to Athenry, the 'Fields of Athenry' [laughs] I came to the … [whispering] to that station with my father and my mother and that was quite sad

to say goodbye to them ... [pause as Brenda wipes tears from her eyes and gathers herself] ... and I was met at Dublin, by some person, a man, and ... there was a lot of other girls from different parts of Ireland but I didn't know any of them and a special hotel we stayed in and we had to have a medical ... and if you were dirty or had lice or anything like that, you had to go for a bath and your clothes would be fumigated ... and all that ... before ... and in the morning, we went to the boat and I was met in Holyhead, by erm ... the people I was going to work for ... because they were in Wales at the time because it was the week of the 12 July, my brother was home from erm ... Belfast, he was living there then, and he was quite upset about me coming as well, yeah ...[27]

In 1943, following an outbreak of typhus in the west of Ireland, the British and Irish authorities established temporary embarkation regulations requiring boat passengers travelling from Ireland to England to be disinfected in Dublin prior to boarding.[28] Narrated as an accelerating stream of consciousness, Brenda's deeply autobiographical recollection of this process recalls it as a procedure of depersonalisation, occasioning disintegration of the first-person voice as she traverses the boundary between home and away, self and other. This loss of self has to do in the first instance with what is being left behind: the poignant image of Brenda, 'only 19', leaving her parents at the station evokes heartbreak at having to leave them and the family-centred world they represent. The raw emotions that seep into Brenda's narrative here, as she laughs nervously then breaks down momentarily, represent the embodied effects of the rupturing of the emotional bonds that tied her to her family, the release of suppressed resistance to leaving a world that had become deeply embedded within the self. The depersonalisation and dissolution that ensues is vividly depicted in the image of a vulnerable young Brenda arriving in Dublin on her own, only to be met by strangers, 'some person' and girls she 'didn't know', and the prospect, 'if you were dirty or had lice', of delousing and fumigation.

Brenda's narrative here summons the semantic field of exile. This is apparent in her depiction of the dehumanising embarkation process, which recalls the notorious treatment of Irish emigrants at Ellis Island, New York, during the post-famine years, and more directly in her reference to the popular ballad 'The Fields of Athenry'. Although this ballad was composed in 1979 and tells of forced departure during the famine, Brenda's reference to it, triggered by her memory of saying goodbye to her parents at Athenry station, is important because it indicates a paradigmatic association between the themes and emotions evoked in the song's lyrics and Brenda's own understanding of her experience:

By the lonely prison wall.
I heard a young girl calling
Michael they are taking you away,
For you stole Trevelyan's corn.
So the young might see the morn.
Now a prison ship lies waiting in the bay.
Low, lie the fields of Athenry,
Where once we watched the small free birds fly.
Our love was on the wing,
We had dreams and songs to sing.
It's so lonely round the fields of Athenry.[29]

For Brenda, the publicly recognised story of exile made available a legitimate subject-position and explanation through which the felt disempowerments, injustices and losses of her own personal predicament could be understood and obliquely expressed without transgressing the prohibition on the expression of individual desire embedded within dominant conceptions of the obedient daughter. Put differently, there is a degree of confluence, based on shared themes of powerlessness, stoic suffering and the glorification of victimhood, between the figure of the exile and that of the martyr that here facilitates the transformation of feelings of jealousy and anger into sadness and loss, and that in turn affords Brenda a means of disclosing these feelings. There is thus a complex strategy of composure at work: despite leaving having been a disempowering experience for Brenda, by framing this experience within the story of exile she is able to make sense of it in a way that connects it with public and shared understandings while preserving a positive memory of her parents and life growing up in rural Ireland. The recognition this affords enables a degree of composure in that the tension between emigration and the regulatory ideals of femininity, however imperfectly, can be narratively mediated, allowing a coherent understanding to be synthesised.

Other migrants, however, negotiated these contradictions in different ways. At first glance, Aileen Walsh's pre-departure biography shares important features in common with that of Brenda. Born in 1929, Aileen grew up in Co. Mayo in the west of Ireland, the fourth-born in a family of six children. Like Brenda, Aileen's childhood was spent on her family's small farm, which formed her family's chief source of income, and like Brenda, Aileen departed the family smallholding for England in the immediate post-war years, travelling, with other girls from her village, to take up employment as a chambermaid in a London hotel in 1945. However, while the timing and form of Aileen and Brenda's migration were closely matched, the ways in which they narrated their departures were strikingly different. Where Brenda accounted for her departure in terms of family needs, Aileen drew simultaneously on two different frameworks to explain her motivations. Within one version of leave-taking, departure was explained in terms of economic compulsion. Drawing on a public narrative of Irish economic stagnation, Aileen left:

> Because there was no work in Ireland, in those times. You couldn't get a job, not unless you went up to Dublin or something. Yes. And I left Ireland because I had to. And ... as I've often said, 'twas just as the war had finished.[30]

On the other hand, and more pervasively within Aileen's account, departure was also related to her experience of everyday life on the family smallholding. From early on in the interview Aileen sought to convey her unhappy memories of rural existence:

Aileen: Well it was very hard. Er ... [pauses] Er ... I didn't get on with my father.
Barry: Why not?
Aileen: Because ... (laughs) shall I say it, I was the fourth girl in the family ... and they wanted a boy. So there was two boys younger than me. Both dead now. And I wasn't [laughs] I wasn't like my older sister, definitely not. I couldn't do the things she ... 'Cos I often said to my husband, that she worked harder than many men. She was a great outdoor worker. But but put her inside and, well leave me inside and I was fine. And ... no, I'd ... my father used to say if there was two ways of doing anything, I'd always do the wrong way, and that's why I've no confidence now. Yeah. So ... erm ...
Barry: What about your mum?
Aileen: My mum was a lovely woman. But she was ... dictated to by my father. He was a bully. That's what I would say. A real bully. Yeah. Erm ... All I could say in his favour was that ... he didn't drink ... he didn't gamble, and he was a good provider. 'Cos he made out where ... another manager died. It was only a little farm.[31]

Where Brenda felt herself 'one of the lucky ones that we had the farm and were kind of well looked after by our parents', Aileen's experience of farm life was 'very hard', this being due to her fraught relationship with her father, who, despite his effectiveness as a land 'manager', was 'a real bully'. Aileen explains this conflict in terms of her failure to meet his expectations: where they had wanted a boy, they had got a girl; unlike her sister, moreover, who could perform the work of a man, Aileen proved to be an unsatisfactory substitute. Thus, on a small subsistence farm where there was a constant need for hard manual labour, not being able to fulfil this role entailed an intrinsic devaluation of Aileen's status and constant subjection to her father's critical gaze. As such, in order to insulate herself from the emotional effects of this devaluation and the transactional character of relations on the land, Aileen sought refuge 'inside', where she felt better equipped to perform a role.

Consequently, given Aileen's negative experience of farm life, so she did not aspire to emulate her mother and marry on the land. On the contrary, where Brenda's mother features as an object of admiration in her narrative, Aileen's mother, although a 'lovely woman', was 'dictated to' by her tyrannical father. In turn, where Brenda conceives of departure in terms of obligation, Aileen associates emigration with opportunity and self-determination:

Aileen: Well I was glad to leave home. Because I never saw any happiness in it. Because ... you had no money, you'd work all week, on the farm, no matter what it was: haymaking, harvesting, no matter what it was. And, you wouldn't get sixpence to go to the dance.
Barry: How did your parents feel about you coming to England?
Aileen: Well, there was nothing there for me. Because I had two brothers, younger than me, coming up behind me. And, they'd take over the farm work, you see, which they were much more suited to than what I was. Because I certainly was not suited to farm work ... And if you went to work for anybody, you might get five shillings a week, and no respect for you ... And that wasn't what I wanted either. Yeah.[32]

Aileen was 'glad to leave home' because she 'never saw any happiness in it'. In part, this was due to a lack of opportunities for leisure and self-expression: despite its arduous nature, 'relatives assisting' with farm labour were rarely remunerated for their exertions, meaning that Aileen 'wouldn't get sixpence to go to the dance'. By implication, emigration represented the possibility of a more enriching social life. More generally, Aileen regarded herself as 'not suited to farm work': in addition to being arduous and poorly remunerated, farm work offered no prospect for the development of a sense of personal self-worth. As Aileen recognised, even if she had gone to work as a domestic servant on another farm, rural gender relations were characterised by a general lack of 'respect' for female labour. Thus, given her own experiences of growing up on a farm, together with those of her subjugated mother, emigration was conceived as a means of pursuing a different form of married life, implicitly associated with greater marital intimacy and equality:

Barry: Did you want to leave Ireland?
Aileen: Did I want to leave Ireland? I did, yes, because I didn't want farm work, and I said I'd never marry a farmer. And I didn't ... My husband,

he was ... so different to my father. He was such a kind, kind man, and he adored his children.[33]

The contradiction between ideal versions of identity and material realities was thus generative of different subjective implications. For Brenda, this contradiction was a source of emotional loss, since emigration removed her from an environment in which she saw her desires reflected. But for Aileen, overcrowding and narrow employment prospects further justified and reinforced her desire to escape rural life. In large measure, what differentiated the two accounts was the differential character of intra-familial relations, the different ways in which parents cared for their children, and the impact of these relations in emotional terms. In each case, the emotional dispositions engendered via different experiences of family life shaped the formation of gendered identifications with place in divergent ways, differentiating attitudes to the world beyond the family smallholding.

These processes were also powerfully mediated through wider shifts in cultural values. What Aileen's narrative helps illustrate is how, during this period, the transactional code governing interpersonal relations within the familial system could lose purchase to alternative discourses of the individuated self. One source for this was the increasing importation and consumption of modern forms of popular culture.[34] While mid-century Ireland is often portrayed as a static and deeply conservative society, during the same period an increasing number of women were abandoning 'traditional', low-status roles within agriculture and domestic service in favour of 'modern' jobs in light industry, secretarial and white-collar work, and in retail and shop service.[35] As in other European countries, this expansion in new forms of female employment fuelled the consumption of popular film and literature, contemporary fashions and teenage dancehalls, fostering thereby the gradual incorporation of heightened expectations of personal freedom and fulfilment within vernacular understandings of femininity.

Emigration fed off this process but it also contributed to it, as representations of emigrant encounters with city life were recirculated back into rural parishes, communicated via informal transnational networks linking sending and receiving societies.[36] During the nineteenth century, these connections were forged via the transmission of emigrant letters from America, but after 1945, given the ease of travel between Britain and Ireland, returned emigrants themselves became the chief vectors of dissemination. Returning home at regular intervals, replete with stories depicting the freedoms of the English city, post-war emigrants engendered increasing awareness of the possibilities for pleasure and self-expression among peers in their home villages. In so doing, they deepened dissatisfaction with the deprivations, restrictions and inequities of rural life, projecting alternative models of individuated selfhood against which the patriarchal transactionalism of the familialist system could be negatively assessed.

These processes of transfer and exchange drew conflicting responses from contemporary observers. For conservative critics, many of whom called for restrictions to be placed on female emigration, young women's apparent rejection of rural life endangered the nation's reproductive capacity, deepening fears of racial depletion. 'There is work, plenty of work,' claimed Senator Helena Concannon in 1951, but 'there is something else, some psychological urge making the girls fly from the country, from the hard work of the farmer's wife.' As a result, 'the young men on the farms cannot get wives', meaning that 'the supply of children will soon be giving out.'[37] Similarly, a columnist for the *Tuam Herald* perceived that:

> Youth today have grown restive and difficult the world over, but here the problem is accentuated ... Of recent years the wound, we hold, has taken a turn for the worse; our girls are leaving now in ever-increasing, if not alarming numbers. Yes, potential mothers of future Church and State leaders, of men and women in all professions and walks of Irish life, are going most of them for ever. Their loss is irreparable in our day. That loss most surely leave some appalling mark on the future Ireland. If their going is not a national scourge, surely it is a sign of decadence, if not degeneration.[38]

For other commentators, however, young Irish women's rejection of rural life formed one component of a more generalised critique of the 'backwardness' of rural society.[39] According to this perspective, accelerating rates of female departure were merely symptomatic of an attitude of 'absolute disregard for women, except as child bearers and unpaid labour'. This attitude

> stains rural life in every way. It emanates from priests, from husbands, from many men with the ability and influence to lessen the boredom and drudgery of women's lot in many parts of Ireland, of which Dublin knows nothing. From this lack of consideration of their needs, the lack of companionship, the lack of status, girls go to places where they can find something better. More power to them![40]

Young women's rejection of rural subjugation and their embrace of 'something better' thus located them as emblematic of a wider post-war cultural transition, whereby young people were developing a much greater sense of 'pride and ambition than their parents'. Prominent within journals such as *The Bell* and *Dublin Opinion*, as well as the *Irish Times*, this narrative of transition expressed the political ambitions of an educated and increasingly vocal urban middle class, discontent with its cultural marginalisation within the Catholic-nationalist settlement. Aligned against the anti-modernism promulgated by cultural nationalists and religious leaders, these urban-based liberal critics were engaged in an attempt to institutionalise an alternative vision of Irish modernity centred on economic modernisation, social liberalisation and greater openness to the external world.[41] Within this discourse, conventional portrayals of the emigrant were powerfully inverted: instead of lamenting emigration as a source of national loss or impugning the emigrant's selfish motivations, many contributors to *The Bell* idealised the independent initiative and ambition of the 'new' emigrant, who rejected the limitations of a culture rendered stagnant by a regressive church and state.[42] In this way, the emigrant was fashioned as a symbol of youthful 'enterprise' and 'vigour':

> One does not wish to remain in a land of ghosts. One wants to live where people are thinking and developing, where there is movement and progress, where new ideas and ideals are being born and fought for, where there is some vision, where in a word there is a future for the young and enterprising, and a chance for the worker, whether he be a labourer or an intellectual, to play a part in shaping a better world. One does not find any of these things in Ireland today, and there does not, at the moment, seem to be any likelihood of finding them in the near future either. Most of the enterprising, the young and vigorous have gone, the less enterprising, the aging and the very young remain.[43]

This construction of the ambitious emigrant, constrained by the limitations of a regressive culture, supplied the narrative framework within which Bill Duffy reconstructed his experience leaving. Born in 1951, the eldest of four siblings, Bill grew up on his family's 50-acre mixed farm in Roscommon in the west of Ireland. After attending the local National School until the age of 13, Bill 'went straight onto the land', while his younger brother completed a vocational education until he was 16, eventually training as an electrician.[44] Thus Bill, as the eldest son, had been chosen to follow in his father's footsteps and inherit the family holding.

For Bill, however, this inheritance was not viewed in a positive light. While inheritance of the family holding had traditionally formed a masculine *rite de passage* in the west of Ireland, enabling the chosen son to achieve adult male status, during the period in question the practice began to wane. In part, this was due to the fact that heirs frequently did not take ownership of the land until well into middle age, meaning that chosen sons lived out an extended 'boyhood' of low status and few personal freedoms in the meantime.[45] At the same time, however, increasing dissatisfaction with these deprivations was also heavily mediated by the availability of alternative routes to masculine status 'across the water'.

Narratives of exit 51

1 Till, 'Wisha, Michilin Pat, you're not the same at all since you emigrated to London', *Dublin Opinion*, December 1954 (Dublin City Archives).

As the report of the 1954 Commission on Emigration observed, although 'a lack of opportunities for employment' represented one major cause of increases in emigration, an enhanced 'desire for improved material standards' represented another, this being a function of 'a widespread awareness of the existence of opportunities abroad and a realisation of differences between conditions at home and in other countries'.[46] Herein, 'the reports of emigrants who returned well dressed and with an air of prosperity' played an important role in reshaping rural perceptions of departure.[47] As the journalist John Healy recalled in 1967, where seasonal migrants were once considered 'an inferior breed' in his native Charlestown, during wartime, when British industrial mobilisation created rising demand for Irish labour, the spectacle of the wealthy returnee recast the male emigrant as a local hero:

> He came home at Christmas dressed to the nines, his style paid, Windsor-knotted in the latest spiv fashion and his wallet full of notes. He was a success. The good rearing. A credit to his mother and father. Yes, the money was good, he admitted. And yes, it could be tough. The tough bit was admitted. It was the male ego, a manifestation of the hero of the day and was in the best Jimmy Cagney style.[48]

Bill's assessment of his own experiences growing up in Roscommon powerfully reflected these changing perceptions of rural life. Where official conceptions of national identity valorised physically arduous 'work on the land' as the essence of Irish manhood, in Bill's narrative farm work is equated with exploitation and backwardness, constraining the young self's desire for play and competitive endeavour:

> Everything was so manual, you didn't have any tractors, you had a donkey and cart and that was it. Every ... everything was done by, you know, by hand, and you know, it was hard work, very, very hard work ... It wasn't enjoyable. It was necessity [laughs], you know. Work had to be done, and ... When you're thirteen, fourteen, fifteen, you want to be out playing football and doing that type of thing.[49]

In Bill's view, the burdens imposed by the difficult nature of farm work were not shared equally among all members of the family. He emphasised that, 'as far as the farming was concerned, if you were the eldest you did most of the work and the milking.'[50] In Bill's case this distribution of responsibility turned out to be particularly burdensome, partly because Bill's father typically spent six months of the year in England working, but also because his father's drinking habits, when he was at home, often meant Bill was left to do all the work on his own: 'I didn't have good memories ... of, you know, even when my father and mother was there, that my father would go out on the beer, and ... day drinking 'til ... ten, twelve, one o'clock in the morning.'[51] Perhaps for these reasons, Bill began to recognise his own ambitions through the masculine image of material success projected by different 'forefathers', men who had 'gone to England' and 'done very well':

> You know ... all you'd seen was your forefathers and your uncles and all that, they'd gone to England, and had made living, and you'd see them

come back on holidays, and other people coming back on holidays and … and doing well, and other people, you know, not doing so well, but lots of them doing very, very well, coming back on holidays and you'd see big cars with them, and well dressed and plenty of money, which I hadn't.[52]

Recalling the image of style and success projected by holidaying forefathers, Bill realised that 'if I worked … as hard as I worked on the farm, I'd make a living, and that's exactly what … you know, what I did'. As such, Bill left for Manchester to take a job in the construction industry in January 1967, aged 16. Bill's narration of this event and those immediately preceding it reveals a distinct form of composure at work in his narrative of leaving:

Well, the days before I left … was … my father had come over from England, home, and we were cleaning out some barns, for to put the cattle in over the winter, was alright, the weather was alright. But, in the … in the barns, from the year before, the … straw and all that was in the barns was gone hard, it was … well you had … that had to be cleaned right down to the bottom. And the only way you could clean that was with the shovel, to cut it all the way round, and throw it out into the cart, and take it away. Myself and my father … he came back as I said about … December the tenth, twelfth, whatever it was, and was about fifteenth or sixteenth of December he says to me, 'We'll clean out that barn today.' I say, 'Sound.' So we went out the two of us and … and he says, 'Now here … look here young fella', he says, 'There's no place for me … me or you here. One of us will have to go. Either you … or I'll go.' And, er … well, 'There's no place for the two of us here.' So I said nothing, and he said, 'Sound, sound.' So … when my mates came back from England, er … at Christmas they came back maybe four, five days before Christmas, I said to them, they took me to the dances and … which was, you know … we weren't sent to the dances, I wouldn't go to the dances that much. But anyway, went out with them and … they were home and they had a … a Mini, you know. A young lad and er … er, plenty of money, and well dressed, suits and all. Anyway. Went to the, what do you call it? And one of them said to me, 'Why don't you come to England with us, when we're going back?' And I says, 'Jeez, I might!' I says. So anyway, that was two or three days, so … on Boxing Night … as they call it, St Stephen's Night, as they call it down in the … west of Ireland, the boys … We went out and … I came back, and my father was obviously out in the pub, and … came back and the two of them was in bed, my father and mother, the Lord have mercy on them. They're dead now. And … I went up to the room and I says, 'Look it. On the seventh of January, I'm going to England.' This was, as I said, three o'clock, two, three o'clock in the morning, 'with … John and Micky Kelso'. My father says, 'Go on down to bed!' he says, 'I'll talk to you in the morning!' Anyway, got up in the morning, and ... he says, er, 'Now then', he says, 'what are you on about?' I says, 'I'm going to England on the seventh.' He says, 'Are you?' 'Yep.' So ... my mother was there, crying, and, and ... yeah, I says, 'Yes, I'm ... I'm going with them on the seventh.' 'Well you've no suit, you'll have to come ... and, and ... clothes.' So I went and cycled, nine mile to Castlerea, which was the ... local, well ... was the postal address town ... and, to get a suit. And er, clothes, and packed everything in the case, and headed on the seventh for Manchester.[53]

Set as the old year gives way to the new, at one level this story is about the transitions from boyhood to manhood, farm labourer to 'modern' worker, where the constraints implied by the former status are overcome, enabling Bill to pursue his personal ambitions. In the first stage of the narrative, set in the outhouses of the family farm which, it may be suggested, symbolise tradition, continuity and Bill's filial duties, Bill is positioned in the subordinate and dependent role of son and farm hand. The action in the scene is controlled by Bill's father, who determines when the barn will be cleaned and who confronts Bill with an ultimatum: 'one of us will have to go'. At this stage in the narrative, Bill does not articulate his desire to leave (though this is implied in the description of the old barn straw, which is suggestive of Bill's sense of his life on the farm as having gone stale and in need of change). One reading of Bill's silence here is that Bill's father's ultimatum conflicts with his need to authorise his own destiny: leaving because your father permits you is not the same as staking your own claim. Alternatively, Bill wants to avoid being characterised as an irresponsible son, who abandons his family the first chance he gets. A third possibility is that Bill, while obviously considering the possibility, has not yet fully made up his mind.

Whatever the case, the scene ends with convention and order intact. However, in the next stage of the narrative this order is disrupted with the return of Bill's friends from England. Symbolising in their appearance ('plenty of money, and well dressed, suits and all') affluence, independence and style, their return activates Bill's desire to leave and moves the action forward, culminating in the drama of Bill's Boxing Night declaration of his intention to leave. The pivotal act of self-assertion in the narrative, this marks the moment when Bill transcends the constraints of the old order and stakes his claim to autonomy: 'I went up to the room and I says, "Look it. On the seventh of January, I'm going to England."' Bill having been ordered to bed by his father, a note of suspense is introduced as the action is held in abeyance until the scheduled reopening of the issue the following morning. The final stage of the narrative resolves this tension as Bill's bid is upheld. Under questioning by his father Bill reasserts his determination to go and his father acquiesces, giving him money for the journey and buying him 'a suit'. This finalises Bill's overcoming of the imposed constraints of life in rural Ireland and his transition from son of a farmer to 'man of the world'.

Bill's leaving narrative is thus similar to Aileen's account in a number of important respects. Where Brenda's narrative expresses a sense of reluctance in relation to departure, for both Bill and Aileen leaving is presented as a personal choice, motivated by a rejection of the constraints of rural life and a desire for self-realisation. In this regard, in order to formulate a coherent understanding of one's desires for leaving, both situate their experiences within a wider liberal narrative of aspirational emigration. This narrative supplies a means of interpreting the tensions and deprivations of their early lives as obstacles they have surmounted to become the people they are. Departure for both Aileen and Bill thus represents a moment of liberation and self-authorship, when they take charge of their personal destiny.

Nevertheless, while the versions of self constructed within Aileen's and Bill's leaving narratives are both defined against the limitations of rural life, this oppositionality articulates in subtly different ways in each account. While both predicate leaving on a rejection of the hardships of farm labour and difficult filial relationships, the forms of identity aspired to through leaving express distinctive sets of values. For Aileen, departure is identified with the pursuit of a modern form of domesticity, associated with greater marital intimacy and equality; for Bill, it is identified with the achievement of wealth and personal success within the sphere of work. Thus, while both Bill and Aileen locate their experiences within a common liberal framework, they adapt this framework in ways that reflect the differentiated subjective effects of the gendered organisation of rural life. Despite Bill's and Aileen's rejection of rural life, therefore, departure does not represent a complete severance of old from new: rather, conventional understandings of gendered selfhood are recalibrated through the process of emigration.

The stigma of desertion: narratives of guilt and shame

Given this recalibration, it is important to emphasise the negotiated character of these narratives of self-realisation. In Bill's case in particular, while his leaving narrative portrays the rejection of one sort of identity for another, this process does not occur without reference to his father. Although Bill's father embodies the constraints he wishes to transgress, his father's facilitation of his departure ultimately relieves him of the obligations of the filial relationship and recognises his right, as an autonomous agent, to choose his own future. Bill's father's supportive actions, in other words, help mediate the oedipal conflict implied by

Bill's rejection of the 'honour' of inheritance, allowing him to remember leaving as both the expression of his own desire and as conforming to his father's wishes. In this way, the problem of guilt is contained and a form of equilibrium achieved: as well as being about the assertion of a new identity, leaving is also an occasion of reconciliation, a *rite de passage* that involves a working-through of the oedipal drama.

Reconciled or not, however, these negotiated aspects of Bill's departure story allude to a further way of understanding emigration within Irish culture: leaving as abandonment. While emigration was a structural feature of rural society, its resilience was always closely tied to the realisation of familial needs. Where, however, departure involved the subversion of familial norms rather than their confirmation, emigration could also be conceived as a selfish act. As Kerby Miller here observes, an important function of the exile myth within post-famine rural society was to mask the extent to which departure was motivated by self-interested desires in conflict with dominant notions of familial duty.[54] In normalising emigration as a passive, unwilled activity, therefore, exile simultaneously inscribed 'wilful' departure as morally suspect, establishing thereby the basis for a more stigmatising construction: the ungrateful and disloyal emigrant who, lacking the moral and physical strength to remain on the land, departs without regard for family or national needs. Hence, in the midst of political struggle with Britain, Patrick Pearse portrayed ongoing departure as 'desertion', condemning the emigrant as 'a traitor to the Irish state' and 'a fool into the bargain'.[55]

After 1922, this trope of desertion was exploited in a variety of ways by conservative critics of emigration. In one formulation, desertion was employed to displace culpability for continuing emigration onto the emigrant, typically as a defensive response to criticism alleging the incoherence of nationalist imperatives. 'Not a week passes', claimed Bernard Butler, Fianna Fail TD for Dublin Townships, 'in which I do not find people ready to leave quite good situations in this country, apparently out of a spirit of adventure.'[56] Mass departure was thus not 'compelled'; it reflected, rather, the self-serving and illogical motivations of the emigrants themselves. Speaking in reference to a 1951 Christian Workers report alleging that Irish workers were subject to 'appalling' living conditions in overcrowded English cities, Taoiseach de Valera questioned the rationality and patriotism of emigrants prepared to endure conditions of 'absolute degradation' damaging to both themselves and 'the prestige of the Irish people'. 'Not only', claimed de Valera,

> do they fail to improve their own circumstances by going abroad, but they leave enterprises for the development of our own national resources without sufficient labour to enable progress to be made as rapidly as we would all desire … The saddest part of all this is that work

is available at home, and in conditions infinitely better from the point of view of both health and morals.[57]

De Valera's suggestion that sufficient work was 'available at home' was difficult to sustain, and his comments drew criticism within the national and local press.[58] Nevertheless, the comments did stir public consciousness, engendering a heated debate in which emigrants' 'degradation' in England served as a measure of their moral debasement and a means of projecting wider fears concerning the cultural implications of mass departure.[59] Not only, claimed the Rev. Dr Durig, did Irish settlement in English cities expose Irish 'boys and girls' to the threat of 'infection from paganism and materialism';[60] mass departure signalled the rejection of traditional rural culture more generally, revealing the contamination and debasement of the Irish racial character. According to Captain Patrick Giles, where people had been 'content' to endure the hardships of rural life in the past, furnishing them with 'well-developed bodies with plenty of muscle, brawn and sinew from hard work', 'emigration and the flowing in of money here from emigrants has made our people slack and soft'.[61] The logical terminus of this physical and moral weakening was the collapse of marriage on the land, and with it 'the vanishing' of 'the Irish nation itself':

> For the rural families are the well-springs from which the towns and cities replenish themselves, and if they are drying up, then inevitably we are doomed to wither as a nation. Aught else it is foolish to hope for and absurd to expect.[62]

In response, in an effort to shore up the boundaries of the Catholic-nationalist nation and inhibit the progress of secularisation among emigrants, the Catholic Church endeavoured to intervene in the practice and conduct of departure. As well as lobbying the government to impose restrictions on particular groups, this regulatory agenda was pursued via the sustained attempt to influence the perceptions of intending emigrants and their parents, a process facilitated by the development, from 1940, of a network of Catholic organisations specifically tailored to the problem of emigrant welfare.[63] From the pulpit and in Lenten pastorals, within local newspapers and emigrant advice literature, priests and bishops sought to constitute the decision to leave as a deeply *moral decision*, entailing serious moral implications. These referred to the welfare of the emigrant's own soul, which was endangered by exposure to the lurid attractions of the city, but also to the welfare of emigrants' parents, village and national community. As late as 1965, Fr R. L. Stevenson continued to rail against the 'top-heavy, out-of-proportion flight from the country of birth'.[64] While 'real economic necessity' was a 'valid' reason for leaving, Stevenson suspected that 'the greater percentage must prove comparatively trivial'.[65] Indeed, in most cases the problem of 'dire need' could 'be solved at home, given the determination and the will to work with enthusiasm and diligence':

> Too often however, contrary to the Christian tradition that all work is noble, there is a background of false pride which labels certain jobs as 'menial', because they entail beginning at the bottom of the ladder.[66]

As Stevenson fumed, such pride was not only mistaken; it amounted to a gross betrayal of God as well as one's parental and national family:

> It was there God gave you life; good, loving parents and a Christian home. There you were surrounded by kindness and consideration, much of which stemmed from the self-sacrifice of your parents ... both your family and the people of Ireland spent thousands of pounds on your housing and clothing, your education and health, and that over a period of seventeen or eighteen years. I don't suppose there is any likelihood of you ever being in a position to repay that debt, even in part. Have you ever thought of putting anything into the town where you claim there is nothing?[67]

This construction of the selfish and ungrateful emigrant played a complex role in shaping the leaving narrative of Paul Quinn. Born in 1938, Paul grew up in rural Galway on his family's smallholding, the eldest son among four siblings. Following attendance at the local National School until the age of 13, like Bill Paul began full time work on the land, combining this with intermittent employment as a local construction worker. However, unlike Bill, Paul recalled this period in his life in highly positive terms. Where Bill 'didn't have good memories' of farm work, Paul's account emphasised the virtues of a simple rural existence where 'work on the land' provided for both basic material needs and deeper spiritual enrichment. While there was 'no good living at them stages', Paul's family were 'definitely never hungry either, like' due to the produce yielded from the soil.[68] And although there 'wasn't much money', farm work supplied unparalleled access to a sense of the oceanic:

Barry: Did you like working on the land?
Paul: Loved it. Loved it. If I could have made a living I'd love to do it even now.
Barry: And what about the building then?
Paul: Liked that as well. When I was getting a few bob. I was getting paid for that. You wouldn't get much money in that, like, but ... You had to eat though, hadn't you?

Barry: You did, yeah. So there wasn't much money obviously involved at that time ...?
Paul: There wasn't. There was very little money. Very little money. Good times though. Good times. Not bad times.
Barry: What were the best things about that sort of work?
Paul: The freedom. Like the bird. You were like the bird. You were free. You were free to roam the fields, and the mountains.[69]

For Bill, farm work was 'not enjoyable'. On the contrary, within his representation of rural life work on the farm was identified with exploitation, backwardness and the limitation of personal desire. By sharp contrast, Paul's account of rural life affirms work on the land as an abiding source of personal selfhood. In this regard, where Bill's narrative of rural existence was framed by a wider liberal critique of the regressive and restrictive character of Irish rural culture, Paul's narrative expressed an identification with an opposing 'traditional' code of rural masculinity. Constructed against an image of the modern industrial worker, this discourse rooted the authenticity of Irish manhood in physical and spiritual closeness to the land, pitting the frugality, self-sufficiency and hard labour of the ideal peasant farmer against the morally corrupting comforts of modern materialism.[70]

Nevertheless, although Paul's narrative embodies an implicit devaluation of modern work, like Bill he leaves for Manchester in 1962, travelling with a friend who has returned home on holiday. In his account of this process, departure is framed in two conflicting ways. Within one version, emigration was a product of economic necessity, rather than a personal aspiration. As Paul states above, he would 'love' to work on the land 'even now', if, back when he was a young man, he 'could have made a living'. The same inability to 'make a living' compelled mass departure more generally in these years:

Paul: A lot of people were emigrating to England, and some to America as well, like. Odd ones to Canada or Australia, but ... but mostly England, like, you know. Some were ... might be going to the cities as well, going to Galway city or Dublin. They were all leaving them smaller places, like.
Barry: Why do you think that was happening? Why was there so many moving away?
Paul: Well there was nothing for them. There was no money, no jobs for them. And there wasn't a big future on the land, like, you know. Happy enough on it, but you never had much money in your pocket.[71]

However, while Paul initially sought to frame departure within a wider narrative of economic compulsion, in a subsequent narrative focused on the personal circumstances of leave-taking he reveals that he 'could have got a job in Galway at the time':

Barry: When did you leave and how did that come about, when you were 23?
Paul: [extended pause] Well I don't know really now. I just took it in the head, and I went off with some fella here and ... set up in Manchester, in Moss Side [pause] for no particular reason, only maybe to get a job, I don't know. Although I [pause] I could have got a job in Galway at the time, in Galway city, but ... There was people going in from ... into Galway at the time.
Barry: What do you think made you want to go?
Paul: [extended pause] Maybe to see a bit of the world or [pauses] to see the things that are supposed to be very good in other places. The grass is always greener on the other side of the fence.
Barry: That's right. Who was the friend that you went over with?
Paul: I can't even think of his name now! I come over with him. He was on holidays, and I went with him.
Barry: He came back for his holidays?
Paul: Yeah. And then ...
Barry: And then you went back with him.
Paul: Yeah. Went down, landed in Moss Side.[72]

Paul's narrative of rural belonging articulated an explicit preference for a version of masculine identity defined in terms of closeness to the land. As such, given this preference, Paul initially, and logically, explains departure as involuntary. Paul's recollection, however, that employment was available in Galway threatens the coherence of this initial account of leave-taking. Alert to this, Paul endeavours to locate an alternative subject-position by which to mediate the tension between the image of rural masculinity he wishes to project and the latent implication that departure embodied a voluntary rejection of Irish culture in favour of the corrupting 'allurements' of modern well-paid work. The fraught character of this renegotiation is suggested, not only by the hesitations and extended pauses which punctuate Paul's narration, but by the reluctant and ambiguous portrayal of the outlook of the younger self. Where Bill's epic narrative of leaving works to validate the younger self's desires for economic betterment and personal self-fulfilment, Paul's narrative embodies an attempt to distance the perspective of the present from the intentions and motivations of the past self. Hence, the perceptions, impulses and calculations of the younger Paul are characterised as unknowable, incomprehensible and, in the end, naïve: the younger self leaves 'for no particular reason', with a friend whose identity cannot be recalled, in order 'maybe' to see 'the things that are supposed to be very good in other places'.

As Paul's account of leaving evolves, the deeper reasons for these features of his narrative become more apparent:

Barry: So what about your parents then? What did they say about you going?
Paul: [pause] Well I think they weren't that happy that I went, but I suppose like every parents, you do what you have to do. [extended pause] Yep [sigh, voice trails off]
Barry: Did they want you to stay on the farm, did they?
Paul: Well I think they did really, yeah. Yeah, yeah, yeah. [extended silence]
Barry: Erm, do you remember the day you ... the day you left?
Paul: I don't really, no. [voice quietens] It was March I think. Early in March.
Barry: Erm, at that time did you think you'd be coming back?
Paul: [pause] Well, when you're young you don't give it much thought, do you?
Barry: You just weren't thinking about it at all?
Paul: No. [extended pause] But funnily enough, the first or second time I ever went home on holidays, I was offered two jobs, and I didn't take them, like, funny enough. But good God, two of the damn things! I suppose I thought I'd make a lot of, a fortune here and ... [trails off]⁷³

Paul's narrative of leaving embodies an internal struggle between two conflicting forms of desire and identification. On the one side, love for and loyalty to his parents and the rural life which they represent. On the other, a personal desire for wealth and adventure, identified with the debased English city. Back in 1962, Paul elected to pursue the latter desire. This was despite multiple employment opportunities in Galway, and against the wishes of his parents, who wanted him to stay and work the family holding.

Consequently, for Paul, departure is implicitly viewed as an act of abandonment, reflection upon which evokes an unresolved sense of guilt. The nostalgia, evasions and inconsistencies of Paul's account are here symptomatic of his efforts, conscious and unconscious, to limit the destructive impact of this guilt upon a deeply internalised image of the self as a loyal son and authentic rural Irishman. Memory production is thus structured by a concern to insulate and preserve this self-image via the disavowal of the 'selfish' aspirations of the younger self. Initially, this process is manifest in Paul's framing of emigration within the public narrative of economic necessity, which backgrounds and submerges the personal motivations for departure. Ultimately, however, once the concept of necessity becomes untenable, disavowal takes the form of splitting past and present selves. By rendering the actions of the past self separate, foreign and irrational, the present self can disclaim ownership of the decision to leave. As Paul puts it: 'when you're young you don't give it much thought'.

However, while this strategy enables the destabilising emotional consequences of departure to be deflected to some degree, by identifying the stigma of desertion with the incomprehensible actions of the younger self the aspirations and ambitions which motivated leaving are inherently devalued. Different parts of the self are segregated, with the result that important forms of experience and desire cannot easily be acknowledged or admitted into the story of one's life. The risk is that, in seeking to preserve one image of self, one of the most important decisions of one's life, the decision to leave, comes to be regarded as a mistake, implying the devaluation of all subsequent experience stemming from that decision

In the final leaving story of this chapter, such processes of disavowal and splitting exercised a similar, if more pronounced, influence over how departure could be remembered. The circumstances of Rosie Long's childhood were in important respects different from those of any of the respondents considered thus far. Born in 1938 and leaving for London in 1954, Rosie grew up in a decaying tenement building in inner-city Cork, the third of six children in a 'very, very poor family'.[74] Such were the conditions of this existence that 'we lost two babies, Patrick and Kathleen, through bad chests' when Rosie was still very young. Nor did things improve with time. While her mother was pregnant with her youngest brother Pat, Rosie's father, an 'obnoxious, horrible man', 'went to England. Left us in other words'. Not only did this leave the family financially dependent upon a weekly 15 shillings benefit and whatever provision was available through local charities such as the Society of St Vincent de Paul; it also conferred upon the family a 'stigma ... about your dad going to England, and a mother who was on her own'.[75]

These circumstances affected the development of Rosie's sense of self in two particular ways. On the one hand, given her family's impoverishment, the Catholic Church formed a vital source of welfare during her childhood. To a much greater extent than the rural narratives of childhood considered hitherto, Rosie's memories of growing up are structured around interactions with religious institutions. Within these environments, religious authority figures are portrayed simultaneously as sources of care and moral condemnation, associated with kindness and shame:

> I was awfully embarrassed, going to school, 'cos I wasn't dressed like the other kids ... But ... most of the nuns kinda liked me, but ... I can ... I mean, it also brings me back to the fact that, erm ... it was all church,

church, priests, nuns. We were led and said by 'em, but they weren't great to the very poor people, I'll tell you that now.[76]

On the other hand, Rosie's father's abandonment of the family also accentuated the intensity of her relationship with her mother:

> The one thing I do remember is, you know we were so poor and hungry and that ... I remember being happy. My mum was just such a lovely lady, and she was a lovely singer, and she's actually passed it on to us – I used to be a pretty good singer until I got my asthma but my daughter is a lovely singer now, and she's also called Rose.[77]

When Rosie's father left, the oldest members of the family were called upon to support their mother in a variety of ways in order to ensure survival. For Rosie this took the form of domestic labour within the home alongside her mother, particularly following her older sister Anne's detention in an Industrial School for stealing when Rosie was 6 years old. One result of this close contact was the development of an especially tender affective bond between mother and daughter, reflected in Rosie's narrative in a recurrent refracting of her own self through images of her mother, blurring the distinction between them. As in the above extract, in which a gift of voice is passed twice from mother to daughter, this intersubjective relation features ubiquitously as a source of cherished personal qualities, idealised in the mother and incorporated into the self.

At other moments, however, the demands associated with the auxiliary role the young Rosie has been assigned also appear as unconscious sources of frustration, even as the successful performance of this role affords her a powerful form of social recognition. Although Rosie repeatedly emphasises how much she enjoyed helping her mother, when her mother finds a job at the School for the Industrious Blind, shortly after her sister Anne has been sent to the Industrial School, her responsibilities at home increase, and signs of strain begin to creep into her depiction of her domestic role:

> So she got a job there, cleaning, which meant I had to look after my brother Pat. I had to do all the work in the house, and ... and I did it, I did it. I remember we had the old washboards and a bar of soap, and my knuckles used to be red raw from the scrubbing, you know. But I used to peg lines of washing out, and I remember one ... one neighbour said, 'Oh, God, I wish I had a daughter like you that would do some work like that for me!' like, you know. So, I didn't mind doing that. I didn't feel resentful at all. I just felt that, you know, I could do it![78]

In ideal constructions of the Irish Catholic family, housekeeperly prowess is conventionally defined as a source of feminine virtue. In Rosie's account, however, representations of domestic routines are repeatedly shot through with ambivalence. From one perspective, Rosie's assigned role supplied an opportunity to support her mother and family: as Rosie's ventriloquisation of the neighbour's perspective suggests, the performance of this supporting role invited recognition as a 'good daughter', a self-image from which Rosie derives a sense of value. On the other hand, however, her insistence that she 'didn't feel resentful' summons, paradoxically, an opposing narrative of subjugated femininity. Against Rosie's claim that she 'didn't mind' her role within the home, her depiction of her knuckles 'red raw from the scrubbing' conveys a visceral image of domestic enslavement, intimating an unarticulated desire to escape the drudgery of her situation.

As Rosie's narrative of childhood progresses, the tension between these opposing images of self becomes increasingly pronounced. Leaving school in particular here formed an important turning point within Rosie's narrative of growing up, in relation to which she became increasingly conscious of the limitations of her situation:

Rosie: Anyway, when it come time for me to leave school, I didn't want to leave. I really didn't want to leave. And the nun said, 'Would you ask your, your mam to come in and see me?' And, er, my mam was so shy, she said, 'Oh I can't do that!' I said, 'Do mum. She just wants to … have a word with you.' So, anyway, what she wanted to say was, was it possible that I could stay on 'til I was sixteen? And my mam said, 'No. No, we need the money. No, she has … she has to get a job, we need the money. We can't afford it.'
Barry: How did you feel about that?
Rosie: [sighs] Oh, again, I was … I was devastated, and there were all my friends staying on, who I'd got to know. And it began to dawn on me that I was getting to be pretty worthless, 'cos, erm …
Barry: In what … what way?
Rosie: In every way, in every way. I w … I began to, erm, I didn't notice throughout my childhood I was, I was very shy. But that … I suppose a lot of people can be shy without, you know … Erm … I just felt, 'Why me?' like, you know, 'Why can't I stay on at school?' and, and that … I should've known, but as a kid you don't. So, no sooner said than done, the nuns actually got me a job in the hospital in Cork, it's a private hospital, still there. And I more or less finished school on the Friday and I started work on the Monday … and the work I was doing, obviously, was down on my hands and knees scrubbing floors, which I didn't mind. Didn't mind it a bit, 'cos I was quite good at cleaning.[79]

Rosie's family's impoverishment imposed a range of constraints upon her personal development when growing up. In addition here to the domestic labour Rosie was expected to perform, Rosie was prevented from completing her schooling due to her family's need for additional income, something which 'devastated' the young Rosie. In response, the imposition of these constraints only intensified Rosie's desire for greater personal freedom; but the repeated thwarting of this desire simultaneously engendered a sense of personal worthlessness: as Rosie put it, 'it began to dawn on me that I was getting to be pretty worthless'.

What made these processes so powerful in Rosie's case was her emotionally complex relationship with her mother. Given Rosie's auxiliary role with the home, one effect of material deprivation was that Rosie was emotionally dependent upon her mother for her own sense of self: while Rosie may have aspired to a life beyond the home, her performance of the roles of surrogate mother and housekeeper shaped an earlier understanding of herself as a 'good daughter', from which she drew a fragile sense of self-worth. At the same time, however, Rosie's mother was also heavily dependent upon her, such that Rosie developed a deep-seated sense of personal responsibility for her mother's welfare and that of her family more generally. This sense of responsibility, together with the need to retain her mother's recognition, rendered self-assertion emotionally costly. Hence Rosie's compliance with the constraints of her role, and once again, the partial sublimation of her personal desires into an image of sacrificial femininity: 'the work I was doing, obviously, was down on my hands and knees scrubbing floors, which I didn't mind. Didn't mind it a bit, 'cos I was quite good at cleaning.'

Rosie's departure for London two years later with her sister Anne represented an attempt to break this pattern of constraint and self-abnegation. However, as her account of this process demonstrates, the emotional legacies of her childhood continued to exercise a powerful influence over how leave-taking was experienced. Where the pursuit of personal self-fulfilment forms a positive source of identity in Bill's and Aileen's narratives of departure, Rosie's narrative of leaving embodies a faltering and convoluted attempt to justify the decision to leave, in an effort to manage the emotional consequences of severing the mother–daughter relationship.

Set over two years, between the ages of 14 and 16, in the first version of this leaving story Rosie constructs an elaborate, fairy-tale-like narrative organised in three successive phases. In the first phase, presented as a period of improvement and harmony in the fortunes of Rosie's family, Rosie recalls her joy at the return of her brother John-Joe from Industrial School and the benefits this brought to the family income when he got a job as a messenger boy. As Rosie put it, 'we were all getting on our feet': 'We were a happy group!'[80] This period of stability and harmony was not to last, however. The second phase of Rosie's leaving narrative concerns the return of her father, who has come into money in England, and the implications his reinstatement within the family home has for the continuity of the 'happy group'. Having only moments ago constructed the return of her brother in idealised terms, Rosie now switches to venting emotions of hate as she recalls her first sighting of her returned father:

> I was coming uphill pushing my bike, and I could see my mum up at the top of the hill, and, I knew … I kinda knew him on sight, and I hated him on sight. I hated him! Still do.[81]

Despite his new-found wealth, Rosie opposed her father's efforts to ingratiate himself with the family: 'We didn't need him, we were all getting on our feet.'[82] Whether he was needed or not, however, Rosie's father stayed. And although Rosie, thanks to a live-in job at a local hospital, was largely autonomous of him, his reinstatement within the family home altered familial dynamics in important ways. Firstly, Rosie saw less and less of her mother. In part, this was because, as Rosie states, 'I didn't want to go home. I didn't want to go home, I … the only reason I went home was to see my mum.'[83] At the same time, however, her father restricted her mother's mobility:

> She didn't kind of go out a lot, 'cos you see, when he wasn't there, we could please ourselves like, if we wanted to go to the pictures, and if we could have afforded it … But she didn't seem to be doing that now he was home. Things like should have been getting better for her, with him having a few bob. But … leopards don't change their spots.[84]

Rosie's father's 'spots' were fully exposed when, having come home drunk one night, he beat her younger brother Pat 'black and blue' with a belt buckle. Such was the degree of his injuries that 'the police had to be involved', resulting in Pat being 'put away for his own safety, into the Industrial School.'[85] While this event confirms Rosie's assessment of her father within the narrative, justifying her autonomous stance and avoidance of the family home, it also meant that, as Rosie states, 'my brother couldn't go home at his confirmation, 'cos my father was there.'[86] Thus, Rosie, together with her older brother and sister, take Pat out for the day after his confirmation. Then, having described the details of the day out, Rosie reveals that she has left her job at the hospital, an event she seems to suggest was immediately temporally antecedent to her leaving for England:

> We got to Blarney, had a fantastic day, and took my brother back into the school before evening. And … because they would … because they didn't want to let me out for my brother's confirmation, in the Home, I says, 'Well I'm very sorry', I said, 'I'm going to my brother's

confirmation.' And I said, 'If I can't have the day off, I'll have to leave!' So I left. That was major! Wherever it came from I don't know, but that was major!⁸⁷

Because it was so 'important' for Rosie 'to be there' for her brother given 'the other fuckin' bastard wouldn't have been there', she is forced to leave her job: family is prioritised over self-interest, justifying the decision to leave (her job).

This leaves the way open for the action of the third phase, initiated by the phrase 'so then', in which Rosie's sister Anne returns from London. After mesmerising Rosie with stories about 'all these dancehalls, and glamour', she asks her to come over: 'why don't you come over?'. Since Rosie had 'already been working two years', she had her National Insurance number, and with no other reason to decline apparent, Rosie, in a deeply resonant phrase, 'succumbed to temptation'.⁸⁸

On closer inspection, revealing inconsistencies are apparent in Rosie's presentation of this third phase. The phrase 'so then' seems to imply that Anne's return coincides with Rosie leaving her job, which in turn coincides with Rosie going to England: these three events are run together, giving an impression of linear temporal coincidence. However, as Rosie realises, in order to receive a National Insurance number she needed to be 16, and she was only 14 when she left her job at the hospital. Thus, when Rosie reveals that she'd 'already been working two years', it becomes apparent that two years, in which Rosie had been working, have elapsed between her leaving her job at the hospital and departing for England, thereby undermining any suggestion of a causal link between the two events. This in turn prompts questions about the role of Rosie's sister in her narrative of leaving. Initially, Rosie seems to suggest her sister's question 'why don't you come over?' was asked at the time when she had lost her job, when she was 14, given the word 'until' in the sentence immediately subsequent: 'well I couldn't go over 'till I was sixteen'. However, the sentence immediately following seems to bring Rosie into contradiction: 'and I'd already been working two years'. Rosie could not have been 14 and have already worked two years when her sister asks the question which 'tempted' her into going to England.

What do these inconsistencies signify? And why does Rosie's narrative of leaving compress time in such a way that two years are effectively excluded from her story? Partial answers to these questions begin to emerge later in the interview when Rosie reveals that during the two years in question she has been working in the Institute for the Industrious Blind, her mother, who also worked there, having found her a position that afforded her accommodation in addition to a 'fantastic' 30-shilling-a-week wage. Thus, not only was a lack of employment not a factor in Rosie's emigration, but she was also able, despite her father's return, to see her mother on a daily basis. Rosie then tells a very different story regarding events immediately preceding leaving for England:

> [T]he night I was leaving they were all giving me cards, I even got references from the matron of the Blind Asylum, they used to call it. Way with words, you know, they used to call the mental hospital 'the mad house'. They have a way with words in Cork. And [coughs] I remember cycling home on my bike and there was a part in Cork city by the bus station, still the same place, and when the tide comes in, the water's almost level ... with the thing ... and it almost crossed my mind to cycle straight into the River Lee. I felt that bad about things. 'Cos, things had really started to get normal for me, and I began to feel, I never, ever wanted to leave home, and things could have only got better, you know. I really was tempted to just carry on cycling in, straight into the River Lee. Didn't. Came home. I had to leave my bike there obviously, 'cos I, 'cos the lady came and took it back, 'cos I was paying for it by the week anyway. And, erm ... so 'twas the next day then that I set off.[89]

One possible reason why Rosie bypasses two years in her initial narrative of leaving is that this period in her life is associated with deep emotional conflict, leading her on the night before her departure to London to contemplate suicide. This event, like the fact that Rosie had a good job working near her mother prior to leaving, needs to be erased from Rosie's preferred account of leaving because it makes apparent an undisclosed personal desire to pursue an independent life in England, the same desire present in sublimated form in earlier images of self-abnegation. Rosie 'felt so bad about things', it is suggested, not because she was being driven against her will to leave her home, but because she felt torn between a sense of devotion to her mother on the one hand, and a countervailing desire to 'succumb' to the 'temptations' of 'dancehalls and glamour' on the other.

The full impact of this conflict finally surfaces in Rosie's deeply autobiographical reconstruction of the moment of departure:

Barry: Do you remember that day, the day you left?
Rosie: I'll never forget it. Never forget it. [quietly crying] I managed to buy this lovely new bike. And I'd started try ... I was getting kind of a, a normal type of life. I was pal-ing round with a friend of mine, who used to live near me in Cork, too. And we used to go off on our bikes, and I felt normal for the first time in years, with the bike, friends, and going places. [crying] In spite of all that I thought, 'No, I'll ... I'll go with our Anne,' you know, thought, 'Oh! They love Irish people in England! Oh! And they even eat potatoes in tins!' and all these ... stories I was hearing. And they bury them under the ground! Must

have been war stuff. So I went over, and again, my mum couldn't come out ... come to the boat to see me off, because of him. So, Jesus knows what I'd put in the suitcase, but whatever I had was shoved in this little suitcase. And it was my Auntie Nellie who used to live across the road from us, my father's sister, who while we were all young, pretended not to know us. I never, ever forgave her for that. But she'd ... came down to see me off at the boat, and I remember her, 'twas one fifty to go on the Innisfallen, single fare. Erm ... she gave me two bars of Cadbury's chocolate. Big ones. 'Jesus!' I thought, you know, delighted like. And I got this old handbag, I'd never had a handbag, and I ... you had to go up this plank on the Innisfallen, and they were singing all these songs: 'Now is the hour we must say goodbye.' And, erm ... my heart was absolutely broke. And erm, the next, next thing I'd seen was my mam on the quay. On her own. She'd, she'd come down ... He must have gone to the pub, or whatever. So I remember waving goodbye to my mum [crying] ... I didn't want to leave her! I didn't want to leave home. And I could just see, she was only small, she had a shawl on her, and she was saying, 'Wave to me!' So I, I had these two bars of chocolate, and the boat set off, and sobbed like.[90]

As she recalls the day of leaving, Rosie is caught up in a blizzard of conflicting emotions and impulses, veering from one pole of understanding to another in a narrative of warring desires, where opposing parts of the self can no longer be kept apart. Rosie begins by recalling, as in the previous extract, the ways in which things were becoming 'normal', once again invoking the image of her 'lovely new bike'. However, 'in spite of all that', Rosie opts to go to England, enticed by 'all these stories I was hearing'. This vacillatory interplay between uncertainty and excitement is well captured in the image of Rosie boarding the ship with her first handbag, walking 'the plank' to the words 'now is the hour we must say goodbye'. The image as a whole depicts Rosie crossing a threshold of femininity, boarding the ship with a new handbag that symbolises the modern, sophisticated femininity she aspires to and associates with England. This new femininity, however, is embodied with uncertainty. In hearing the words of the song, which reinterpret the scene in terms of loss rather than new beginnings, Rosie's 'heart was absolutely broke'. Her sister absent from the scene, it is at this point that Rosie poignantly recalls the diminutive, solitary figure of her mother waving on the quayside. The scene now becomes a metaphor for the irresolvable emotional conflict leaving represents for her. At the scene of the new departure, the moment of self-realisation, the past does not recede into the background; the figure of the mother returns, a searing symbol of guilt, love and loss. Rosie denies once more the desire to leave. The boat sets sail.

Disparity at the origin

> What is found at the beginning of things is not the inviolable identity of their origin; it is the dissension of other things. It is disparity.[91]

Linear histories of migration journeys typically begin in the place left behind. In such narratives the 'homeland' constitutes a point of origin, the anchor of a shared lineage and descent, and a discrete narrative moment explaining the decision to leave and upon which the meaning of subsequent events may be predicated. Representations of this moment in interpretations of Irish emigration typically deploy an aesthetics of exile to highlight the shared despair and injustice suffered by successive generations of migrants. Referring to the post-war 'exodus', Tim Pat Coogan begins his history of the Irish diaspora with a recollection of 'the shabby, set-faced horde' he regularly observed making their way to 'the mailboat' in Dun Laoghaire when he was a boy:

> Like nearly every other Irish person of my generation, some of my closest relatives were forced into unwilling emigration. I have always lived near Dun Laoghaire where 'the mailboat' left for Holyhead, in Wales, and the sight of the shabby, set-faced horde pouring down Marine Road and on to those uncomfortable, vomit-producing ferries for dead-end jobs, punctuated by pub and prejudice, was one of the haunting memories of childhood. Nobody talked about those people, nobody did anything for them. Theirs was a fate that did not speak its name ...[92]

Coogan's point concerning the cultural awkwardness of post-war emigration remains salient. For although Ireland's current economic success is typically measured against the failures of the post-independent state, there remains a reluctance to acknowledge the extent to which the evolution of twentieth-century Irish society depended upon the agency of post-war emigrants, whether through the vast remittances they sent home, or through the 'British' tastes and values they transmitted into Irish culture. On the other hand, however, the mythology of exile evoked by Coogan greatly simplifies the experience of post-war departure. By illuminating the diversity of circumstances and motivations shaping emigrants' leave-taking, the personal accounts examined in this chapter further substantiate Enda Delaney's contention that there was no uniform Irish experience of emigration to post-war England. Moreover, however, while the chapter has endeavoured to point up the discrepancies between popular understandings and lived experiences, it has also shown how popular constructions were implicated in the constitution of emigrant subjectivities, without necessarily being descriptive of them.

The post-war discourse of national crisis in Ireland did not reflect the emigrant experience in any direct or unmediated way, but it did define the discursive possibilities for migrant self-understanding: as Clair Wills has put it, 'the experiences of individual Irish emigrants were overlaid by and fed back into fantasies ...which helped shape the way those experiences could be understood'.[93]

What migrants' personal accounts here indicate is that the discursive possibilities set by these fantasies were never as limited as historical narratives of post-war emigration suggest. Coogan's popular story of forced displacement simplifies and overlays a more dynamic post-war politics of exit wherein debates around emigration were centrally implicated in the contestation of Catholic-nationalist hegemony. This politics contributed to the replenishment of an aesthetics of exile, but it also generated and amplified an internally divided discourse on the meanings of departure, where competing images of the emigrant served as vehicles for the reimagining of the goals of nation-building. Migrants were historical agents in this process, in that their actions and desires contributed to both the transformation of social relations in post-war Ireland and the discursive contestation of dominant narratives of national identity. But this agency was itself mediated via migrants' active negotiation of the matrix of conflicting representations their actions helped produce.

Herein, the ways in which migrants interacted with available constructions were differentiated by the specificity of personal circumstances. It was not that individuals consciously selected a particular subject-position inscribed within public discourse based on how closely it fitted with or resembled their personal experience of leave-taking; rather, these subject-positions supplied a means of expressing and negotiating the complex and often difficult emotions associated with departure. A close reading of how migrants incorporate significant others within their leaving narratives here suggests that the emotionality of departure is heavily conditioned by migrants' pre-departure enmeshment within complex forms of affective relations. In particular, what differentiated the form, content and functions of the accounts was the differential character of intra-familial relations, the different ways in which parents cared for their children and the impact of these relations in emotional terms. In each case, the emotional dispositions engendered via different experiences of family life shaped the desire to stay or leave, and migrants' creative investment in available narratives of departure formed a means of making sense of and managing the emotional ramifications of those desires.

In some instances, available constructions provided a means of processing the emotional tensions reflections upon leaving evoked; for other migrants, negative constructions of the emigrant played into and exacerbated unresolved feelings of guilt and shame. What is true of both cases, however, is that departure involved emotional conflict, rather than being governed by wholly rational considerations. In turn, just as these conflicts shaped experiences of leaving at the time, so they continued to exercise a complex influence over how each respondent could reflect upon these experiences. Whatever the particular significance of leaving within each narrative, such are the emotional stakes involved in departure that recollections of the experience are often deeply autobiographical: leaving is an event in relation to which the present self continues to evaluate the path taken, where the interpretation of one's past is directly implicated in ongoing emotional adaption to the personal effects of migration. The importance of narratives of leaving thus lies not only in what they can tell us about the causation of emigration; it lies too in what they reveal about the emotional legacies of departure and the memory strategies migrants evolve to manage and resolve them.

Notes

1 John Moher, Fianna Fail TD for Cork East, quoted in *Dáil Éireann Deb.*, CXLVIII, No. 3, 16 February 1955.
2 N. Green, 'The Politics of Exit: Reversing the Immigration Paradigm', *Journal of Modern History* 77 (2005), 266.
3 In Patrick Fitzgerald's estimate some 8 million men and women left Ireland between 1801 and 1921. See P. Fitzgerald, *Irish Emigration 1801–1921* (Dublin, 1984), 1.
4 On Ireland's culture of 'exile' see K. Miller, *Emigrants and Exiles: Ireland and the Irish Exodus to North America* (New York, 1985); P. Ward, *Exile, Emigration and Irish Writing* (Dublin, 2002).
5 Taken from E. Delaney, 'State, Politics and Demography: The Case of Irish Emigration, 1921–71', *Irish Political Studies* 13:1 (1998), 26.
6 Estimates vary. According to Delaney, some 150,000 departed during the Second World War alone, while some scholars suggest that around 1.3 million left between 1946 and 1971. See E. Delaney, *The Irish in Post-War Britain* (Oxford, 2007), 12–13, 17.
7 Patrick Cogan, Clann na Talmhan TD for Wicklow, quoted in *Dáil Éireann Deb.*, CIV, 12 March 1947, col. 1950. On the variable meanings of what constituted 'the best' in post-war Irish culture, see C. Wills, *The Best Are Leaving: Emigration and Post-War Irish Culture* (Cambridge, 2015), ch. 1. See also M. Daly, *The Slow Failure: Population Decline and Independent Ireland, 1920–73* (Madison, WI, 2006).
8 William Norton, Labour TD for Carlow-Kilkenny, quoted in *Dáil Éireann Deb.*, XCIX, 8 May 1946, cols 2381–2382.
9 Peadar O'Donnell, 'Call the Exiles Home', *The Bell* 9:5 (1945), 383; Dr T. F. O'Higgins Snr, Fine Gael TD for Leix-Offaly, quoted in *Dáil Éireann Deb.*, XCIX, 7 March 1946, col. 2152.
10 *Commission on Emigration and Other Population Problems 1948–1954, Reports* (Dublin [1955]), 138.

11 Captain Patrick Giles, Fine Gael TD for Meath-Westmeath, quoted in *Dáil Éireann Deb.*, CI, 2 July 1946, col. 70.
12 Fr Culhane quoted in *Sligo Champion*, 16 August 1952.
13 O. J. Flanagan, Independent TD for Leix-Offaly, *Dáil Éireann Deb.*, XCVII, 12 July 1945, col. 2411; J. M. Dillon, Independent TD for Monaghan, *Dáil Éireann Deb.*, XCVII, 12 July 1945, col. 2422.
14 *Commission on Emigration*, 138.
15 S. O'Faolain, 'Love among the Irish', in J. O'Brien (ed.), *The Vanishing Irish* (London, 1954), 112.
16 Green, 'The Politics of Exit', 266.
17 H. Böll, *Irish Journal* (Evanston, IL, 1957), 4.
18 F. O'Toole, 'The Ex-Isle of Erin: Emigration and Irish Culture', in J. Mac Laughlin (ed.), *Location and Dislocation in Contemporary Irish Society: Emigration and Irish Identities* (Cork, 1997), 158–178.
19 T. Inglis, *Moral Monopoly: The Catholic Church in Modern Irish History* (Dublin, 1993), 187–214.
20 Fitzpatrick, *Irish Emigration*, 29–30, 37–42.
21 Brenda Grady (b. Galway, 1927) PI/SA/5, 2.
22 Ibid., 4.
23 Ibid., 3.
24 Ibid., 4.
25 Ibid.
26 Ibid.
27 Ibid., 5.
28 C. Wills, *That Neutral Island: A History of Ireland during the Second World War* (London, 2008), 319–320.
29 Pete St John, 'Fields of Athenry' (Waltons Publishing Ltd, 1985).
30 Aileen Walsh (b. Mayo, 1929) PI/SA/10, 4.
31 Ibid., 1.
32 Ibid., 2.
33 Ibid., 3.
34 See C. Wills, 'Women, Domesticity and the Family: Recent Feminist Work in Irish Cultural Studies', *Cultural Studies* 15:1 (2001), 33–57, 51.
35 C. Clear, 'Too Fond of Going: Female Emigration and Change for Women in Ireland, 1946–1961', in D. Keogh, F. O'Shea and C. Quinlan (eds), *The Lost Decade: Ireland in the 1950s* (Cork, 2004), 142–156.
36 On the relationship between emigration and the 'Americanisation' of Irish culture see G. Meaney, M. O'Dowd and B. Whelan, *Reading the Irish Woman: Studies in Cultural Encounter and Exchange, 1714–1960* (Oxford, 2013), chs 3 and 4.
37 Senator Helena Concannon, Fianna Fail, quoted in *Seanad Éireann Deb.*, XXXIX, No. 16, 4 July 1951.
38 'Leaving on Tuesday ...', *Tuam Herald*, 29 December 1951.
39 See, for example, B. MacMahon, 'Getting on the High Road Again', 207, and K. Norris, 'Muted Wedding Bells', both in O'Brien, *The Vanishing Irish*, 144–145.
40 'Letters to the Editor: Emigration', *Irish Times*, 11 September 1951.
41 On the sources of this modernising discourse see T. Finn, *Tuairim: Intellectual Debate and Policy Formulation in Ireland, 1954–1975* (Manchester, 2012),

esp. ch. 5. See also, T. Garvin, *Preventing the Future: Why Was Ireland So Poor for So Long?* (London, 2004).
42 See, for example, O'Faolain, 'Love among the Irish', 105–116.
43 V. McGuire, 'Will Our People Come Home?', *The Bell* 11:2 (1946), 723–724.
44 Bill Duffy (b. Roscommon, 1951) PI/SA/4, 1.
45 C. Arensberg, *The Irish Countryman* (New York, 1937), 145.
46 *Commission on Emigration*, 135.
47 Ibid., 137
48 J. Healy, *No One Shouted Stop! The Death of an Irish Town* (Achill, 1968), 44.
49 Bill Duffy (b. Roscommon, 1951) PI/SA/4, 2.
50 Ibid., 1.
51 Ibid., 9.
52 Ibid., 5.
53 Ibid., 7–8.
54 K. Miller, 'Emigration, Ideology and Identity in Post-Famine Ireland', *Studies: An Irish Quarterly Review*, 75:300 (1986), 525.
55 Taken from C. Ó Gráda, *A Rocky Road: The Irish Economy since the 1920s* (Manchester, 1997), 212.
56 Bernard Butler, Fianna Fail TD for Dublin Townships, quoted in *Dáil Éireann Deb.*, XCVII, 12 July 1945, col. 2430.
57 Eamon de Valera, quoted in, 'Emigrants Living in "absolute degradation" in parts of Britain', *Irish Times*, 30 August 1951.
58 Peadar O'Connell, 'Emigration', *Irish Independent*, 1 September 1951; 'Letters', *Irish Independent*, 3 September 1951; 'Irish Workers in England: Letters to the Editor', *Irish Independent*, 4 September 1951; 'Letter to the Editor', *Irish Independent*, 9 September 1951; 'The Exodus', *Irish Examiner*, 6 September 1951; 'The Workers in Britain Controversy', *Munster Express*, 7 September 1951; 'When Will It End?', *Donegal News*, 8 September 1951.
59 'Irish Workers in England Degraded', *Irish Independent*, 30 August 1951; 'Mr De Valera Affirms His Charges', *Irish Independent*, 31 August 1951; 'Fifteen Sleep in One Room', *Irish Examiner*, 30 August 1951; 'Irish Workers in England', *Irish Examiner*, 31 August 1951; 'The Emigrants in England', *Irish Press*, 31 August 1951; 'Grim Revelations on Plight of Emigrants', *Connacht Tribune*, 1 September 1951; 'Warning to Workers', *Evening Herald*, 30 August 1951.
60 Rev. Dr Durig, quoted in 'Irish Youth Told: Don't Emigrate', *Irish Press*, 15 August 1950.
61 Captain Patrick Giles, Fine Gael TD for Meath-Westmeath, quoted in *Dáil Éireann Deb.*, CV, 9 May 1947, cols 2540–2541.
62 Rev. Dr Lucey, 'Vanishing Nation', *Southern Star*, 3 May 1952; M. Connolly, 'Rural Depopulation', *Irish Monthly* 79:942 (December 1951), 514–517.
63 H. Ewart, *Caring for Migrants: Policy Responses to Irish Migration to England, 1940–1972* (Liverpool, 2017), ch. 1.
64 R. L. Stevenson, *Shall I Emigrate?* (Dublin, 1965), 3.
65 Ibid., 8.
66 Ibid., 9.
67 Ibid., 10.
68 Paul Quinn (b. Galway, 1938) PI/SA/9, 1.

69 Ibid., 2.
70 Fr Basil, 'A Revolution in Education', *Irish Monthly* 83:968 (April 1954), 140–145.
71 Paul Quinn (b. Galway, 1938) PI/SA/9, 3.
72 Ibid., 4.
73 Ibid., 6.
74 Rosie Long (b. Cork, 1938) PI/SA/8, 1.
75 Ibid., 2.
76 Ibid., 3.
77 Ibid., 2.
78 Ibid., 5.
79 Ibid.
80 Ibid., 8.
81 Ibid., 9.
82 Ibid., 10.
83 Ibid.
84 Ibid.
85 Ibid.
86 Ibid., 11.
87 Ibid., 12.
88 Ibid., 11.
89 Ibid., 14.
90 Ibid., 12.
91 M. Foucault, 'Nietzsche, Genealogy, History', in P. Rabinow (ed.), *The Foucault Reader* (London, 1991), 79.
92 T. P. Coogan, *Wherever Green is Worn: The Story of the Irish Diaspora* (London, 2000), ix.
93 Wills, *The Best Are Leaving*, 10.

2

In-between places: liminality and the dis/composure of migrant femininities in the post-war English city

Liminal femininities

After working in London as a nurse during the war, Elizabeth Reegan, the central character in John McGahern's *The Barracks*, returns to the small rural village of her childhood to marry the local police sergeant. Confined now to the undeviating daily rhythms of the barracks, and to the roles of wife and mother within a marriage lacking the intimacy she had always craved, Elizabeth spends her days reflecting upon the events of her life, leading her back time and again to wartime London. At one point, bored and simmering with frustration at Mrs Casey's efforts to draw her into tedious conversation in the barracks day room, Elizabeth begins to remember that:

> She used to love watching the young girls home from the city parade to Communion, especially at Easter, when many came; it used to excite her envy and curiosity, so much so that when she'd come home from Mass she'd always want to talk about them to Reegan; it gave her back the time when she too was one of them, but he'd never care to listen.[1]

At another moment, after Elizabeth has discovered she has cancer and is travelling with her husband into Dublin to have a life-threatening operation, the train journey into Westland Row throws her mind back to the years when the station had been the scene of youthful leave-takings:

> How the lights of this city used to glow in the night when the little boat train taking her back to London after Christmas came in and out of the countryside and winter dark. The putting-on of overcoats and the taking of cases off the racks and the scramble across the platform to get

on the train that went the last eight miles out to the boat. Always girls weeping, as she had wept the first time too, hard to know you cannot hide for ever in the womb and the home, you have to get out to face the world.[2]

Historiographical representations of Irish women's migration to Britain are structured by a sharp dichotomy. While some writers portray migration as a context in which 'Irish patriarchal culture'[3] was reproduced, signalling women's 'enduring ethnic affiliation',[4] an opposing narrative presents emigration as a route to material betterment and greater independence.[5] Within John McGahern's portrayal of the inner life of Elizabeth Reegan, however, the relation between family, emigration and the city has neither a fixed nor straightforward meaning. In her reflections upon the conflicting desires of the younger self, the English city is neither a place of independence and self-realisation, nor of loneliness and familial loss, but all these things, at different times, in relation to different situations.

Following John McGahern's lead, this chapter develops a more ambivalent conception of the relation between mobility, power and gendered selfhood. As Louise Ryan has observed in her studies of Irish women's migration to twentieth-century England, women's narratives rarely disclosed a singular perspective on issues of empowerment: evidence of 'individual agency' and 'familial obligation' coexisted within women's accounts.[6] Pushing this tension further, this chapter conceives power, not as an externally imposed constraint, but as a generative force, centrally implicated in the production of gendered subjectivity as a divided formation, riven by conflicting emotional investments in competing constructions of femininity.[7] Migration was never only an 'escape from patriarchy' or an extension of its obligations, but a context in which adaption to the transition between cultures and places destabilised the contradictions on which identity is based. Iain Chambers puts it thus:

> Cut off from the homelands of tradition, experiencing a constantly challenged identity, the stranger is perpetually required to make herself at home in an interminable discussion between a scattered historical inheritance and a heterogeneous present.[8]

As Alistair Thomson observes, this 'discussion' engenders a pressing need for narrative coherence, registered within the stories told about migration:

> [T]he experience of migration, which by definition is centred around a process of acute disjuncture, presents both an urgent need for, and

particular difficulties in, the construction of coherent identities and life stories, a past we can live by.[9]

This chapter explores the construction of gendered subjectivities within the early settlement process, focusing on a key moment of 'liminality' within the migration journeys of three women. This early period of arrival and settlement is liminal because the women are caught between places: while they have departed their homeland, they have not yet 'put down roots' in their new environment. It is also liminal because the women are caught between phases in the life cycle: while they are no longer house-bound daughters, living under the supervision of parents, neither are they yet married. The chapter analyses women's ambivalent representation of this interstitial moment to explore the ways in which gendered migrant subjectivities are produced in the spaces 'in-between' coherently constituted subject-positions. Where Mary Chamberlain suggests that migration is a process via which women 'achieve' a sense of autonomous selfhood, the chapter offers a snapshot of the difficult process of 'becoming', illuminating the conflicting forms of gendered re/identification produced through migration and the strategies of 'composure' implicated in their management and reconciliation.[10] Instead of a linear narrative about the rejection or reproduction of patriarchy, what emerges is an account of the re/formation of gendered migrant subjectivities as the unstable and incomplete product of competing discourses and conflictual desires.

Redemption story

In post-Second World War Britain women's position did not undergo the transformation predicted by some contemporaries during the war.[11] Yet such was the demand for 'manpower' within the post-war economy that the state would be forced into continued reliance on female labour in the decades after 1945, ensuring that opportunities for female work continued to expand in the post-war period even if these were generally only realisable at particular moments in women's life cycle. As Fitzgerald and Lambkin note, such conditions opened new opportunities for Irish female migrants, around 30,000 of whom, the majority single and under 25, arrived in Britain each year between 1946 and 1961.[12] According to the census, although over 30 per cent of Irish-born working women in England and Wales were still working in 'personal service' in 1951, over 60 per cent were spread across 20 different categories of employment, with over 5 per cent employed in 'commerce', 9 per cent in clerical work and over 22 per cent in 'professions'.[13]

Occurring at a time when Irish society was itself undergoing demographic transition, for many Irish observers young Irish women's mass entry into the post-war British labour market signalled their rejection of 'traditional' rural life in favour of enhanced personal freedoms and material betterment. Yet, if liberals such as Sean O'Faolain promoted such a view during the period, it did not supply a framework within which Brenda, whom we met in the last chapter, gave form to her memories of early settlement in England. Born in 1927 in Co. Galway, the third-born in a family of six siblings, Brenda emphasised a 'happy' if frugal childhood growing up on her family's small farm. Indeed, so content was Brenda with her life in rural Galway that she harboured a desire to emulate her mother and marry on the land. This option, however, proved unavailable, as Brenda's older sister received the family dowry, enabling her to 'go into a farmhouse'. As such, Brenda 'had to go out to work', but since local employment opportunities were limited and poorly remunerated, in July 1946, aged 19, she migrated to Lymm in Cheshire in order to take up work in domestic service as part of a government labour recruitment scheme.[14]

Instead of a story of escape to freedom, Brenda's account of this process hinted at suppressed feelings of loss. Although Brenda affirmed that she 'wanted to go' to England, the reasons she gave in support of this constantly referred back to the needs and desires of familial others, suggesting that leaving was understood as a form of duty rather than an object of personal desire.[15] To the extent Brenda's personal feelings were audible, these emerged indirectly, through sighs and silences as well as depictions of aspects of her external environment that intimated interior feelings of alienation. As well as in her story of leaving, Brenda's memories of arrival spoke repeatedly of 'disappointment', inciting reflections upon the place left behind:

> Well I was a bit disappointed because really, it was Wales, we came over here to look after ... they were children, they was up there during the war, and they were going to Grammar school and all that, this special Matron was looking after them, they were in Wales on holidays ... and they were telling me how lovely Wales was and stopping every so often looking at this, that and the other and well, I just said I'd left a place more beautiful than that, which I did, I was a bit disappointed.[16]

Because Brenda migrated as part of a centrally organised labour recruitment scheme, she was liable to be directed where female labour was then most in demand. In her case, before actually taking up residence in Lymm, this involved a period in rural Wales, where the children of the family she was going to work for were then on holiday. Rural Wales, however, did not evoke the familiar in Brenda's memories; although stopping to look at the Welsh scenery provoked backwards-glancing at the place left behind, this only served to confirm Brenda's 'disappointment': 'I'd left a place more beautiful than that.'

Such memories evoke Brenda's continuing emotional ties with the place she has had to leave, but, at certain points, they also hint at other dissatisfactions linked to the context of arrival. Questions regarding Brenda's early encounters with 'English people', for example, did not elicit voluminous narration:

Barry: So what about the English people? What were your first impressions of them?
Brenda: They were alright, I never ... I never ... got anything to say about them.
Barry: Never nothing to say?
Brenda: No, no, no [pause].
Barry: Was it easy to settle, when you first arrived?
Brenda: Well it wasn't a case of settling, you couldn't go back for a year [laughs].
Barry: So you had to?
Brenda: Well, you had to, you had to ...[17]

As Brenda reticently states, 'settling' was not the issue. Although Brenda may have 'wanted' to go to England in order to aid her family's economic situation, she ultimately had very limited control over the decision to leave or the migration process itself. Where Brenda migrated to, who she worked for and the work she actually performed were largely determined by the recruitment needs of the British state. And, whether she liked where she was sent or not, she 'had to' stay: if she broke her contract she was obliged to pay back her travel costs, which the state had funded in order to facilitate rapid labour movement during wartime and immediately after.

The muted character of Brenda's responses to my questions insinuates that, in fact, she retained no special fondness for the place she was sent to. As she reveals a little further on, her employers were 'quite strict':

> The people where I worked in then were quite strict and hard work as well, you know, they'd expect you to wash the walls down and in fact there was a lady who was supposed to come in to do the cleaning and that and then this little group of Irish girls came, the cleaners was let off and we had to do it.[18]

As in Ireland, domestic service went into steep decline in Britain in the decades after 1945 due in part to the unattractive nature of the work relative to the new employment opportunities opening for young women within the labour market during the period.[19] As well as being poorly remunerated and characteristically arduous, living-in was frequently associated with the loss of personal freedoms since employers, if they were particularly 'strict', could monitor and regulate the behaviour of servants because of the way the overlapping of places of work and residence confused servants' status as employees and members of the household. Young women such as Brenda were thus being recruited to fill vacancies in a sector which British women were evacuating as alternative possibilities opened in the post-war labour market.[20]

Brenda's references to these aspects of her first job in England indicate that, like the process of leaving Ireland, this phase in the migration process was tacitly associated with compulsion and unfairness, experienced as something one 'had to' endure. This section of her narrative thus depicts a decline, from happy recollections of an idyllic rural childhood to muted expressions of unhappiness associated with leaving her family and the exploitative circumstances of her employment in Lymm. However, this arc of descent did have a turning point in Brenda's pre-marriage narrative. Asked about what was important in eventually aiding her settlement in England, Brenda moved the narrative forwards and eastwards to Manchester:

> Well, when I came into Manchester ... we first came into Manchester because there are places to go, socialising and all that, and I worked for a very nice Jewish woman that was a medical herbalist ... and she was very good to me, she had no family of her own, and I was a receptionist and I used to live in digs but with her living on her own, and I wasn't keen on my digs, I lived in with her, there was a girl coming in every day to do the cleaning and that and it was quite a nice place ... so ... I was quite happy in Manchester, and that was where I met my husband, here in Manchester ...[21]

Following the completion of her one-year contract as a domestic servant in Lymm, Brenda returned home to Ireland for a holiday in July 1947. Thereafter, instead of returning to Lymm, Brenda moved into nearby Manchester, where she initially took up residence in 'digs' run by a private landlady.[22] While living here, one of her friends alerted her to the possibility of work at the home of a medical herbalist based in Cheetham Hill, then a working-class district on the northern boundary of the inner city.[23] Soon after taking up employment as a receptionist at the herbalist's, run by 'a very nice Jewish woman' with 'no family of her own', Brenda moved into her new place of work, having not been 'keen' on the digs where she was then staying. This move marked a shift in the tone of Brenda's narrative, from stoic resolve to endure her situation at Lymm, conveyed through a language of reticence, to relative happiness: 'it was quite a nice place ... so ... I was quite happy in Manchester'.

This shift appears to be linked to various aspects of her conditions of employment at her new place of work and residence. In contrast to her depiction of her experiences of leaving, her living-in job at Lymm and her first digs in Manchester, the language Brenda uses to describe her new working environment and her new employer suggests a much stronger emotional relationship with place. Indeed, where Brenda's earlier narratives emphasised the impersonal character of the environments she was passing through, her recollection that the 'very nice Jewish woman' she worked for 'had no family of her own' intimates that she saw herself as a surrogate daughter to her childless employer and her new situation at the herbalist's more generally as resembling the familial dynamics she had been used to at home in Ireland. In addition, Brenda also preferred her new job at the herbalist's. Where Brenda's work as a domestic had been arduous, exploitative and low-status, working as a receptionist marked a step upwards on the employment ladder, distinguishing her from the 'girl coming in every day to do the cleaning'.

As well as liking her new place of employment and residence, the tonal shift discernible in this phase of Brenda's narrative was also related to new possibilities for 'socialising' and, as we shall see, to meeting her husband. Although Brenda and her co-workers in Lymm had often travelled together into nearby Warrington and Altrincham for nights out, Manchester offered much greater opportunities for dancing:

> Well we used to go dancin', there was dances here, or there used to be erm ... some parochial halls attached to the church and then they was a lot down near the university and around that area there was piles and piles of Irish dance halls.[24]

As Alan Kidd has noted, one of the reasons for the relative buoyancy of Manchester's economy during the middle decades of the twentieth century was the existence of a large and developing manufacturing sector which cushioned the effects of the decline of the textile industry.[25] A corollary of this growth in 'light industry' and other areas such as retail and clerical work was the advent of the young, single wage-earner within the local economy, an event which heralded the emergence of a youth-based commercial leisure culture within the city.[26] As well as growing rates of cinema attendance and the consumption of new popular fashions, this burgeoning of commercial forms encompassed a 'craze' for dancing, inciting a proliferation in dancing venues in various parts of the city.[27] In the post-war period the number of venues would continue to rise and were augmented by a growth in various kinds of Irish dance venue, providing migrants like Brenda with opportunities for 'socialising' with other

Irish people in their new city of residence. As such, Brenda's use of such spaces represented participation in a form of commercial leisure that simultaneously formed part of what Enda Delaney has termed migrant 'cultures of adjustment'.[28]

Additionally, however, such spaces were also part of a pre-established Catholic culture in Manchester, their function related to the preservation of the Catholic community in the city.[29] As Irish migration to Britain began to rise during the 1940s, clerics and Catholic social workers in both England and Ireland repeatedly advised young migrants to spend their leisure time in these spaces as a form of religious and national duty, warning against the myriad 'difficulties and dangers' young Catholic migrants were likely to encounter in English urban environments.[30] In 'An Open Letter to Irish Girls about to Emigrate' published in *Christus Rex* in 1949, Olive Mary Garrigan, Wartime Welfare Adviser at the London Rest Centre, outlined a comprehensive list of potential pitfalls facing 'young Irish girls' arriving in England at a time of 'much moral unrest as well as resentment at the restraints of society'.[31] One of the most serious, according to Garrigan, was 'loneliness', because:

> [I]f you are lonely you are likely to accept *any* companionship rather than none – and that way trouble lies. Oh, and don't think because there is a dancehall in the town that it is the very thing for you. There are dancehalls, and dancehalls – some of them no girl of good character would be seen entering – so try to get the advice of those able to judge of the matter.[32]

Such advice, and indeed leisure itself, should be sought within one's local parish:

> The socials and dances run by the Parish Church to which you come will give you recreation. Do attend them. You are perhaps a child of Mary in Ireland. Bring your medal and office book with you. The Sodality in your English parish will welcome you as a friend ... I should mention too that there may be a suitable Irish Club in your new district. If so, do join it. The sound of your native accents is most comforting when you are feeling a long way from home I do assure you.[33]

While the post-war influx of Irish migrants was sometimes viewed as an opportunity to expand numbers by the Church in England, Catholic observers repeatedly expressed concerns over rural migrants' ability to navigate the moral dangers of English culture at a time when the Church was anxious about the combined effects of welfarism, suburbanisation and rising affluence upon the cohesion of working-class Catholic life.[34] Involving the activities of parish priests and Catholic welfare workers, lay groups such as the Legion of Mary and the Young Christian Workers, post-war migrants formed the object of a regulatory discourse which emphasised the dangers of everyday life in a materialistic urban culture, but that also instructed migrants on how to achieve a distinctive version of migration success. In the case of female migrants, whom observers viewed as 'well-intentioned, homesick, and painfully inexperienced', anxieties accumulated around issues of sex and marriage.[35] Cautionary stories in welfare reports and prescriptive tracts warned of the dangers of pre-marital sex, contraception, flirtations with 'non-Catholics' and 'miscegenation'. The good female emigrant would exercise vigilance at all times in relation to such dangers, while ensuring she maintained her religious observances and practices.[36] As Garrigan stressed, crucial in this respect was securing 'suitable' employment:

> Many Irish girls, indeed, I believe most, are coming here either to be trained as nurses or to undertake domestic work, and there is very great need of them. Particularly are girls welcomed in homes where there are young children, and they will be doing a great work of Christian service by helping mothers of families. But care must be taken in deciding on a first place ... Before finally agreeing to take a position it is wise to make sure that the prospective employer appreciates the necessity of allowing you to be free to attend mass regularly; this will save you embarrassment and difficulty after you arrive, and it will be understood as a condition of your employment.[37]

As well as being sites of leisure, used by the Church as a way of generating revenue, Catholic dance venues were sites of moral regulation, one of whose functions was to disseminate a regulatory construct of the 'good girl emigrant'. In her narrative of this phase of her settlement story Brenda sought to present her young self as in conformity with the prescriptions embedded within this construct, stressing in particular her employer's commitment to moral supervision. Although Brenda knew that drinking and fighting occurred at the dancehalls she attended, for example, she did not 'see' these activities firsthand because her employer imposed a strict curfew:

Barry: And was there much drinking that went on?
Brenda: Erm yes, the drinking used to go on and the fighting used to go on as well ...
Barry: And did you see any fights yourself?
Brenda: No, no, I didn't, I didn't see ... because we weren't allowed to be out late so we had to be in at 11 or half-eleven and ... we didn't see a lot of it, no.[38]

And although some employers were lax in their obligations, Brenda's employer ensured she attended mass:

> [W]here I worked for the herbalist, the church was only a few yards away down the road, St Chad's and ... there was no ... it was important to us and it was important to the people we worked for that we did go ... to church.³⁹

Yet the ideal figure of the 'good girl emigrant' was not merely proscriptive or segregative; she attends church regularly and frequents Irish Catholic dancehalls because these are the spaces in which she will meet a suitable future husband. Catholic discourse did not counsel emigrants to return to Ireland at the earliest opportunity, but viewed marriage and the creation of a family within the Catholic Church as ultimately the most effective way of safeguarding migrants' spiritual welfare in England. A 'confidential' 1948 *Report on Irish Workers in London*, produced by a London parish priests' committee, argued for the creation of a new London Irish centre staffed by priests on the grounds that 'they [migrants] are very anxious to be among their own sort, who understand them. After marriage they more easily fit into ordinary parish life, especially if there are children.'⁴⁰

Advice manuals and prescriptive letters in Catholic journals thus presented Catholic marriage and family as the ultimate goals of settlement in England, and gave precise instructions about the form marriage should take. A 1953 tract by the Catholic Truth Society explained that:

> In Ireland, it is the accepted thing to look on marriage as a gift from God. In England, this gift is constantly degraded on the radio and in films, newspapers and daily conversation. The Catholics in England must therefore be very careful in choosing a partner or accepting an offer of marriage. The boy should not think simply of good looks or appearance or charm; he will, if he wants to be happy, judge which girl will make the best wife and mother. The girl should not be swept off her feet by glamour or ready money or sweet words; she will want a good husband and father who will be hardworking and faithful. Each will want to marry not only a Catholic but a good Catholic.⁴¹

Although Catholic discourse lamented the post-war Irish 'flight from the land' and constantly denigrated English culture, it nevertheless encouraged migrants to settle in England, so long as they married 'a good Catholic'. And although such discourse repeatedly stressed the differences between English and Irish attitudes to marriage and family, it's sanctification of these institutions as the goals of settlement resonated closely with the wider aims of social reconstruction in England, which valorised the re-establishment of family life as necessary for the moral and social rebuilding of the English social order following the disruptions of wartime.[42] Catholic discourses on femininity, which positioned women as mothers and housewives at the centre of the family home, thus complemented rather than contradicted English conceptions, and in Brenda's case supplied the main ideal in terms of which she composed a positive memory of her early settlement experiences:

Barry: Tell me about your husband?
Brenda: Yes, I met my husband here in Manchester soon after I came over, because I was very friendly with his sister, she was one of the ladies that was, am, used to come where we were living in the digs, and eh, met him here and, eh, we were married within two years. I met him at a dance, he came from the midlands, Abbeyleix, not far from ... what do you call it now Marlborough it was, Portlaoise, that's where he came from, now he was a man that was reared inside the town, he knew the difference between rich and poor, he was a very very good worker, and we were quite ... we had our ups and downs like everybody does but just soon after retiring he had a massive brain haemorrhage and died overnight, eh, our life was alright and, we reared our children and we worked hard and so did I, of course I had to stay off during the years that my children were young, but every one of them passed the eleven-plus ... and every one of them university ...[43]

Brenda's reconstruction of her pre-marriage years in England is ordered according to the arc of a redemption story. If Brenda's account of leaving and arrival in Britain manifests signs of loneliness and loss, on moving to Manchester these emotions are replaced by expressions of happiness and a more purposeful style of narration. This tonal shift was not only related to her new circumstances of employment or greater opportunities for dancing, but to the way these things were associated in her memory with meeting her husband. Arrival in Manchester coincided with the beginning of a two-year courtship, leading ultimately, in Brenda's account, to the successful realisation of the prescribed ideals of marriage and family. In part, the significance of these events referred to the re-establishment of a sense of belonging: marriage consolidated a process of re-identification by which the feelings of loss and dislocation occasioned by departure were mastered through re-incorporation within a new family. This process was foreshadowed in the security provided through Brenda's relationship with her herbalist employer, but culminated in meeting and marrying her husband, in whose figure Brenda's desire to emulate her mother and establish a family of her own could be rediscovered and pursued. Regulatory Catholic discourse clarified, affirmed and facilitated this process.

At the same time, Brenda's framing of her marriage as a redemptive event may also be related to that fact that, as she mentions, her husband had now passed away. Freudian theories of mourning contend that, in the experience of losing a loved one, the loss of the other is overcome through a process of internalisation whereby the lost object is incorporated within the self in order to sustain love for it after death. In terms of the composure of memory stories, such a process may accentuate the tendency to remember lost loved ones in idealised terms, so as to reinforce the identification set up through internalisation. In Brenda's case, framing her marriage as a redemptive moment registers its implication in negotiating the destabilising effects of migration back when she was 19, but it may also reflect her present need to preserve her love for her departed husband. The interview process thus supplies an opportunity to consolidate the work of mourning.

Opportunity, self-expression and the return of the past

Within the overall context of Brenda's narrative of settlement, the significance of the three years between migrating to Lymm and getting married lay in their relation to meeting her husband. These years represent a prelude to the more important events of marriage and family, and as such, although Brenda's account includes stories about work and leisure, these themes are ultimately secondary in importance. However, to numerous contemporary observers, both Irish and English, it was precisely the opportunities English urban centres provided for work, excitement and consumption that enticed young migrants to cities like London, Birmingham and Manchester. Established in 1948 by the incoming coalition government to 'investigate the causes and consequences of the present level and trend in population', the Irish Commission on Emigration suggested in 1954 that 'economic necessity' was not the only factor influencing migration to Britain:[44]

> A natural desire for adventure or change, an eagerness to travel, to see the world and share the enjoyments of modern city life, to secure financial independence by having pocket money and by being free to spend it in one's own way, to obtain freedom from parental control and a privacy not obtainable in one's home environment, to be free to choose one's own way of life – such matters affect a proportion of young people everywhere and they appeal strongly in a country where there has been, for so many years, an established tradition of emigration.[45]

The anxious rhetoric of religious observers in this period was underpinned by the realisation that the post-war English city potentially provided migrants with new possibilities for self-development and the performance of alternative cultural identities. Such 'opportunities' were premised not only on having more money, but on greater freedom of movement, less pervasive parental supervision and on enhanced access to spaces of leisure and social interaction, most obviously pubs, cinemas and dancehalls. By the mid-1950s, rising wages, full employment, technological advance and the institutionalisation of the 'welfare state' had helped foster the development of an increasingly consumer-driven culture in major urban centres, one effect of which was the increased public availability of relatively 'permissive' and assertive images of femininity. Linked to the dissemination of Freudian discourses on sex and the increased use of sex as a selling tool by advertisers and the popular media, new sexual knowledges helped popularise images of young, assertive and glamorous femininity, 'socially mobile young women who appeared able to cross the city's social boundaries, and drew on the resources of the sex industry as a form of empowerment'.[46]

Representations of Irish female migrants' relationship to such opportunities have taken divergent forms. For contemporary Catholic observers the sinful enticements of the post-war city posed a threat to young women's future roles as wife and mother within the ideal Catholic family.[47] In his Lenten pastoral of November 1945, for example, Bishop Henry Marshall of Salford warned that 'many marriages are fore-doomed to failure by reason of sinful courtships, and much of that distrust which husbands manifest towards their wives in later life is due to the fact that during the days of courtship they found that these same wives were so easily tempted by them.'[48] In sharp contrast, however, other forms of representation have contributed a more assertive and adventurous image of migrant femininity to the communal imaginary of the Irish in Britain. Although primarily an epic tale about Irish masculine achievement within the post-war British construction industry, John B. Keane's novel *The Contractors* engages in its portrayal of female characters with the idea of 1950s London as a space of self-construction and experimentation for young Irish women. In chapter 2, we are introduced to Margo Cullagan, a nurse in Newsham General Hospital, originally from Wexford, who 'had no particular ambition beyond being a staff nurse' and who 'enjoyed life where possible'. Margo, we are told,

> could not get out of Ireland quickly enough, out of the 'sexless morass' as she called it, out of the 'dreary strictures of nunneries' … She wanted escape from the unnatural physical restrictions as she had so often confided to her best friend in the convent. She was forever delighting and shocking this fascinated listener with threats and promises of what she would do as soon as she established herself in England.[49]

True to her word, once 'established' Margo uses her new-found freedom to explore her sexuality with a number of men. In our second encounter with Margo in the same chapter she is envisioned in 'the Colorado Hotel', 'sat in the dim light of the residents' lounge with a glass of gin in her hand'.[50] Her other hand is 'entwined around' that of a new intern doctor, Angus McLernon from Alloway, who has just made a proposal:

> 'I've never gone to bed with anyone before.' She sounded aggrieved.
> 'I'm sorry,' he said, 'I didn't mean to offend you.'
> 'You didn't. You said what was on your mind and I like a person for that. I suppose you're a Protestant?'
> 'Yes. A Presbyterian.'
> Margo smiled to herself. She had never gone to bed with a Presbyterian.
> 'Why don't you ask the night porter if he has a double room with a bath?' The question caught him by surprise.[51]

Although Margo initially presents to Angus an image of feminine innocence, the interaction, which she controls, is ultimately as much a vehicle for the satisfaction of her desires as it is for Angus's. These, moreover, extend beyond the purely sexual: Margo's pleasure derives from her self-conscious manipulation of competing versions of femininity and the power this affords her, and from the prospect that sleeping with Angus, a Presbyterian, will enable her to perform a double transgression. It also has to do with Angus's status, socially and economically, as a doctor: the phrase 'a double room with a bath' is suggestive of the ways in which Irish feminine 'ambitions' in post-war England could involve an interplay between issues of mobility and affluence simultaneously with those of romance and sexual experimentation.

Post-war discourses of feminine 'opportunity' supplied a discursive framework within which Clare reconstructed her experiences of pre-marriage years in 1950s London. Clare was born in 1940 and grew up in rural north Cork, the youngest daughter in a family of four children. Clare's memories of growing up in north Cork were ambivalent. Although she reflected nostalgically on the quaint otherworldliness of the rural villages she knew as a child, her home life was not a happy one due to the unpredictable and often violent moods of her father, who was a guard in the Garda Siochana (Civic Guards).[52] Alongside memories which articulated a desire to achieve, like her older sisters, academic success, Clare also told stories in which such desires were persistently thwarted by the inefficiency of local institutions and the stifling prescriptions of authoritative others. Indeed, as one such story relates, it was the desire to escape her father's control, to 'see something else', which ultimately confirmed Clare's resolve to leave:

> My father wouldn't allow me to go anywhere. This was one of the reasons I left home really. I can really say I didn't leave to find a job. I just wanted to get away, and wanted to get away from him. And I wanted to see the bright lights of London. I thought it was so ... you know ... just so ... I just wanted to do rid of it, to get away, to see something else, you know ... travel ... so, I never really looked for a job.[53]

Aged 17, Clare left for 'the bright lights of London' in the summer of 1957, travelling by Rosslare to Fishguard along with her older sister. Clare's sister, who was returning from holiday, was 'a qualified nurse' in London, and having recently moved into 'her own flat' was able to provide Clare with an immediate source of accommodation. 'Within a week', Clare, who had undertaken secretarial training in Ireland after leaving school, had found a job in Lloyd's bank because "'twas very easy to get work then, you know. You could pick and choose."[54]

Work, however, was not the central focus of this part of Clare's narrative. Within a year of arriving Clare had met her future husband, Sean, at a popular Irish dancehall, 'the Shamrock in Elephant and Castle'. Sean, who was from Roscommon and had recently finished national service in the British army, then worked for the large Irish building contractor Kilrow, though not, as Clare informed me, as 'a manual worker': 'he was the plant and transport ... in the management side, always.'[55]

As a man of experience in the ways of the metropolis, Sean was able to guide Clare to its wonders:

Clare: He introduced me to, like, some days we'd go to the Tower of London, we'd go to Buckingham Palace, we'd go to the War Museum, so it was a great place, because all these things were relatively free, you know, on a Sunday you wouldn't need much money, you'd go up to Hyde Park and just sit there, and the Serpentine, and at Trafalgar Square, or you'd go up to ... is, is Speakers' Corner still in London? Er, that was tremendous. Have you been?
Barry: Er, I've never been, but it's near ... it's in Hyde Park.
Clare: Yeah. I don't know whether it's still going on, but that's ... was tremendous, 'cos you could get up there and speak about anything or anybody, or run anyone down, and just, 'twas just amazing. And there was always something to ... you know, it was really good. And, I ... he used to take me to the shows, and the pictures, and as I say that was the best thing, having a boyfriend, then you never paid for anything, you had the boyfriend paying for everything [laughs]. In retrospect it was awful, I often think of that! But, you know ... you thought, you could save more money when you have a boyfriend, you know![56]

In this courtship narrative the young self is envisioned achieving her aspiration to experience 'the bright lights of London'. The iconic monuments and landmarks of the metropolis, in particular 'Speakers' Corner', here become symbols of personal development and self-expression, themes central to the discourse of opportunity. At the same time, this experience incorporates Sean, here positioned in two different ways. Initially, Sean is presented as a guide or teacher, someone from whom Clare, positioned as a student, learns. Yet, as with Margo in *The Contractors*, if the teacher–student relation implies a power imbalance, by the end of the narrative it becomes apparent this could be inverted: 'you had the boyfriend paying for everything'.

Thus far, the mode of exposition adopted has tended to amplify one story: that of the independent young women who escapes a restrictive familial regime in pursuit of personal fulfilment and romance in the city. Yet closer scrutiny, particularly of the period prior to Clare's courtship, makes audible a different, less self-assured voice:

> Well, my first job I got in Lloyd's bank in, er … up the City of London, and I remember getting out of … and these hu … huge buildings, where everything was so grimy, and you'd, you'd get on the Tube and you know, you'd … you'd, in those days all the women used to wear your gloves and everything and they'd be all smuts and everything after just one trip to work. It was really quite grimy, and dirty, you know.[57]

In this narrative what is recalled is not the city's iconic landmarks and possibilities for leisure, but its 'dirt' and 'grime', which 'after just one trip' would besmirch Clare's gloves. The 'dirt' and 'grime', which had to be negotiated on a daily basis as Clare made her way through the city, between work and her sister's home, may be read as unconscious markers of an unease with her new projected identity and environment, here metonymised through the reference to wearing gloves. The unconscious surfacing of this unease is suggestive of a prior muting of personal experience:

> I was, like, excited, at the idea of coming to London and all this, and seeing all these places. You only … you just heard of or read of. I was very homesick, but I didn't pretend it, you know, you just kind of always did … we, we were brought up not to show our emotions very much, you know. We, we didn't cry. We, we didn't do anything. You kept all your emotions inside. Everything was a bit suppressed …[58]

Although Clare was 'excited' about coming to London, she was also 'very homesick', but family protocol dictated that such feelings be concealed. The collective 'we' here returns to Clare's account, not as a positive sign of 'ties that bind', but of suppression and unresolved conflict. Underlying the preferred narrative of the independent young woman we begin to glimpse emotions of rejection and abandonment as 'family' displaces 'opportunity' as the frame of memory:

They never sat you down and tried to advise you, or say, 'Try it and come back if you don't like it', there was never any of that. You went, and that was it. There was no return, you know. And then, when you went, you know, you'd be writing a letter sometimes, and you'd put an odd pound in for your mum and that, you know, when you got your wages and things, you know. But ... it ... I think it's ...we were ... like, I was 17, I was out there, and then when my sister, she got married, and I moved into a flat with a friend. Then when I think when you got your wage, we ... you put so much by for your rent, so much by for your fares to work, and so much by for ... to buy some clothes and so on ... and I, I ne ... never had any experience of doing it, you just did it. And there was no one to borrow from if you couldn't have the fare to work, would have never happened. That is, we always used to sort ourselves out, you know.[59]

'Family', more specifically Clare's parents, remains an important motif in her narrative of pre-marriage years in England, but not as an evocation of continuity, support or belonging. It is rather the lack of these things that is remembered, resulting in the production of a competing version of experience which works to subvert the process of subjective composure: instead of the self-confident, independent young women spurred on by the desire for urban excitement, we are left in this instance with an image of a 17-year-old fending for herself far from home, with 'no one to borrow from', with no option of return.

Set within the context of this narrative Clare's courtship with Sean takes on a new significance. Clare met Sean in December 1957, only four months after arriving in London, and married him two years later, when Clare was still only 19. Unlike Margo Cullagan, Clare does not therefore 'play the field'. Rather, like Brenda, she became attached early on to one person whom she later married. From this perspective, as well as being about romance, personal development and, indeed, financial prudence, Clare's courtship may also have been a response to emotional loss, reflecting a desire for the emotional closeness so lacking at home in Ireland. Migration to London thus involved identification with an image of assertive femininity, defined in opposition to patriarchal control and evoked in Clare's presentation of how she managed her relationship with her future husband to her own advantage. But because this identification was itself the outcome of an ambivalent relationship with parental figures, so it was vulnerable to the re-emergence of the underlying forms of resentment, desire and loss it temporarily resolved. Where memory production for Brenda was structured around the need to consolidate and preserve her courtship and marriage as redemptive experiences, for Clare the post-war city is a locus of competing desires, the tensions between which memory labours to resolve.

A cautionary tale

At least initially, similar images of self seem to shape the pre-marriage narrative of Rosie, whom we met in the last chapter. Rosie was born in 1938 in Cork city, the third of six children, into a desperately poor family. To a much greater extent than in Clare's case, Rosie's memories of this period of her life were fraught with tensions. Although she remembered her mother, brothers and sisters with affection, her father's abandonment of the family when she was a young girl both stigmatised and further impoverished her family in her account.[60] Having developed an intense hatred of her father in his absence, when he decided to reinstate himself in the family home when Rosie was 15, Rosie took a live-in position as an orderly in a local mental institution and became estranged from the family home.[61] It was against this backdrop that Rosie was persuaded by her older sister Anne's stories of 'dancehalls and glamour' to come to London in 1954, aged 16, to take up employment as a maid in a West End hotel.[62]

Rosie's narrative of leaving, however, was not a straightforward story of escape to a better life. One of the consequences of her father's abandonment of the family was that Rosie became an indispensable aide to her mother within the home.[63] While this led to the development of a close emotional bond between Rosie and her struggling mother, and to Rosie's internalisation of a self-image of the dutiful daughter, the practical constraints involved in realising this image also engendered competing desires for experiences beyond the home, as she watched her sisters and school friends follow their own individualised paths into adulthood. Rosie's decision to follow her older sister to London in 1954 represented an attempt to realise these desires for a more independent life, but her narrative of this process was deeply fraught, revealing an inability to reconcile such a desire with counterposed feelings of love and duty towards her mother and family.[64]

Signs of this emotional conflict continued to permeate Rosie's narrative of her early experiences working and living with her sister in London's West End. On the one hand, Rosie relates stories that evoke the glamour and excitement of the district;[65] on the other, Rosie emphasised how much she missed her mother, recalling that she 'cried every night. I wrote home practically every day to my mum.'[66] In addition, however, a third voice also becomes audible, one that speaks of the dangers of the West End as well as the religiosity of the young self:

> My sister met me at Paddington station, and in those days as well, the Legion of Mary used to be down there, catching girls coming over, because like Mary said, there'd used to be what we'd call 'wideboys', who'd know, they'd know straight away you were just over from Ireland,

> although the city girls were better at dressing up than the country girls, you know, because we were more in style. Erm ... and I did, I joined the Legion of Mary.[67]

As Frank Mort has argued, although London's West End had long-standing popular associations with crime and immorality, the decades after 1945 witnessed an intensification of public concerns around perceptions of the district as a transient 'twilight' zone and hotbed of 'vice'. The site of a flourishing post-war sex industry and scene to large rises in a variety of sexual crimes, the West End came to epitomise deteriorating British moral standards in a wide-ranging national debate involving journalists and police chiefs, politicians and representatives of the tourist industry.[68] Predictably, given that the district's hotels, bars and restaurants were major employers of Irish female labour in this period, so the area also featured prominently as a source of anxiety within the Catholic discourse on Irish immigration. Writing in 1958, Fr A. P. Boland reported on the exceptional difficulties faced by Our Lady of the Assumption and St Gregory, a parish at the very heart of the district. As well as around 2,000 permanent residents, the parish catered for a 'floating population' of around 8,000–10,000 who worked and lived in the district's many bars, night-clubs and restaurants.[69] Of these, Boland estimated that around 85 per cent were Irish Catholics, the majority of whom were women. In his view, not only was the parish ill-equipped to track the movements of this transient population, but more disturbing still, many of the young migrants were 'inadequately prepared' for the dizzying spectacle of glamour and sin daily on display in the district's streets and thoroughfares:

> The fact that more than 50 per cent of the immigrants have their first contact with a city when they come to London might well appal us. The glamour and the bright lights, the endless train and diversity of amusements, many of them unwholesome, the new sense of freedom for which many are inadequately prepared, each exacts its toll. Coupled with this is the stark fact that the agents of immorality are constantly recruiting, seeking to enmesh the weak and unwary. There is easy money to be made. The commercial value of sin is in daily evidence at every street corner.[70]

As Boland went on to note, the Legion of Mary, the apostolic lay organisation that staffed the emigrant section of the Catholic Welfare Bureau, represented one means by which the Church might manage the problem of 'the weak and unwary' within London's West End. In addition to disseminating literature and advice manuals in the district's hotels and restaurants, Legion members awaited new arrivals at train and bus stations, 'catching girls coming over' as Rosie put it, before they came under the predatory gaze of local 'wideboys', poised to exploit their sexual innocence.

As Rosie's description of the function of the Legion here suggests, the Legion promulgated a cautionary narrative of sexual danger which positioned the female migrant as a vulnerable innocent in need of protection. Yet, if Rosie identified with this construction, one of the assumptions embedded within it, that the naïve innocents arriving from Ireland were all 'country girls', is actively rejected by Rosie, who, being from Cork, identifies herself with the 'style' of the 'city girls'. In a pattern that echoes the competing identifications with family and 'glamour' articulated through her leaving narrative, Rosie's memory of arrival seems to project opposing self-images of innocence and sophistication relating to competing versions of Catholic and 'modern' femininity. Stimulated through recollections of 'mortifying' spectatorship, time and again this competition gave rise to strange tensions in this phase of her narrative:

> In Park Lane Hotel, you were plonked in the middle of the West End of London, and there used to be prostitutes walking up and down the front outside, and I used to say to our Anne, 'What are they doing there?!' And she said, 'Oh, I'll explain that to you another time.' You know. And, erm, she did eventually, and I thought … was mortified! You know, 'cos they'd be, they'd just get picked up with a taxi, and they'd go off, and all glamour and furs and all that type of thing. And again, like a lot of Cork people I was kind of starstruck, you know.[71]

According to a range of contemporary observers, the visibility of public prostitution in the West End increased dramatically in the years after the war, and the figure of the glamorously enrobed female prostitute became a prominent character in the flourishing public discourse on metropolitan 'vice'.[72] In Rosie's narrative, these figures appear as highly conflictual phantasy objects, embodying ideals of sophistication and fallen womanhood simultaneously, triggering competing desires and anxieties. Evoking both disavowal and idealisation, Rosie recalls being both 'mortified' and 'starstruck' by the image of 'prostitutes walking up and down the front outside'. Set amidst the moral chaos of the West End, the confusing spectacle of the glamorous prostitutes provides a means of portraying the innocence and hubris of the misguided younger self as it attempts to make sense of its new environment. In the process, the narrating self is laying down the narrative tracks for the younger self's own moral fall:

> I got a room with this friend, who was older than me, and was like … streetwise, I suppose you could say. And erm … [long pause] … and I got in trouble. Erm … [pause] … I had a child. A little boy. Really, I don't know if I should be telling you this? Er … [pause] … [sigh] …

and again of course, that made things ten times worse. Anyway, the father married me. We got, actually got married, in a Catholic church, I think. And, he was an Anglo-Indian. So in other words he was a foreigner. And ... and I think the reason that came about was because nobody had ever shown me any kind of affection, or even interest. And this man did. He was, oh! Just lovely, couldn't do enough for me. And erm, I didn't, like ... stupid, probably, didn't see nothing in ... no harm in having a, a foreigner, so to speak. But again, you see, I'd shamed the family. What family there was. I mean the major one would only have been like cousins and that, you know. But, it didn't bother me, actually. It didn't bother me, because I thought, 'I have to make the best of what's ... what's here now' you know, so ... I got married. We lived in a flat ... a basement flat. It wasn't, wasn't a happy relationship at all. He was a lot older than I was anyway. A lot. Erm ... and then had a little girl, so, that was two children I had.[73]

Having parted company with her sister, who she felt had become overbearing, Rosie moves in with a girl she describes as 'older' and more 'streetwise', the proverbial 'bad company', and before long she has been 'led astray': as she hesitantly reveals, 'I got into trouble'. Reflecting on this event from the distance of the present, Rosie explains its occurrence in terms of flattery and the low self-esteem of the younger self. Her relationship with the man she would marry appeared to offer the prospect of romantic love and affection, things of which the young self had no prior experience, yet desperately yearned for. As it turned out, the relationship only served to enhance her sense of isolation and alienation. Despite marrying the child's father in a Catholic church, Rosie had 'shamed the family' by becoming pregnant and entering into marriage with, as she revealingly puts it, 'a foreigner'. Her family ties all but severed, Rosie resolved to 'make the best of it', and moved into a basement flat with her new husband. Isolated and hidden away, family life in the subterranean dwelling, however, proved intolerable, and after having a second child Rosie made her escape to Oldham in 1966, taking her two children with her.[74]

In this narrative the tensions between competing models of femininity are worked out in terms of the fate of the naïve/wilful emigrant prophesised within cautionary religious narratives. But this mode of resolution, involving Rosie's take-up of the identity of 'the fallen woman', has highly ambivalent results in terms of subjective composure. The narrative, as a means of articulating the personal in terms of the general, facilitates the emotional and cognitive processing of an experience whose impact is intimated through the deep pauses that punctuate Rosie's tentative confession. More precisely, the construct of the naïve and vulnerable emigrant girl enables Rosie to project responsibility for her transgression onto a range of external others, collectively embodied in the alluring figure of the West End prostitute, the unsettling symbol of urban moral disorder. Yet, given the concept of original sin, the 'naïve emigrant girl' was never a blameless victim: the journey from vulnerable emigrant to 'unmarried mother' assumed a degree of agency on the part of the emigrant, however 'unworldly' she might be within cautionary stories about English popular culture. Prescriptive literature advising on the duties of the emigrant girl in England emphasised responsibility concomitantly with vulnerability: according to one such pamphlet:

> The sixth commandment forbids whatever is contrary to Holy purity in looks, words or deeds. It is here that the Irish girl has a great responsibility. She it is who dictates whether sin is to be committed or not. She is failing in her solemn duty if she allows a man to be impure with her by word or action.[75]

In Rosie's case, the issue of 'purity' and the boundaries it signified was further complicated by the fact that her 'illegitimate' child was the product of intimacy with 'a foreigner'. Within Catholic discourses on the emigrant, intimacy with a 'non-Catholic' had long been viewed as one of the principal mechanisms by which secularisation proceeded among migrants since the children of such a union were potentially 'lost' to the church. As Fr Leonard Sheil lamented in an article in *The Furrow* in 1958, 'an appalling tragedy is taking place now in England':

> *The cause is mainly bad marriages.* The Catholic married someone who had no religion, who never knelt down in the house to pray and never went to any church on Sunday. As the children grew up, this example from a parent whom they loved and admired destroyed their religion. Whether this marriage took place in a Catholic church or in a registrar's office does not seem to make much difference, as far as the children are concerned.[76]

Traditionally, concerns about 'leakage' in Britain had centred on intermarriage between Catholics and Protestants, but during the post-war period new anxieties emerged in relation to mixing with immigrants from other countries. As early as 1951, Catholic social workers were reporting with alarm on the intermixing of Irish Catholics which such immigrants in the inner-city lodging houses of major urban centres, and in particular, on the phenomenon of 'Irish girls' forming romantic liaisons with 'black men'.[77] Recounting the experiences of a priest out on his rounds in a London parish, Fr Sheil drew out the implications of such relationships in his article 'Marriage and the Leakage':

> The door was opened by a lovely young Irish girl. Beside her stood a little mite of perhaps three years, with a ribbon in her hair. The girl admitted that she was married in the registry.

> 'Is that little girl yours?'
> 'Yes.'
> 'What's her name?'
> 'Fatima.'
> 'That's a nice Catholic name.'
> 'Not at all; it's the name of the Prophet's daughter.'
> She was married to a Mohammedan from Fiji![78]

Articulated at a time when simmering racial tensions in England were beginning to erupt into popular violence, Sheil's depiction of the 'lovely young Irish girl' draws implicitly on contemporary pathologisations of mixed-race relationships, in which white womanhood, symbolising the boundaries of the British race as whole, was portrayed as under threat from black desire.[79] For Rosie, this complex discursive formation, in which discourses on religious 'leakage', sexual transgression and endangered whiteness competed with and reinforced one another, proved difficult to negotiate because it offered ways of understanding the events of her pre-marriage years which repeatedly threatened to bring the self into contradiction:

Rosie: I even went to the priest and I said, 'I'm leaving', I said, you know, 'I just can't live this life.' It got so as like he was bringing his mates in, like I said he was older than I was, and he'd bring his mates in, and I'd be sitting up in bed, and he said, 'There she is, she's good for nothing!' You know. And, that's another thing, another man in my life, sort of ... pulling me down, kind of thing, you know. So I thought, my sister, God rest her soul, had got a letter from an auntie who had moved up to Oldham in Lancashire, me Auntie Kitty – the Auntie Kitty who was our saviour as kids. So I, 'Oh I'd love to see Auntie Kitty!' So I came up for a weekend, one weekend, and I said, 'That's it!' Next weekend I was there, lock, stock and barrel. So I just left, with my two children. And went to Oldham.
Barry: What year was this?
Rosie: 1966. 1966, yeah. So, and my son had ... just made his communion, so ... we'd moved up to Oldham, and again you see I ... my, erm ... my son kinda looked foreign, if you like. My daughter didn't, you know. It never bothered me. But it did a lot of other people. I got a lot of, erm ... [sighs]. Again, didn't help my situation and my confidence, or ... you know what I mean? A... again, I was different. I was that one who was different, you know?[80]

This memory of escape to Oldham depicts a self struggling to negotiate a maze of subject-positions as it strives for redemption in the face of competing prohibitions and designations. In response to the figure of the priest, who presumably counselled against the break-up of the family, Rosie seems to invoke the image of the victimised white woman to justify her escape to Aunt Kitty's, 'our saviour when we were kids'. Oldham, however, does not provide the desired redemption but becomes the site of further discomposure, marking the reopening of a fraught conversation with the longer, pre-migration history of the self. Although she has escaped the domestic misery of her marriage to a 'foreign' husband in London, the powerful definitional effects of racial norms inhibit Rosie's transcendence of the consequences of that liaison. Rosie's first-born son 'kinda looked foreign', and although it 'never bothered' her, 'it did a lot of other people'. Instead of the hoped-for new beginning, the reflection ends on a note of dejection, bringing together episodes from distinct phases of Rosie's life as proof of the inescapable otherness of the self: 'again, I was different. I was the one who was different.'

Ambivalent horizons

In the twentieth-century discourse of Irish nationalists and religious elites, the English industrial city has often been denigrated as the antithesis of Irish rurality and tradition. In the post-1945 period, however, as the Irish economy stagnated while the British economy boomed, various Irish observers of the dense traffic of emigrants crossing the Irish Sea came to acknowledge that post-war British reconstruction offered young Irish people, and young women in particular, very real opportunities. Writing in 1954, the Irish novelist Bryan MacMahon recalled the impact the return of a young emigrant from England had upon the 'young girls' of his parish congregation one Sunday morning:

> Last Sunday at church, just as the priest was about to come to the altar, a girl, faultlessly dressed, minced up the passageway seeking a place, her young, well-dressed husband close behind her. With a start I recognized her. She was a maid who had left our town for England some years before, being then gawkish and shy. To all intents she was now a lady! As she passed the pews, the young girls of our town became brilliantly alert. The incident was a sermon without words.[81]

On one reading, the 'sermon' embodied in the young emigrant's striking performance of return spoke of England as a place of alternative self-fashionings. The transformations which English society underwent in the post-war period not only opened new opportunities for Irish women within the labour market, but created too new possibilities for the consumption of modern fashions, for leisure and social interaction and for romantic adventure. In short, English cities such as London, Birmingham and Manchester potentially constituted spaces where, beyond the censorious gaze of parents and priests, young single Irish women had access to the resources, freedoms and leisure venues which might enable them to live out the fantasy of feminine independence so prevalent in contemporary constructions of 'modern' femininity and implicit in MacMahon's 'sermon'.

This fantasy, in different ways and at different moments, shaped the memories analysed in this chapter. Its themes of affluence and empowerment, fashion and romance, echo through the stories these women told about their lives as young Irish migrants in the post-war English city, informing how they understood their experiences and the images of identity they wished to project. Yet these were not the only themes invoked in their stories. One of the things that MacMahon's depiction of the young emigrant omits is the complex negotiations and reworkings presupposed in the young woman's transformation from a 'gawkish and shy' young 'girl' to 'faultlessly dressed' young 'lady'. The post-war English city could be a space of exciting new possibilities and pleasures, but, as the narratives here examined suggest, it could also be a place of loneliness and isolation, danger and guilt. Attuned to the destabilising effects the city could have on new arrivals, and concerned more generally for the future of the Catholic family in an England that was undergoing major change, Catholic priests and welfare workers, working through a complex network of societies and organisations, sought to warn young female migrants of the dangers of the city while reminding them of their ultimate vocation as wives and mothers. And indeed, some part of that message appears to have informed MacMahon's young emigrant, whose performance of accomplishment includes the acquisition of a (docile) husband and takes place within the space of a church.

What this meant was that, as young migrants attempted to negotiate the losses associated with leaving home and the challenges and opportunities of their new environments, they were confronted with an interplay of competing ideals and images. In MacMahon's depiction of the young emigrant these potentially conflicting ideals appear to be cohesively married together; her self-assured passage down the aisle of the church, 'mincing' with husband in tow, projects a vision of femininity in which 'traditional' and 'modern' ideals of womanhood appear to be smoothly integrated. As the three narratives examined here suggest, however, in practice identity construction in the years between leaving for England and getting married was often a difficult and problematic process, shot through with anxiety and loss as well as excitement and satisfaction, and rarely arriving smoothly at a predestined point of self-realisation. Ideals of 'independence' and 'family' were not necessarily mutually exclusive poles, but elements embedded within competing constructions of femininity which subjects' took up and distanced themselves from in different ways, at different points in their narratives. Even with the passing of many years, however, memories of this period continued to arouse complicated emotions, indicating that the conflicts associated with this liminal moment in the migration journey remained to some extent unresolved and that the stories being constructed were implicated in, and shaped by, the present self's ongoing quest for psychic 'composure'.

As the oral historian Alistair Thomson has observed, 'a central and abiding claim of oral historians of migration' has been that 'oral evidence provides an essential record of the hidden history of migration'.[82] Like any other 'record', however, oral narrative does not simply reflect the experiences and events to which it refers. As Penny Summerfield suggests, it is 'necessary to encompass within oral history analysis and interpretation, not only the voice that speaks for itself, but also the voices that speak to it, the discursive formulations from which understandings are selected and within which accounts are made'.[83] The narratives analysed in this chapter underline the importance of attempting to decipher the multiple voices which echo through migrants' stories. These voices allude to the complexity and power-laden character of the environments migrant women inhabited, to the competing roles of different institutions and agencies in confronting women both with regulatory prescriptions and alternative possibilities for self-construction. Listened to for their variability, as texts in which the traces of a specific personal history are inscribed, these voices also make apparent the distinctive ways in which different women negotiated the conflicts and possibilities which the post-war English city presented to them. As well as the strategies women employed to manage the disruptions of early settlement in an unfamiliar place, 'negotiation' here refers to the ongoing psychic process by which women incorporated and displaced, affirmed and elided, different aspects of their pasts in order to integrate the self situated in the present. Such processes complicate the tendency to read oral narrative as a 'record'. Yet as evidence of the shifting interplay between social discourse and the psychic dimensions of subjectivity, the analysis of such negotiations forms a crucial element in any attempt to understand how the self is challenged, shaped and transformed through the process of migration.

Notes

1 J. McGahern, *The Barracks* (London, 2009), 52.
2 Ibid., 113.
3 S. Lambert, 'Irish Women's Emigration to England, 1922–60: The Lengthening of Family Ties', in A. Hayes and D. Urquhart (eds), *Irish Women's History* (Dublin, 2004), 152; S. Lambert, *Irish Women in Lancashire, 1922–1960: Their Story* (Lancaster, 2001), 102.

4 M. Buckley, 'Sitting on Your Politics: The Irish among the British and the Women among the Irish', in J. MacLaughlin (ed.), *Location and Dislocation in Contemporary Irish Society: Emigration and Irish Identities* (Cork, 1997), 111.
5 C. Clear, 'Too Fond of Going: Female Emigration and Change for Women in Ireland, 1946–1961', in D. Keogh, F. O'Shea and C. Quinlan (eds), *The Lost Decade: Ireland in the 1950s* (Cork, 2004), 142; I. O'Carroll, *Models for Movers: Irish Women's Emigration to America* (Dublin, 1991); M. Daniels, 'Exile or Opportunity? Irish Nurses and Wirral Midwives', *Irish Studies Review* 2:5 (1993), 4.
6 L. Ryan, 'Family Matters: (E)migration, Familial Networks and Irish Women in Britain', *Sociological Review* 52:3 (2004), 351–370; L. Ryan, 'Migrant Women, Social Networks and Motherhood: The Experiences of Irish Nurses in Britain', *Sociology* 41:2 (2007), 295–312; L. Ryan, '"I Had a Sister in England": Family-Led Migration, Social Networks and Irish Nurses', *Journal of Ethnic and Migration Studies* 34:3 (2008), 453–470.
7 This conception of the relation between gendered subjectivity and power draws on J. Butler, *Gender Trouble: Feminism and the Subversion of Identity* (London, 1990), chs 1 and 2.
8 I. Chambers, *Migrancy, Culture, Identity* (London, 1994), 6.
9 A. Thomson, 'Moving Stories: Oral History and Migration Studies', *Oral History* 27:1 (1999), 35.
10 M. Chamberlain, 'Gender and the Narratives of Migration', *History Workshop Journal* 43 (1997), 105
11 See, for example, Mass Observation, *The Journey Home: A Mass-Observation Report on the Problems of Demobilisation* (London, 1944), 57–58.
12 P. Fitzgerald and B. Lambkin, *Migration in Irish History, 1607–2007* (London, 2008), 245. Estimates of the number of Irish migrants entering the post-war British labour market vary. The estimate quoted derives from K. Paul, 'A Case of Mistaken Identity: The Irish in Post-War Britain', *International Labour and Working-Class History* 49 (1996), 117
13 Figures from J. A. Jackson, *The Irish in Britain* (London, 1963), 199.
14 Brenda Grady (b. Galway, 1927) PI/SA/5, 1–4. Labour recruitment schemes were common in the immediate post-war period. See E. Delaney, *The Irish in Post-War Britain* (Oxford, 2007), 48.
15 Brenda Grady (b. Galway, 1927) PI/SA/5, 5.
16 Ibid.
17 Ibid.
18 Ibid., 6.
19 P. Summerfield, 'Women in Britain since 1945: Companionate Marriage and the Double Burden', in J. Obelkevich and P. Catterall (eds), *Understanding Post-War British Society* (London, 1994), 60–61.
20 The same observation has been made by L. Ryan, 'Moving Spaces and Changing Places: Irish Women's Memories of Emigration to Britain in the 1930s', *Journal of Ethnic and Migration Studies* 29:1 (2003), 75.
21 Brenda Grady (b. Galway, 1927) PI/SA/5, 6.
22 Ibid.
23 A. Kidd, *Manchester: A History* (Edinburgh, 2002), 224.
24 Brenda Grady (b. Galway, 1927) PI/SA/5, 7.

25 Kidd, *Manchester*, 187–198.
26 A. Davies, *Leisure, Gender and Poverty: Working-Class Culture in Salford and Manchester, 1900–1939* (Buckingham, 1992), 81.
27 C. Langhamer, *Women's Leisure in England: 1920–60* (Manchester, 2000), 64.
28 Delaney, *The Irish in Post-War Britain*, 170–172.
29 The most comprehensive study of this culture for the pre-1939 period remains S. Fielding, *Class and Ethnicity: Irish Catholics in England, 1880–1939* (Buckingham, 1993). See also C. Wildman, 'Religious Selfhoods and the City in Inter-War Manchester', *Urban History* 38:1 (2011), 103–123.
30 'Irish Warned of "Dangers"', *The Observer*, 5 June 1955.
31 Olive Mary Garrigan, '"So You Are Going to England". An Open Letter to Irish Girls about to Emigrate', *Christus Rex* 3:2 (1949), 49.
32 Ibid., 53.
33 Ibid.
34 See J. Keating, 'Faith and Community Threatened? Roman Catholic Responses to the Welfare State, Materialism and Social Mobility, 1945–62', *Twentieth Century British History* 9:1 (1998), 86–108.
35 N. Roberts, 'Irish Girls in England: I – A Pathetic Immigration', *Manchester Guardian*, 1 April 1955.
36 Catholic Truth Society of Ireland, *A Catholic Handbook for Irish Men and Women Going to England* (Dublin, 1953); E. Gaynor, *The Shamrock Express* (Dublin, 1962); Robert L. Stevenson, *Shall I Emigrate?* (Dublin, 1965); 'Irish Labour Emigration', 23 July 1951, National Archives of Ireland, Dublin (hereafter NAI), DT/S/11582/C; E. Hopkins, 'Irish Workers in England', *Christus Rex* 2:2 (1948), 17–24; R. Culhane, J. F. Duggan, E. Hopkins, G. Brady and D. O'Leary, 'Irish Catholics in Britain', *The Furrow* 1:8 (1950), 387–414.
37 Garrigan, '"So You Are Going to England"', 50–51.
38 Brenda Grady (b. Galway, 1927) PI/SA/5, 7.
39 Ibid.
40 Parish Priests' Committee London, *Report on Irish Workers in London and Proposed Plan*, May 1948, AIB/ICIB/1.
41 CTS, *A Catholic Handbook*, 22.
42 Summerfield, 'Women in Britain since 1945', 60–66; A. Thomson, '"Tied to the Kitchen Sink"? Women's Lives and Women's History in Mid-Twentieth Century Britain and Australia', *Women's History Review* 22:1 (2013), 134.
43 Brenda Grady (b. Galway, 1927) PI/SA/5, 9.
44 Commission on Emigration, *Reports*, 1.
45 Ibid., 138.
46 F. Mort, *Capital Affairs: London and the Making of the Permissive Society* (London, 2010), 16.
47 See, for example, J. J. Gray, 'Caring for Our Emigrants', *Christus Rex* 9:1 (1955), 15.
48 'An Advent Pastoral Letter on Christian Marriage', Bishop Henry Vincent Marshall, 19 November 1948, Salford Diocesan Archives, Manchester, Box 226, Marshall Papers.
49 J. B. Keane, *The Contractors* (Dublin, 1993), 16.
50 Ibid., 18.
51 Ibid., 19.
52 Clare Cullen (b. Cork, 1940) PI/SA/1, 2.

53 Ibid., 7.
54 Ibid., 10.
55 Ibid., 13.
56 Ibid., 14.
57 Ibid., 10.
58 Ibid.
59 Ibid., 11.
60 Rosie Long (b. Cork, 1938) PI/SA/8, 2.
61 Ibid., 10.
62 Ibid., 11.
63 Ibid., 2.
64 Ibid., 12.
65 Ibid., 15.
66 Ibid., 14.
67 Ibid., 12.
68 Mort, *Capital Affairs*, 41–48.
69 A. P. Boland, 'A London Parish', *The Furrow* 9:4 (1958), 240.
70 Ibid., 241.
71 Rosie Long (b. Cork, 1938) PI/SA/8, 15.
72 Mort, *Capital Affairs*, 42–45.
73 Rosie Long (b. Cork, 1938) PI/SA/8, 16.
74 Ibid., 17.
75 CTS, *A Catholic Handbook*, 17.
76 L. Sheil, 'Marriage and the Leakage', *The Furrow* 9:8 (1958), 522–523.
77 'Irish Labour Emigration', 23 July 1951, NAI/DT/S/11582/C. See also Gerard Brady, 'Irish Catholics in Britain', *The Furrow* 1:8 (1950), 407–408; M. Foley, 'Some Notes on the Situation of Irish Workers in Birmingham', July 1951, Birmingham Archdiocesan Archives (hereafter BAA), AP/J6j.
78 Sheil, 'Marriage and the Leakage', 523.
79 On defensive British discourses on whiteness see B. Schwarz, 'The Only White Man in There': The Re-Racialisation of England, 1956–1968', *Race & Class* 38:1 (1996), 65–78; C. Waters, '"Dark Strangers" in Our Midst: Discourses of Race and Nation in Britain, 1947–1963', *Journal of British Studies* 36:2 (1997), 207–238; W. Webster, '"There'll Always be an England": Representations of Colonial Wars and Immigration, 1948–1968', *Journal of British Studies* 40:4 (2001), 557–584.
80 Rosie Long (b. Cork, 1938) PI/SA/8, 17.
81 B. MacMahon, 'Getting on the High Road Again', in J. O'Brien (ed.), *The Vanishing Irish* (London, 1954), 207.
82 Thomson, 'Moving Stories', 26.
83 P. Summerfield, *Reconstructing Women's Wartime Lives* (Manchester, 1998), 15.

3

Lives in re/construction: myth, memory and masculinity in Irish men's narratives of work in the British construction industry

The derided but mobile Paddy

Given the dire state of Britain's finances at the end of the Second World War, raising national productivity levels became a basic premise of post-war economic recovery for the newly elected Labour government. As the fuel crisis of 1947 demonstrated, however, acute labour shortages seriously threatened the realisation of this goal. As the *Economic Survey for 1947* made clear, a central problem for economic planners concerned how 'to expand the nation's labour force, to increase its output per man-year and, above all, to get men and women where they are needed most'.[1] Immigration, facilitated by labour recruitment schemes and the flexible understanding of citizenship enshrined by the 1948 British Nationality Act, represented one means by which state and industry sought to manage the problem of labour supply. Favoured above all others in this respect were Irish migrants, who, despite Eire's complete withdrawal from the Commonwealth in 1949, were granted the same rights as British citizens under the 1948 Act, enabling the entry of between 50,000 and 60,000 a year into the British labour market between 1946 and 1961.[2]

As a number of scholars have pointed out, Britain's post-war labour crisis may be seen to mark an important shift in the work history of the Irish in Britain.[3] Beginning with Irish labour recruitment into new industries during wartime, the contemporary sociologist J. A. Jackson identified a process whereby the changing labour needs of the British economy opened 'the way for far greater occupational choice and mobility for the Irish immigrant to Britain and paved the way for direct Irish infiltration into almost every branch of industry in the period since the end of the war'.[4] Yet if post-war labour demands fostered a greater diffusion of Irish labour within the British economy, contemporary representations of the Irish migrant continued to associate him with heavy, 'unskilled' labour and with brutish propensities for drinking and fighting at odds with the domestication of masculinity valorised within discourses on post-war moral reconstruction.[5] This was apparent, not only in the observations of Catholic social scientists, concerned priests and Catholic welfare workers, but in local press reportage, parodic cartoons and popular television series.[6]

Such representations reflected the resilience of long-established stereotypes, but they also pointed to continuities in the work profile of the Irish migrant in the post-war period. If such migrants were in high demand, they were needed most in Britain's 'undermanned' industries, for the performance of 'dirty jobs' the state could not persuade native Britons to undertake. Despite relative occupational diffusion, the majority of Irish migrants arrived in Britain lacking the forms of capital necessary for entry into the more lucrative and prestigious fields of employment within the labour market, and so continued to gravitate towards arduous, low-status and frequently hazardous forms of work in domestic or 'personal' service, metal manufacturing, agriculture and construction. Concerning the last of these, and according to the 1951 census, almost 18 per cent of the total Irish-born male population resident in England and Wales worked in 'building', with an additional 13.8 per cent classified as 'unskilled'. In Scotland this rose to almost 25 per cent and 14.3 per cent respectively.[7]

Viewed thus, the Irish in post-war England constituted a flow of commodified labour, a 'replacement population' whose function was to inhabit those segments of the division of labour hastily evacuated by Britons. Such was the view of Donal Foley, whose own migration from Kilkenny to London in 1944 would ultimately lead to a career in journalism, first on Fleet Street and later with the *Irish Times*:

> The Irish in Britain were always hewers of wood and drawers of water, and so they have remained to this day ... This was much in evidence during the war and post-war years in Britain, when it was the derided but mobile Paddy who willingly did all the dirty jobs for clean money ... Often they had no tax cards, no insurance stamps. In fact, there were no records at all of many of them. They were hard-working, well-paid slaves, exactly what Britain wanted to rebuild their devastated country.[8]

In highlighting these continuities in the work experiences of Irish migrants in twentieth-century England, such views constitute a crucial corrective to narratives which position Irish migrants unproblematically within the newly 'affluent' working class.[9] This, indeed, has been a chief function of the figure of the Irish construction worker across a range of discourses in post-1945 English culture: inscribed within a tragic myth of exile and exploitation, the Irish construction worker has been mobilised repeatedly to point up the limitations and contradictions of post-war modernisation. In some versions, such as Phillip Donnellan's 1965 documentary *The Irishmen: An Impression of Exile*, the exile of Irish construction workers from their rural homeland resonates with a wider post-war nostalgia for 'community' amidst rapid reconstruction.[10] More recently, the same themes of exile and exploitation have been coupled with ideas of abandonment, isolation and forgetting in documentaries, fiction and an expanding community literature seeking to draw public attention to the present-day circumstances of many Irishmen who 'built Britain's cities'.[11] Based in part on research carried out in the mid-1990s, for example, Enda Hughes's 2011 documentary *The Men of Arlington House* offers a powerful portrayal of the plight of thousands of post-war construction workers who, having spent the best part of their adult lives working as labourers in the industry, now found themselves homeless, forgotten and, in many instances, struggling with multiple physical and mental health problems.[12]

Such images of the migrant experience have supplied one particularly influential means of representing the journey of the Irish construction worker in post-1945 England. A limitation, however, of inscribing this journey within a tragic mode is that the workplace is grasped only as a site of alienation. While work is inextricably linked with processes of economic positioning, it is also central to 'how one earns or acquires a sense of identity and moral worth through interaction with others'.[13] For men in particular, studies of masculinity stress the importance of men's interactions with the work process, and participation in work-based cultures, as sources of masculine selfhood.[14] As Collinson and Hearn observe:

> For many men, employment provides the interrelated economic resources and symbolic benefits of wages/salaries, skills and experience, career progress and positions of power, authority and high discretion. Typically, it seems, men's gender identities are constructed, compared and evaluated by self and others according to a whole variety of criteria indicating personal 'success' in the workplace.[15]

Using the personal work histories of three male migrants who spent the bulk of their working lives in construction, together with migrant diaries, memoirs and autobiographies, this chapter investigates the industry as a site for the construction of migrant identities, exploring this process in terms of three interrelated dynamics. Setting the analysis within the broader contexts of the post-war English economy and culture, the first project of the chapter is to examine the specificity of respondents' experiences within the industry, exploring how their performance of distinct roles, different occupational trajectories and changing conditions within the industry shaped different kinds of gendered identification with construction within their work histories. Alongside and intersecting with this, the chapter also explores the different ways in which the experiences of Irish men in the construction industry have been represented and disseminated by a variety of actors in the second half of the twentieth century, such that a set of common tropes, images and formulas have become available at the level of communal/public memory for popular consumption. The chapter examines the different ways these images are implicated in the dialectic by which respondents endeavour to make their experiences within the industry and the identifications engendered through them cohere with the psychological needs of the narrating self.

Finally, the chapter also explores the diverse ways issues of belonging and subjective change play into these processes of self-construction. As Liam Harte has put it:

> The 'ex-isled' self is forever prone to reading 'here' in relation to 'there'. It is a truism that migration, whether coerced or freely chosen, typically entails the loss of a familiar, sustaining community and demands a fresh orientation towards a new and often discomfiting world of chance and change. Yet the past is never entirely left behind, even by those who devoutly desire it, any more than the present is seamlessly embraced, once and for all.[16]

Within the historiography of the Irish in Britain questions of belonging have often been addressed in dichotomous terms. As Harte's point suggests, however, migrant belongings are much more ambivalent, contingent and pluralised than such frameworks permit. Migrants rarely invest exclusively in either a sending or receiving society, but often sustain, in variable and graduated ways, both forms of attachment, modulating between one and the other at different times, in different spaces, for different reasons. Indeed, as Fitzgerald and Lambkin point out:

> For most migrants it was never a simple choice between old world and new world because they effectively belonged to 'three different worlds': that of the immigrants, that of the receiving country and that of the old country. This means that outcomes of migration at the level of individual migrants are highly diverse, varying over time according to changing circumstances and attitudes in all 'three worlds'.[17]

For Irish migrants in the post-war construction industry, the industry was never only an arena for the construction of masculine identities, or even class identities, but a space in which masculinity, class position and diasporic belongings intersected in complex ways. This chapter explores this intersectionality through the distinct forms of dialogue that take place between 'here' and 'there' within subjects' accounts of work within the industry.

Going outside

Denis was born in 1927 and grew up near Listowel, Kerry, on his family's 25-acre farm. After leaving school in 1941, aged 14, Denis began work on a local council-managed bog, where he drove a horse and cart transporting turf. Although Denis liked this job, by 1947 work on Lyrecrumpane bog where he was employed had become increasingly irregular. As such, given the lack of alternative forms of employment in the immediate vicinity and the fact that he was not in line to inherit the family farm, Denis migrated to London in September 1948 in order to keep 'working and making a living'.[18] Arriving in England during a period of acute labour shortages, Denis did not have to wait long to achieve his aim. Having got 'a set of cards', Denis found work almost immediately in a foundry in Ealing, moulding doors for electric trains.[19]

Despite Denis's rapid success in finding work, his memories of this period in his work history contrast with the nostalgicised account he offered earlier of working on the bog back in Ireland. Where Denis 'loved working everyday' on 'the bog', equating this time in his life with 'freedom' and 'craic', his recollection of the period immediately following arrival in England registers a shift in tone:

Barry: And that would have been a few years after the war then?
Denis: Well it was. Well, the war was finished in 1945. And then that was 1948. So that was all the immigration, you see. The [pauses] they come over here and they ... you had to ... you had to work, because there was no other way to get a living.
Barry: So what was your first job, whenever you arrived?
Denis: My first job was working in a foundry, in Ealing. In London.
Barry: What did you think of that sort of work?
Denis: Oh I ... 'twas the wintertime, when you come on the winter it changed, it changed with the winter. And it was, er, it was very dusty, which was ... No, I enjoyed it. Really. But I wanted to go outside and the first chance I got I went outside then. Working on the roads and sewers and all that craic.[20]

As noted above, a necessary condition of British economic recovery in the immediate post-war period was a significant increase in output levels in staple industries. The popular rhetoric of post-war 'austerity' did not only call upon citizens to conserve scarce resources, but emphasised too the importance of their role as producers in 'winning the peace'. However, while conditions of full employment were maintained during the period and productivity levels had undergone significant increases by 1949, state and industry continued to have problems directing labour into 'essential industries', necessitating the use of migrant labour from abroad. Irish migrants, their entry to the British labour market predicated on the expectation that they would make up the 'manpower' deficit in such industries, thus became key targets of post-war producerist discourse, even as popular perceptions of Irish workers continued to be affected by Ireland's neutrality stance during the war and longer-standing stereotypes identifying Irishness with unreliability and idleness.[21] This was reflected in the lengths to which the Ministry of Labour went in order to ensure the safe arrival of assisted migrants to Britain, providing food, travel and shelter, and more generally, in the continuation of wartime landing controls, to which all male migrants were subject.[22] Through this latter mechanism, via which male migrants acquired their working papers, the government was able to direct 'suitable migrants' – 'fit men between 18 and 35' – into approved employment, typically the 'undermanned' 'essential industries'.[23] As Denis, alluding to the lack of alternative means of subsistence, thus put it: 'you had to work'.

Yet, if Denis's memories are here related through a language of compulsion, intimating that this early phase of his work history was a difficult one, a sense of agency returns to his narrative when he recalls his ambition 'to go outside'. While metal manufacturing was a chronically 'undermanned' industry during the early post-war period, the construction industry too had persistent problems satisfying its expanding labour needs. Given the aggregate effects of pre-war shortages, wartime blitzing and a post-war spurt in marriage and fertility rates, a central policy aim for post-war governments was to dramatically increase Britain's depleted housing stock, alongside the large-scale development of urban infrastructure. Demand, however, consistently outstripped supply in terms of both houses built and the available labour force, which stood at a third of its pre-war level in the immediate post-war years.[24] Thus, although the industry would undergo sustained expansion throughout the 1940s and 1950s, it did so under tight labour market conditions such that the industry could provide for regular employment at relatively good rates of remuneration up until the 1960s, whether one was working on public housing schemes or 'the roads and sewers'.[25]

The 'first chance' he got after arriving in England, Denis took up work in the industry as a groundworker or labourer. Although Denis insists that he 'enjoyed' working in the foundry, his account of his decision to change employment contrasts the 'dusty', confined environment of this workplace with the desire, articulated through the first-person voice, 'to go outside', establishing overlapping evaluative oppositions between outdoors/indoors and clean/dirty. Approached through Bourdieu's notion of habitus, this preference may be seen as a function of the ways in which Denis's earlier work experiences on the farm and bog have engendered a particular 'sense of one's place'. In a rural context where popular discourses on Irish masculinity linked authenticity with work on the land, Denis's youthful work experiences have engendered an equation between 'outside' and 'freedom', disposing him in England to seek out work contexts where these images of self can be re-embodied. Bog work and farm work are not of course identical with 'working on the roads and sewers', but all take place in the open air and involve similar sorts of bodily competencies, in particular shovel work. One way of reading Denis's desire 'to go outside' is thus to see it as shaped by the way habitus disposes one to familiar spaces and forms of practice.

This 'sense of one's place' was not only related to material features of the form of the workplace, however:

> But that was only for a while, because then we moved out to the country, and I was in digs down in Felixstowe in Suffolk. Worked there for a bit and then we went to pulling beet down in Nottingham in the wintertime. And we came back again to Suffolk again, then took the same job, you know. And I went from that job to London with them. Then ... and I was with them until I left, came down here. They were Kerry. They were the same county as myself and my mate was ... my mate and myself that I ... we worked as partners after, and working ... we, that's how we done it, you know.[26]

Although the post-war construction industry would see growing numbers of 'company men' who contracted to work for one of the large building firms for the duration of their working lives, for many Irish migrants during this period and before the war employment in construction took a more casual form, where workers moved from job to job when one contract finished or there was preferable employment elsewhere.[27] This casualism fostered a particular rhythm of itinerancy, characterised by ongoing movement and travel between jobs in different parts of the country, phases of being in-between jobs, where other forms of 'unskilled' labour were performed as a stop-gap, and the repeated taking up of new residences, either in makeshift on-site accommodation or private local lodging houses.

As migrant diaries, memoirs and fictionalised accounts of the period suggest, this transient lifestyle frequently marked such workers as outsiders among local populations, as marginal to the practices of 'ordinary' domesticity inscribed at the heart of post-war fantasies of Englishness.[28] As such sources also show, however, this itinerancy structured the practices of a distinctive homosocial milieu, based around the construction site, the temporary lodging house and particular local pubs, in which Irish men worked, lived and socialised with other men from similar backgrounds in rural Ireland. Where contemporary industrial sociologists emphasised the individualism of construction workers, whether on civil engineering projects or residential developments, the networks formed through this pattern of itinerary performed important practical functions in terms of disseminating crucial information about jobs, wages and lodgings, much of which was unavailable at the labour exchange office.[29] At the same time, moreover, they delineated the contours, however fluid, of a social space in urban England that could enable the recovery of 'a sense of one's place' in a broader context of disruption and discontinuity, and in many instances, native hostility; where habituated ways of relating to oneself and others could be reaffirmed through interaction with others possessing similar emotional needs and ways of conceptualising the world. Whereas there were only 'three or four'[30] Irish men employed in the foundry at Ealing, the casual labour culture of the construction industry offered Denis the opportunity to interact with other Irish men, indeed, to form a work gang with men from his home county, one of whom would become his life-long 'mate' and work 'partner'. In this way, certain gendered practices of Irish rural communality were transposed into the English post-war urban environment.

The pickaxe, the shovel and the graft

On this reading, then, the construction industry appears as a kind of refuge, where ties of community belonging could be re-established. It remains a brute fact, however, that work within the industry was particularly arduous and dangerous during the period.[31] House-building, and urban reconstruction more generally, was an urgent policy issue for both the Labour and Conservative parties in the decades after the war, and the scale of demand sustained expansion in construction up to the late 1960s and beyond. However, while this helped keep wages relatively high for particular categories of worker, it also contributed to an intensification of the labour process and rising fatalities.

In part, this had to do with the relative lack of mechanisation within the industry, particularly at the level of groundworkers. Because much of the industry was heavily dependent on credit over the period, so it was highly sensitive to demand regulation at the macroeconomic level, with the result that the stop-go fluctuations of the wider economy were particularly pronounced within construction. In turn, although the industry continued to expand up until the late 1960s, outside of the largest companies this was not accompanied by increased mechanisation, since smaller firms were reluctant to invest in new machinery that would lie idle during the next trough in demand. Instead, when the next 'go' phase was initiated firms responded by rehiring labour, employed on 'the lump', which was worked intensively in order to capitalise on the rising wave of demand.[32]

At the same time, such fluctuations also contributed to the spread of payment-by-results methods of remuneration. Although pay and incentive schemes were in fact first introduced in 1947 under the Labour government, it was the returned Conservative Party's active monetary policies and deregulation of the construction industry in the mid-1950s which stimulated the growth of private contractors and labour-only subcontractors within the industry. Aiming to maximise profits while demand was high and money cheap, many such firms negotiated piece-rates directly with 'self-employed' labourers, who would compete against one another within casual labour pools for 'a start'.[33] However, although piece-work might enable some labourers to achieve relatively good wages, the remuneration/effort ratio was in fact increasingly tilted in favour of the contractors. Increases in productivity within the industry from the 1950s were not achieved through the hiring of greater numbers of labour or rapid increases in mechanisation, but via an intensification of the labour process, as fewer labourers were employed to do a greater quantity of work in a shorter space of time. During the 1958–1969 period in particular, the industry underwent a boom, with the average rate of houses built rising from 249,000 to 340,000 per annum, at a time when unemployment was on the increase.[34] Inevitably, as foremen incited labourers to exceed what was physically manageable in order to capitalise on conditions of high demand, fatalities rose, and employment within the industry gained a reputation as hazardous. For construction unions, whose strength had been severely weakened by the spread of 'the lump', industry safety, together with decasualisation and nationally agreed rates of pay, became key issues in this period.[35]

In the diaries, memoirs and fictionalised accounts of Irish men who worked in post-war construction, the intensity of work processes within the industry forms a recurrent motif, around which a range of meanings are generated. For John O'Donoghue, for example, who was recruited to work as a labourer on an aerodrome site during wartime, the strenuousness of the work tasks he was obliged to perform pushed his 40-year-old body to its limits, so that the building site was recalled as site of pain and suffering:

> I poured shovel after shovel into the vessel again, each shovel putting a dreadful soreness all over my limbs. It was a relief when the hopper was raised and I got a few minutes' rest. But down it came again and it

had to be filled in a wild hurry each time. I was ready to drop, but I had to go on. I was by no means lazy, but quite willing to work, only that I had so little strength left in me for it.[36]

For other men who worked in the industry during the post-war period, however, the meanings attached to the work process were much less straightforward. Donall MacAmhlaigh came to England initially to work as an orderly in a hospital, but left after two weeks to work as a general labourer on a building site in Towcester. Transported by the contractor to the site 'on spec', soon after arrival he 'got the job', and was immediately set to work picking the ground with Mike Ned, a seasoned navvy from Cornamona he had met the previous day in Northampton:

> Mike Ned showed me how to go about it properly – not to lift the pick too high and to hit in the same place always and not to be hitting haphazardly with it. I worked better after that and I tried hard because I didn't want any of the lads saying: 'What kind of a man is that that can't work like a proper navvy?' We worked away and when the first break came at ten o'clock I had blisters on my hands and my back felt as if somebody had been laying about it with a stick.[37]

On the construction site workers were subjected to harsh regimes of physical labour that frequently threatened the integrity of their bodies and minds. As MacAmhlaigh describes, by 10 o'clock on his first morning his hands were blistered and his back wracked with pain. But in these accounts such regimes were never simply metaphors for exploitation, but corporeal mechanisms of subjectification through which distinctive conceptualisations of work-based masculinity were generated. If the heavy, arduous, dangerous character of the work regime threatens the viability of the body and self, those traits and competencies which enable conquest of the regime may become encoded as valorised ideals of manliness. As the contemporary sociologist A. J. M. Sykes observed of labourers on a large civil engineering project, 'to be known as a hard worker was something to be proud of. Men who worked hard were praised, while poor workers were regarded with contempt.'[38] In this way, status and inclusion within the homosocial world of the construction worker was governed by one's ability to embody *machismo* ideals of strength, power, endurance and risk-taking; weakness, idleness and cautious self-preservation, as traits associated with the ever-present threat of castration posed by the regime, become anathema. The work process is thus simultaneously a site of self-construction and mutilation, able to 'make or break a man', and MacAmhlaigh's anxiety concerns the recognition of his fellow workers as much as the effects of the work task upon his body: he 'tried hard' to embody the image of 'a proper navvy' lest his manhood be called into question.

Issues of ethnic and national identity played into this culture of masculinity in various ways. As Sykes also observed, navvies as group had long been regarded as an 'outcast' population within wider society; local people in the regions where they were encamped 'despised' the navvies 'for the rough work they did and for their reputation for drinking, fighting and behaving anti-socially'.[39] The concentration of post-war Irish migrants within the industry tended, unsurprisingly, to reinforce the agency of these associations in shaping perceptions of Irish manhood.[40] Within the post-war English imagination, constructions of Irish masculinity thus encoded languages of class and ethnic difference simultaneously, eliding the brutish appetites of the rough navvy with historic tropes of Irish irrationality and hypersensitivity.[41]

2 Joseph Lee, 'Sure an' it's himself miscalling the dacent Oirish-American President o' the U.S.A. an American-Oirishman that'll be starting the throubles all over again ... lemme admonish him!', *Evening News*, 26 June 1963, BCA/03673. The cartoon refers to reaction to US President Kennedy's visit to his ancestral home in Co. Wexford.

If, however, such associations betrayed the enduring legacies of Anglo-Irish conflict within wider popular culture, within the construction industry itself Irish masculinity could also function as a form of social and cultural capital. Because migrant Irish labour was plentiful, mobile and flexible, it was valued by English and Irish contractors operating under conditions of fluctuating demand, and such firms developed distinctive ways of recruiting, managing and remunerating it. As well as employing much Irish labour on 'the lump', a system which enabled both contractors and labourers to defraud the tax system, firms might seek to coax Irish men into ever-greater feats of work through appeals to a mythology which valorised rural migrants as the purest specimens of 'a hardworking and energetic race', conditioned by 'hard living over the years' to glory in the performance of punishing labour.[42]

Irish gangers and foremen, drawn by contractors from the most ambitious and robust of the Irish labour army to manage it at the point of production, were themselves incorporated into this racial mythology as merciless figures who exploited young Irish men in order to secure their own bonus. While working on the Kilsby tunnel near Rugby in 1957, Donall MacAmhlaigh encountered an 'ill-mannered buck from county Mayo', whom, it seemed, 'nobody could satisfy':

> Three wagons of concrete pipes came along with each pipe weighing about a hundredweight and, when we started to lift them out of the wagons at two men to a pipe, he nearly burst with rage.
>
> 'Two men to carry one of those things', he bellowed, 'I'd lift one of them with my little finger on a bad day. I don't know what kind of shrimps they're sending over from Mary Horan's since the war. When I came over, they were sending men not women.'
>
> With that, he grabbed one of the pipes and swung it up over his head just as if it had been a sod of peat. If you only saw the arms that man had when he took hold of the pipe with the muscles standing out like huge thick ropes, you'd say that no man on earth could ever stand up to him.[43]

MacAmhlaigh's account of this episode provides a good example of the ways in which Irish hypermasculinity could be employed to secure hierarchical discipline and enhance productivity on the site. At the same time, however, his representation of the foreman's actions belie admiration for the display of power and strength being projected, linking it through the simile 'a sod of peat' with the bog-lands of the rural west of Ireland. As well as a description of a form of regulation, the representation thus inscribes the ganger's performance of physical prowess within a revivalist myth of the Irish peasant farmer, in which the harsh rural milieu of the west is implicitly equated with a superior Irish fitness to work.[44]

In turn, such images of Irish hypermasculinity have been generalised within the communal memory of post-war settlement in competing ways. In one strand of representations, the themes of physical strength and fearlessness articulate within a story of itinerant adventure coupling the exertions of the work regime with practices of heavy drinking, fighting and gambling. As Sykes observed, navvies valued hard work, but they also liked to see themselves as 'wild men':

> The most socially reprehensible feature of the navvies, so they believed, was their wildness: their drinking, gambling and fighting. But this was a feature that they boasted of and told exaggerated stories about: stories of famous drinking bouts, of gambling schools that have gone on day and night until thousands of pounds had been won and lost, of great battles in which whole camps had been wrecked. The navvies had a romantic view of this aspect of their lives as something glamorous, something with the appeal of the Foreign Legion, and liked to visualise themselves as 'hard' men.[45]

Such stories have become part of the popular mythology of the Irish navvy in England, a process fostered by the emergence of a navvy literature over the twentieth century, and by the incorporation of stock features of this into popular song. As Richard Hall has documented, while Irish music-making practices in the post-war English city were based initially on the replication of pre-existing Irish forms, new ballads about the Irishman's experiences in the construction industry began to emerge in the 1960s within the context of the British folk revival.[46] Although songs such as Eoin MacColl's 'Tunnel Tigers', Christy Moore's 'Paddy on the Railroad' and Dominic Behan's 'McAlpine's Fusiliers' differed in tone, they all made use of a recognisable image of authentic rural Irish masculinity, recast in an urban setting, which proved popular with Irish audiences in Britain. 'McAlpine's Fusiliers' in particular has become a staple of The Dubliners' live sets when touring in Britain, and construction workers themselves are reported to have sung the song while travelling on lorries to and from sites:

> As down the glen came McAlpine's men
> With their shovels slung behind them
> 'Twas in the pub they drank the sub
> And out in the spike you'll find them.
> They sweated blood and they washed down mud
> With pints and quarts of beer
> And now we're on the road again
> With McAlpine's fusiliers.[47]

For other actors concerned with the public reputation of Irish migrants, however, this 'wild man' image was more problematic. Where writers and folk balladeers sought to mobilise Irish male roughness as a subversion of English cultural norms, within post-war Irish associational culture more generally self-representational practices were governed by the twin concerns of the Catholic Church, which was centrally involved in the inception, financing and everyday running of such bodies, and a growing community of socially ambitious migrants committed to long-term settlement in England. Against popular characterisations of the Irish as a 'ghetto' community, given to rough behaviours, and through the intersecting activities of local Irish centres, county associations and the *Irish Post*, these self-appointed leaders of the Irish community endeavoured to 'raise the status and reputation of the Irish community' through the promotion of a semi-official code of Irish respectability.[48]

As part of this, the Irish propensity for hard, honest labour continued to be valorised as a moral virtue: internal discussions on the welfare functions of Irish bodies repeatedly drew a distinction between 'those who have responsibly decided to emigrate' and were capable of reaching 'worthy positions in Britain', and 'those who come on the off-chance of an easier life', deteriorating into 'welfare cases with social and personality problems'.[49] The council of Camden Irish Centre was at pains to point out to fee-paying members and donors that:

> The Irish Centre does not cater nor encourage 'layabouts'. No able-bodied man or woman is ever given financial assistance until he first accepts employment, and this assistance is only ever given after thorough investigation.[50]

At the same time, however, commentary on the social functions of Irish centres and associations also decoupled the performance of work from its association with excessive consumption: the governing committees of Irish bodies envisioned their associations as providing 'recreation and sport in a Christian atmosphere', where members could enjoy a 'quiet drink' in a setting heavily staffed by priests.[51]

Over the second half of the twentieth century, as large swathes of the migrant population have departed the urban reception areas and established suburban homes, this narrative of Irish respectability has become an important framework for communal remembrance of post-war settlement. At the turn of the century in particular, when the 'contribution' of immigration to 'rebuilding Britain' after the war became a major focus of popular memory in England, commemorative histories have foregrounded the myth of a formidable Irish work ethic rooted in the hardships of a rural farming background. While Irish nurses' contribution to 'building the NHS' has attracted increasing attention in recent years, the figure of the male construction worker has here formed the most iconic metaphor for the qualities, attributes and achievements of a post-war generation of 'grafters' who rebuilt modern Britain and established a better life for themselves and their families.[52] In order to mark the twenty-fifth anniversary of Chorlton Irish Club in south Manchester, for example, John O'Dowd, one of its founding members, produced a history of the club, which he read out at a meeting of the founding members on 22 February 1985. The following extract was read out again at the author's funeral mass in 1997, and subsequently reproduced in a 2006 popular photographic history of *Irish Manchester*, published as part of a 'Britain in Old Photographs' series by Sutton Publishing:

> Immediately after we arrived in England was the hardest time. We had no reserves of money and we had to find work. We didn't go queuing at the labour exchange looking for benefits, we travelled to get work. Wherever there was muscle needed for the job the Irish were hired. It didn't matter how menial or poor the conditions, we were conditioned by the rigours of life to work, which proved a very valuable form of education during these times.[53]

Set against the backdrop of this collective myth of the Irish work ethic, Denis's earlier assertion, 'you had to work', begins to take on new connotations. As Denis's personal narrative of work within the construction industry evolves, what becomes apparent is that this myth forms a key framework within which Denis sought to compose a valued image of self:

Barry: What was the construction industry like to work in?
Denis: Well, way harder than it is now. Because you had no compressors or nothing. You had no hydraulic … there was no hydraulics. The hydraulics hadn't come in for a bit after. We only, the only thing we did have, the pick-axe, the shovel and the graft, and that was it.[54]

Read as description, Denis's account of what the industry was 'like to work in' is factually accurate: low levels of investment within the industry right up until the mid-1970s meant that work was highly labour-intensive. At the same time, however, Denis's decision to highlight this particular aspect of his experience may be seen to establish a contrast between past and present on the basis of how 'hard' the work process was and, by proxy, the men embedded within it. The 'pick-axe' and 'the shovel' is not only a description of the tools then available, but constitute affective objects, narratively rendered here as symbols expressive of the greater toughness of a generational 'we' into which the first-person voice is blended. A strategy of composure is thus at work whereby the very rigours of the work regime are mobilised in order to secure recognition for the self's past achievements, measured here in terms of the ideal of 'graft' embodied in 'the pick-axe' and 'the shovel'.

As Denis's narrative of work evolved, this theme of graft became increasingly prominent. While Denis agreed, for example, that ganger men could be 'ruthless' with their workers, this did not form an object of criticism, but was employed, rather, to establish a contrast been good and bad workers:

Denis: Oh, well, they were. They were. They were ruthless with you. The bloke I was working ... when I worked in London I was working with that fella, brothers, three brothers. Well, not all three but I was working with one of the brothers. He had the big say, and I was working with him all the time, and I couldn't go wrong, because if you worked he'd protect you, and I'd always worked. And we were the best of mates, and still is, you know.

Barry: So if you worked hard ...

Denis: If you worked hard and did a day's work then there'd be no complaint, but a lot of lads had been slacking, and he'd sack them then.[55]

Other Irishmen, however, were not the only workers not up to the task:

Denis: No, no. I had a fella of my own ... and we moved up here, and I've had him up to four, five years ago. Six years, maybe six, seven years ago. But, I never seen an English man before that.

Barry: Why do you think that was? Why do you think there wasn't so many of them working?

Denis: Well, because they couldn't work with the Irish. I mean, in our job, they weren't good enough.

Barry: The Irish men were better workers?

Denis: Better workers, yeah. Way better groundworkers.

Barry: Why do you think the Irish men were such good workers?

Denis: Brought up to it, weren't they? Brought up to ... we were brought up to it in school, and when we left school we were brought up cutting turf, cutting ... everything. Work all the time. So that ... that's what I would say was it, you know. Yeah, yeah.

Barry: And did you like working in the construction industry, or would you have preferred ...

Denis: Oh, no, construction, yeah. That's all I was used to all my life, that's it. Digging and everything else.[56]

Although Irish and English men often worked with and alongside each other, particularly when employed for large British firms, the casual nature of work within the industry, together with the development of the subcontracting system from the 1950s, meant that Irish labourers often worked together in gangs, frequently, as in Denis's case, composed of men from the same county. As this implies, an explanation of such clustering would need to take account of the ways in which Irish migrant's habitus disposed them to work in ethnically homogenous work-groups, and the ways in which contracting firms, navigating the fluctuations of the market, recruited and utilised Irish labour in a context where English-born construction workers typically occupied traded positions within the industry.

For Denis, however, the absence of Englishmen was more simply explained: 'they weren't good enough'. In responding thus, Denis here draws on the communal myth of 'Irish muscle', not only to make sense of the life lived, but to construct a positive image of self from which he can derive a sense of personal distinction. The myth makes this possible due to the way it backgrounds negative aspects of the construction industry, enabling exploitative work relations to be viewed as a test of masculinity which Irish men easily pass because of their superior capacity for work. This capacity, moreover, is explained in terms of Irish men's rural origins: such men were 'conditioned by the rigours of life to work'; or as Denis put it: 'we were brought up to it'. As well as a sense of achievement, then, the way in which the myth renders Irish men's physical prowess within the industry continuous with the place left behind enables an integration of past and present, there and here: if migration necessarily disrupts and destabilises one's sense of belonging, splitting identity between different places, the myth enables Denis's experiences 'here' to be viewed as an extension of his experiences 'there', so that the past can remain a present truth of the self, so that 'there' can remain part of 'here'.

The luck of the game

Denis's investment in the trope of 'Irish muscle' thus enables him to view his past in a positive light, facilitating the composure of the self in the present. A hitherto unaddressed effect of this investment, however, is that the performance of work itself tends to be idealised within his narrative, to the exclusion of issues of remuneration, wealth and mobility. Such an exclusion is notable given the popular view of the period as one of growing 'affluence'. Although the British economy's rate of growth was sluggish relative to that of other European countries in the second half of the twentieth century, the post-war period witnessed rising incomes and the development of new patterns of consumption, inducing contemporary social scientists to proclaim the arrival of an epochal 'affluent society' defined in terms of enhanced purchase power, widespread availability of diverse consumer products and rising social mobility and aspirations.[57] As noted, Irish construction workers stood to benefit economically from these processes, even if their 'working lives were primarily orientated towards facilitating homebuilding for the English population'.[58] If increases in home-ownership were most concentrated among the English middle and upper-working classes, it was nevertheless the very demand for housing, coupled with the privatisation and deregulation of the construction industry in the 1950s, which enabled relatively high rates of pay and plentiful overtime for 'unskilled' labourers. As with other manual workers in England, such wages helped transform Irish construction workers into consumers in this period, an observation made time and again by numerous contemporaries.

One such was Donall MacAmhlaigh. Around midday one Saturday in April 1957 he called in to the *Admiral Rodney*, a pub in Northampton, only to find a group of young Irish piece-workers talking incessantly about 'work and money':

> The Irish at home, so far as I know, haven't got this ugly habit – always talking about work and money – but they get as materialistic as the rest when they have been here a while. I've often been with workmen in a pub in Ireland and we always had plenty to talk about besides the daily job. They had all the best stories and traditional lore at the tips of their tongues – as you might expect of the Irish – but this crowd are interested in nothing beyond jobs and horses. What harm but most of them are from the West of Ireland![59]

For MacAmhlaigh, piously evoking the ideal of west of Ireland masculinity, the materialism he associated within English culture did not represent an aspirational ideal, and the preoccupation with 'work and wages' he observed of young Irishmen in the 1950s seemed to him an ugly disfigurement of the Irish racial character. But as his own observations suggest, for many other Irishmen England represented an opportunity to enhance purchasing power and engage in popular forms of consumption. The construction industry was important here, not only because it enabled 'unskilled' migrants to earn good wages through piece-work, but because deregulation and the availability of cheap money created conditions under which those who could save a relatively modest sum might go into business for themselves as private contractors.

Among the firms of contractors and subcontractors that began to proliferate in the 1950s were numerous Irish firms, started by migrants who arrived in England without qualifications, prior business expertise or a skilled trade. And while many such firms would ultimately flounder in the face of market fluctuations, others would grow into successful businesses in the second half of the twentieth century. Around London in particular, Irish-owned 'subbies' like McGinley, Gulmanda, O'Keefe, O'Rourke, and the Byrne Brothers became familiar names on the local scene and eight-figure-turnover businesses in the 1980s. According to a survey of wealth within the industry in *Construction News* in 2000, first- and second-generation Irish-owned firms then accounted for over 10 per cent of the industry's estimated £10 billion wealth, leading industry analyst Paul Fletcher to describe 'the Irish' as 'a powerhouse in the construction industry'.[60]

As well as constituting a particularly dangerous and heavy form of work, the post-war construction industry thus provided some Irish migrants with the opportunity to acquire considerable wealth, and conceptions of masculinity engendered within the industry inscribed ideals of 'affluence' and material success as well as 'graft' and physical prowess. Although Denis does not explicitly make reference to material advancement in describing his experiences within the industry, a number of disclosures insinuate this was an underlying aspiration. At one point, Denis mentions that two of his sisters emigrated to America, prompting a question about whether he ever had aspirations to move there himself to be near them:

Denis: [Laughs]. No. But if you're ... if you'd emigrated there [America] first, it would be the best country to work, to go to.
Barry: Why do you say that?
Denis: Well, the people that moved there the same time as me, they done very well for themselves.
Barry: There was there a lot of men ... I know in Manchester a lot of men came over here and done ... done well as well.
Denis: Oh yeah. Bloody hell.
Barry: In construction and haulage, and things like that.
Denis: Done very ... done ... they've done marvellous. Awful lot of people, many people have done marvellous.
Barry: And why do you think that was?
Denis: Well they ... they had a go at it and that was it. Look at the ... all the wagons and all of that, and the ... Some have gone very big and then some, you know ... [pause] ... And they got the break as well, you know. Some of them were groundworkers and they're doing well as well, you know. Still, luck of the game, isn't it?[61]

In designating America as 'the best country to work' in because 'the people that moved there the same time as me, they done very well for themselves', Denis makes audible a voice that evaluates the migration project in terms of economic advancement. Denis's eagerness to work in construction was not only prompted by a desire 'to go outside' and to work among other Irish men, but by a desire to improve earnings, a motivation which presumably underlay his later decision to start 'working for myself' as a small subcontractor with his partner from Kerry. At the same time, however, designating America as 'the best country' also implies that Denis has not fully achieved his own ambitions in this respect, and that he views a disparity in opportunities between England and America as responsible for this. This idea, that to do 'very well' presupposes conditions of opportunity beyond Denis's control to secure, emerges again in response to the suggestion that 'a lot of men came over here and done well ... done well as well'. Where the superiority of Irish workers was earlier ascribed to their rural upbringing and formidable work ethic, the notable economic success of some of these workers is now explained in terms of chance: 'they had a go'; 'they got the break'; 'luck of the game'.

These responses reveal a new aspect to the process of composure enacted through Denis's narrative. If a culture of economic advancement within the industry encouraged Denis to introject this as an aspirational ideal, the failure to realise this in the communally valorised way complicates the self's relation to it. By explaining the success of other Irish men in terms of luck, Denis diminishes the importance of the ideal their success embodies to him as a measure of status and self-worth, buffering the self from feelings of inadequacy activated by reference to other Irish men's success. This defensive dynamic may explain why the issue of material advancement is largely absent from Denis's narrative, and may also be seen to shape his effort to compose his work identity in terms of the described myth of 'Irish muscle'. On this reading, a split-off desire for status based on material success re-emerges as an investment in notions of superior Irish capacity for work.

It is important to add that this process of splitting is here conditioned by the way in which success within the construction industry has become a marker of status within the particular public of the Irish in England. Irish contractors have not only become powerful within the English construction industry, but symbols of status and success within the particular public of the Irish in England, and efforts to represent the experiences of post-war migrants have repeatedly seized upon the life stories of such men as paradigm instances of the 'rags-to-riches' tale.[62] The central story line of John B. Keane's bestselling epic novel *The Contractors* is here exemplary, making use of this formula to chart the protagonist's quest for wealth, status and recognition within the construction industry in 1950s London. Hailing from a small farming family in Kerry, Dan Murray arrives in London in 1952 with only 'a few inadequate shillings' and a powerful sense of ambition:

> He knew something about London from listening to other young men who had come back home to Kerry on holiday. If a fellow worked his head he could get on in England, be promoted to chargehand or foreman or even become a subcontractor. This was where the real money was.[63]

Having begun work as a bricklayer's labourer the day after arrival, Dan soon establishes himself as 'a good man', and, through closely monitoring how things are done on site, quickly acquires the skill of bricklaying and a grasp of how the industry works.[64] After a few years of hard work and careful saving Dan is able to put this knowledge into practice when he and his friend Eddie Carey start their own subcontracting firm. Through hard work and dedication the firm establishes 'a good reputation', and in four years Eddie and Dan have amassed £2,000.[65] Ever ambitious, Dan now refocuses on buying up and developing his own sites, and soon expands his business to the point where he 'no longer worried about money'.[66] Around this time Dan takes a trip back to his home village, where his transformation from poor farmer's son to self-made tycoon is ordained and celebrated in the local pub:

> Later that night when Dan and his father went to the pub in Ballynahaun the after-hours customers wondered at Dan's expensive suit, his suede shoes, his immaculate white shirt and silver grey tie. They pondered the exposure of white cuff, the teeth obviously well cared for, the unconscious ease and air of opulence that exuded from the man. Dan stood a round of drinks to the house and placing a twenty pound note on the counter instructed the publican to keep refilling as required. In whispers, the locals boasted about him to each other. A decent man. One of the richest men in the country. England must be a great bloody country. They listed off the other Kerrymen who had become millionaires from humble beginnings, who had boarded the emigrant ships at the North Wall, Dun Laoghaire and Rosslare with worn suitcases, no money and limited education.[67]

As with the figure of the hardworking navvy, the self-made tycoon has also become embedded within the communal imaginary of the Irish in post-war England, and is repeatedly deployed in popular community histories and by journalists writing for local newspapers and the *Irish Post*. However, while this figure may provide a means of projecting an image of Irish achievement to audiences in Ireland as well as England, the constant rendering of successful Irish contractors as symbols of the mobility of an Irish community in England also works to solidify wealth and business success as norms by which the value of the migration journey is measured. For those who fail to attain this ideal, in particular those who work in the field of construction, the valorisation of Irish success in the construction industry may induce feelings of personal inadequacy.

Bill, whom we met in Chapter 1, interacts with this narrative of the self-made man in a very different way in his memories of work in the construction industry. Born in 1951 in Roscommon, Bill grew up on his family's 50-acre farm, the eldest of four siblings. After attending the local National School until the age of 13, Bill 'went straight onto the land', which, as the eldest, he had been chosen to inherit.[68] Bill, however, did not aspire to the life of the farmer. In contrast to Denis, who employed an idealised image of work on the land to authenticate a narrative of Irish fitness to work, farm labour in Bill's narrative was associated with exploitation, backwardness and constraint, frustrating the young self's desire for play and competitive endeavour.[69] Bill's desire to escape life on the farm here came to focus on the alternative image of masculine success projected by emigrants returned home on holidays: 'all you'd seen was your forefathers and your uncles and all that, they'd gone to England, and had a made living'. Arriving in the village with 'big cars', 'well dressed' and with 'plenty of money', Bill realised that 'if I worked … as hard as I worked on the farm, I'd make a living, and that's exactly what … you know, what I did'.[70]

In fact, Bill did more than 'make a living'. Leaving in January 1967, aged 16, Bill immediately began work in the construction industry, taking a job with his uncle's Manchester-based contacting firm. At this stage, Bill worked 'as a labourer, 'cos I had no qualifications, I had no skills'.[71] Eventually, however, Bill took a job with Kennedy's, another Irish-owned, Manchester-based contracting firm with whom he would work 'all the way through', and where he was soon promoted to 'jointer', a job that, although relatively unskilled, was nevertheless 'a trade' that carried with it greater responsibility: ''cos if you left a leak, there was serious consequences'.[72]

After working as a jointer for three to four years, Bill's progression up the occupational ladder accelerated: 'then I was made up to a gangerman … I then became a foreman, after a number of years … and then I became a site agent, at 22'.[73] Becoming a site agent brought with it, not only increased wealth, but greater responsibility: 'that entailed … you know, controlling men, gangs … responsible for profitability, for keeping the operation going, at times I had up to, 400 men working under me'.[74] The level of responsibility and authority increased again when Bill became a contracts manager: 'then I became a contracts manager. So I moved up along … A contracts manager then means that … you have a higher responsibility again … And I was only one of three, there was three of us'.[75]

Nor did Bill's progression stop at the position of contracts manager. In 1992, a number of years after Bill's promotion, the company's chairman and majority shareholder 'wanted to go'. The ultimate result of this was that Bill, along with two other men and the aid of a venture capitalist, bought out the chairman, becoming shareholding executive directors of the company. Thereafter, and despite deep reservations about the prudence of involving 'vulture capitalists' in the company, the company went from strength to strength:

Anyway, we ran the company under this new chairman and this new finance director, and we went from ... whatever the turnover, thirty-five, fort... thirty million or thirty-five million, to a hundred and five million, in four years. You know, we just hit it right.[76]

As a consequence of this steady expansion, Balfour Beatty, the parent company to the venture capitalists, made a bid of 48 million to buy the company, which Bill and his co-directors accepted. After staying on as director of Kennedy's for a further three years, Bill finally took early retirement on a 'final salary pension':

'Cos I was ... 38 years' service, with one company, from the labour trench to the board, ... executive director one step up. And the pension, we had a final salary pension, which was the best thing ever! If ever you get a chance to go on to a pension, they're hard to get now, is a final salary pension, it's the best thing ever we did, and I had one, a pension off the company. So I retired, and ... got out to hell. So that's my working history![77]

Where Denis tended to background the theme of economic advancement in his narrative, Bill tells a story about upward progression and material success, using the 'rags-to-riches' formula to organise his experiences and project an image of the self-made man. These differences in narrative strategy are not difficult to explain. If both Denis and Bill arrived in England with ambitions to 'do well' in construction, Bill has realised such ambitions to a much greater degree. Although Bill arrived in Manchester in 1967, at a time when the boom in construction was coming to an end, he has been able to reproduce the success he identified with his uncles and 'forefathers' who came to England before him, not by starting his own private subcontracting firm, but by working his way up within an established firm. Thus, although Denis and Bill both arrived in England from similar farming backgrounds and without qualifications, they entered the construction industry at different stages of development and had access to different kinds of opportunities. Whereas the standard route to economic advancement in the 1940s and 1950s was through private subcontracting, the success and expansion of firms such as Kennedy's by the late 1960s meant that an additional route had opened for later unqualified young migrants, namely through the internal company structure of established firms.

The establishment of social networks, which enabled the acquirement of forms of social and cultural capital of value in the Irish-owned sections of the industry, may also have been important in Bill's case. Not only did the success of Bill's uncles and 'forefathers' in the 1940s and 1950s set an example which the young Bill aspired to emulate, but these men established companies and contacts which the young Bill could make use of when he migrated to England. Although Bill would eventually take up employment with Kennedy's, a rival firm to his uncle's, Bill's decision to migrate to Manchester rather than London was itself based on the fact that he could 'walk straight into a job' with his uncle's firm, while his uncle's experience in the industry, in the form of learned knowledges and competencies, constituted a transmittable resource to which Bill had access. Bill's upward trajectory within Kennedy's, in other words, may have been aided by the fact that he already knew something about how the construction industry worked, and most importantly, knew what qualities and attitudes impressed foremen and bosses scouting for promotable workers.

Learning from yourself

These points concerning the relationship between particular aspects of Bill's habitus and changes in the field of construction in the later 1960s help explain important differences in Denis's and Bill's experiences within the industry, conditioning the latter's take-up of the 'rags-to-riches' formula within the interview. As other parts of Bill's narrative indicate, however, becoming 'self-made' was by no means a linear, unproblematic progression. Most important here was education, a recurrent theme throughout Bill's narrative. At each stage of Bill's progression up the occupational ladder he makes reference either to his lack of skills or qualifications, or to the new tasks and skills he had to learn as he assumed new roles and responsibilities within an industry where clerical, administrative and technical occupations grew exponentially over the post-1945 period.[78] As well as highlighting his increasing importance and status, Bill's account of his progression through Kennedy's often includes detailed descriptions of technical and administrative processes, illustrated through technical idioms designed to demonstrate a comprehensive grasp of such processes. More so than material wealth, Bill strove in the interview to demonstrate the acquirement of knowledge and learning, this being an object he placed much value on:

> And ... I think it was achievement as well, was that certain things that you did, in producing this and producing that, and ... I think something that I never ... at, at school, or ... anything like that, was, you know, sitting in a board meeting, and ... predicting something, and then doing a PowerPoint presentation or saying what you're going to do, and then actually produce it. And producing reports for the board, and ... you know, what your turnover was last month, or what your profitability'd be then, reporting going forward, and that type of thing.

That was hard. That was hard, because you wouldn't ... You know, you didn't go to university, you weren't brought up with that. You had to learn that from yourself.[79]

As Bill climbs the company ladder, moving from the construction site to the office and boardroom, it becomes necessary to acquire new competencies and ways of thinking. If the dangerous, arduous character of the work regime on the building site engendered conceptions of masculinity that idealised *machismo* virtues of strength, toughness and 'graft', the very different work processes of the office, requiring new proficiencies in the use of electronic technology and business-related conceptual schemas, fostered the inscription of technocratic and managerial ideals within work-based conceptions of masculinity within the industry. In this respect, the distinction between 'the Irish navvy' and the 'Irish businessman' evokes differences in forms of embodied human and cultural capital, and suggests a subjective transformation entwining stories of social mobility and the cultural assimilation of middle-class technocratic ideals.[80]

As the above extract also indicates, however, ambivalence still attaches to this transformation. After narrating his progressive story of success in the first-person voice, in the above extract Bill shifts to the more awkward second person when describing the technologies and processes of the boardroom, making visible a sensitive relation to the image of self these objects represent. This sensitivity derives from an insecurity about one's ability to master the new forms of knowledge necessary for competency within the boardroom, an insecurity itself based on the fact that 'you weren't brought up with that'. Indeed, not only did Bill not attend secondary school, having left school at 13 to work on the land, but the schooling he did receive was marred by the brutal teaching practices he encountered in the National School classroom. Recurrent here, in Bill's memories of both childhood and of work in England, were embittered stories about Bill's National School teacher, who had regularly caned him for spelling mistakes:

> I went home on holidays from ... England, and I had reason to go to the post office, to see ... he had retired at this stage ... and er ... who did I walk into, but ... Tony McDaid. And a big shake hands and a big smile. So ... he says to me, 'How are you Bill?' And I says, 'Not too bad.' He says, 'I believe you're doing very well in England.' I says, 'I'm not doing too bad.' He says, 'Bill', ... he says, 'You have a lovely car.' I had a ... 2000T Cortina, brand new, it was ... it was ... a lovely car. And he'd just bought a 2000, it wasn't a 2000T, and the difference was the vinyl roof, and ... all this. He says, 'Well, the', he says, 'I've just bought a car that's similar', he says, and ... he says, 'I believe', he says, 'from the grapevine,

that you're doing very well.' And I says, 'Tony, it's like this', I said, 'it's no thanks to you.' I says, 'You didn't teach us', I says, 'you tried to beat it into us.' And I says, 'That's not teaching.' And ... I was going to give him another ... And I says, 'No, I'll leave it at that.' And I walked out. Well, I got my stamps and I walked out, and left him at that. But it put a bit of thought in his head; it wasn't teaching, it was ... he was ... he wasn't trained properly ...[81]

As Bill's career in England progresses, his struggle to learn the competencies of the boardroom threatens the internal image of the businessman with which the self is now identified, threatening regression to the feelings of humiliation and inadequacy he associates with the classroom. In the story of the Ford Cortina, however, this image is preserved as a valued aspect of the self through the displacement of aggressive impulses onto Bill's old teacher, who becomes an object of contempt. In this process, the thing at the root of Bill's anxiety, namely his lack of education, is implicitly idealised, becoming a measure of Bill's ability to succeed without the help of others, through his own hard work. The Cortina 2000T, with all its phallic connotations, does not just symbolise Bill's material success or upward mobility; it signifies the *self-made* character of the newly fashioned identity and stands as a rebuke to those who doubted Bill's ability to 'make something of himself' in the past.

Nevertheless, at a psychic level, the story of the Ford Cortina rests on a basic contradiction. Although the memory works to establish the autonomy of the self from the deformations of its past, by displacing aggression onto his old teacher Bill implicitly makes him responsible for the anxieties he seeks to manage. So while Bill endeavours to deny the dependence of the self upon the denigrated object, the displacement of aggression onto it demonstrates how the internal psychic landscape remains structured through relation to it, a relation which continues to unsettle the self in the present.

This act of displacement in turn plays into a broader tension concerning the interplay between issues of mobility, assimilation and belonging within Bill's narrative. In Denis's narrative we saw how 'there' could reinforce the present truth of the self 'here'. In accordance with a communal myth of 'Irish muscle', Denis presented his experiences of working on the farm and bog in Ireland as underpinning his formidable capacity for work in England, enabling integration of past and present, there and here. By contrast, 'there' repeatedly figures as an object of bitterness and contempt in Bill's narrative, limiting in turn the self's efforts to realise ideals identified with 'here'. In his memories of growing up in Roscommon Bill denigrates, not only the local school, but work on the farm, his father's drinking and the strangle-hold a village hierarchy of priest, teacher, postmaster and pension officer had over local affairs.

In this way, Bill's narrative registers a powerful disidentification with Ireland as a site of belonging, propelling him dialectically to locate 'here' as an alternative source. All the same, this did not mean the 'here' was constituted as a place free from ambivalence within his narrative. In response to the notion that Irish contractors were 'ruthless and exploitative' in relation to their workers, Bill stated that: 'sometimes you had to be ruthless':

> 'Right', I says, 'vans and wagons has to be in the yard at two o' clock, locked up.' And I said, 'You can please yourself what you do then, it's Friday or Saturday, you can drink or do what you like. But', I says, 'the vans and stuff has to be all tidied up.' These two gangs or three gangs, no, they stayed in the beer hall, so, the next day … out I come, and I says, 'Come here. Come on. On your way.' Had to sack them … had to show an example because … thing is that, if you lose control … of, you know, especially construction workers, er … they'll, they'll control you. And … you know, you're the pay master, you pay them, you agree their wages, you agree this, you give them subs, and that was another thing that was done, on a daily basis, was the subs. You know, you had to be ruthless.[82]

As well as requiring him to learn new skills, Bill's occupational advancement within construction has positioned him within the role of manager within the workplace, necessitating the acquisition and deployment of forms of discipline that enable him to maintain control over the men under him. This in turn establishes a division between Bill and the men: rather than deny the view of contractors as 'ruthless', Bill endeavours to justify the deployment of ruthless managerial practices as necessary for the maintenance of authority within the work environment, setting in play a differentiating logic that assigns Bill and those working under him into opposing 'you'/'them' categories. As the associated opposition between the workplace and pub in this story implies, differences based on relations within the space of work potentially extended to social and cultural practices beyond it. As Bill states a little further on:

> That's something I would never do, is … even at Christmastime or any time, was to go into the pub with any of the lads I employed. I would always keep that completely … If I met them out, yeah, I'd buy them a drink and so-and-so. But I would never socialise with them, because if there's any bit of, er … aggro, that's the time it'll come up, er … when they've about … the sixth … sixth pint, it'll surface.[83]

As well as complicating Bill's relation with his home village in Roscommon, advancement within the construction industry has also encouraged a process of social differentiation from sections of the Irish 'over here', involving avoidance of those spaces, such as the pub, dancehall and Irish centre, typically frequented by Irish labourers in cities like Manchester. As Bill acknowledges at various points in the interview, this sharp separation between work and social life not only entails a distancing from aspects of the Irish community in England, but simultaneously implies a convergence with post-war 'English' values and ways of life:

Barry: Do you think you've changed?
Bill: Aye. I suppose I have, yes. Because, you know, coming from a farming background, and you have to change. You know, you have to come more of a city ... dweller, and yeah, I suppose I have.
Barry: Good changes or bad changes, or ...?
Bill: You'll have to ask her that! [Laughs] Aye, I think it's for the good. It's, yes, we can, we've set out our stall to ... have our own house, paid for, and have it the way we want it, and done the extension she wanted, and set out the way ... we wanted it together, and ... quite comfortable. It's too big. I keep telling her but she doesn't want to sell it! And er ... you can ... you know if you were in Ireland, you'd be out farming or doing something like that. At seven o' clock in the evening you can come in and sit down and watch the ... football or watch whatever we watch, and relax or go on the computer, or do whatever you ... If you want to go for a meal, you go for a meal. If you want to ... cook, or whatever. Yeah. It's er ... I have changed in that line. I suppose I've come more ... English...fied, or English whatever you call it ... in that way. 'Cos I suppose when you're ... you're with them long enough, 'cos I'm forty ... three, forty-four years now, forty-three, forty-four years here now, so ... That's a long time.[84]

In composing his memories of work in England, Denis drew on a narrative of 'Irish muscle' as a means of establishing a form of continuity between past and present, there and here. When Denis is asked if he thought he had changed since he came to England he answered in the negative: 'I don't think I changed ... [laughs] I don't think I changed too much! [laughs].'[85] By contrast, Bill draws on a narrative of the self-made man to construct the experience of migration as transformative. This transformation concerns economic status, but it also involves a linked distancing from the place left behind and a positive identification with the place of settlement. Particularly following retirement, this positive identification has come to focus, not on the urban spaces associated with the Irish community 'over here', but on a home-centred vision of 'affluence'. Prompted to elaborate on his understanding of how he has changed, Bill offers a privatised image of domesticity in which he is envisioned relaxing at home and which he associates with 'Englishness'. Yet Bill's very recognition of this domesticity as 'English' reveals the doubled character of belonging in his narrative. In order to respond to the question, to make sense of change, here must be read in relation to there, a comparison must be drawn between the rural life of the Irish farmer and the English city dweller. However great the social and cultural distance travelled, however long 'you're with them', the transformation is thus never total, the severing of the past never complete.

The money was good, the work was hard

Like Bill, my final respondent, Joe, sought to compose his experiences of settlement in England in the form of a progressive story of ambition and success. Born in 1944, Joe grew up in Longford on his family's 14-acre farm, the eldest of four brothers. After attending the local National School until the age of 14, Joe took a two-year course in woodwork at a local vocational college, before working for around 18 months on Moor Glamona, a local turf-cutting plant. When, however, Joe's younger brother came home from Birmingham for Christmas in 1962, Joe was struck by the transformation in his appearance, prompting him to return with his brother to England at the end of the holidays: 'I saw he had lovely clothes, nice new watch, well dressed 'n' everythin' like that, and I decided to take the emigrant boat along with him.'[86]

Joe went first to Birmingham, a major centre of manufacturing in this period, where he took a job in the paper factory where his brother was working. Neither the job nor the city, however, was to Joe's liking, in part because he considered 'the Irish' were 'never' 'accepted' in the city.[87] Yet, despite this, and the severity of the famous winter of 1963 (by which point he had taken a job in the construction industry), Joe was determined not to give up his ambition of 'making it':

Barry: Did you ever think of going back?
Joe: [pause] Er ... I had the choice of going back, one time, 1963 ... it was a very, very bad winter here, 1963, terribly bad winter ... cold, the frost was that bad, on the ground, two foot it was a that time, terribly, terribly bad winter, it lasted to the month of May ... my father, God be good to him, he was on to us to come home but pride would not let us.
Barry: Why not?
Joe: [pause] I dunno, we just had our mind made up, I had my mind made up I was going to make it here and that was it ... I come here, I'm not going back.[88]

Joe did, however, move to Manchester in 1964, where he eventually found work with a contractor as a tunnel-digger, a form of employment he would remain in until retirement. It was this work, which Joe emphasised 'paid well' but was 'hard', that was responsible for the ultimate success of the migration venture:

> England was good to me, very good to me, I have to say that like you know, brought up my family, brought up here, everything like that and … I worked in the construction industry then for a lot of years, I worked underground, tunnel work and all that … so I did, erm, earned good money and made a good home and a good livin' for myself.[89]

Bill's and Joe's narratives thus have important features in common: both tell progressive stories about the realisation of personal ambitions which work to construct the migration project as a success. Yet, there are also important differences. Material success was not the only, nor even the most, valued aspect of Bill's experiences in England: his narrative was filled with lengthy, detailed descriptions of different work tasks and the changing roles he performed as his career progressed. By contrast, Joe's narrative of success tends to bypass his experiences as a tunnel-digger to focus on the material rewards. Even when prompted, Joe condenses his work experiences into the curt evaluative phrase 'the money was good, the work was hard':

Barry: So you worked in the construction industry then?
Joe: I did, yeah.
Barry: And what was that like?
Joe: It was … it was, alright like, you know, the money where I worked as a job, I was in like where I worked a lot, I worked a lot on the railway tunnel, worked on that you know, the money was good, the work was hard.
Barry: And was that Irish contractors?
Joe: Yeah, it was, Irish contractors but they paid well, but the work was hard.[90]

One way of explaining differences in how Joe and Bill talk about their experiences of work concerns the very different kinds of work they did within the industry. Although Joe has, as he emphasises, 'done very well' from his work in the construction industry, he has not ascended the career ladder in the same way as Bill, but has worked for the most part as a tunnel-digger, a non-managerial if relatively lucrative role. This has meant that, although Joe has not had to negotiate the difficult process of learning boardroom skills, neither has he had access to the same forms of capital or discourses of identity associated with the acquirement of such skills: the image of the high-flying, worldly businessman, who has acquired learning and culture as well as wealth, is not available to Joe for self-construction in the way that it is to Bill.

For Joe, work, and England more generally, is not valued in itself, but constitutes a means to an end.

However, Joe's devaluation of 'work' in the phrase 'the money was good, the work was hard' concerns more than a lack of occupational mobility:

> It's been a ... fairly ... a fairly good life to me but unfortunately for ... the last ten years I've ... I've got arthritis in the base of the spine ... and that was through mostly working in tunnel work and ... getting wet and everythin' like that so ... I haven't been workin' for the last ten years ... and I'm registered disabled as well like, y'know so ... I haven't been able to ... to work ... but er life has been good yeah, it has been good except it's worse for the last ten years, I could say that ... but er ... I've had a really good life.[91]

Involving long hours of intensive labour in often damp conditions, and remunerated by piece-work methods that encouraged workers to push their bodies to their limits, tunnel work constituted one of the most precarious and physically demanding forms of work within the construction industry.[92] As in other forms of heavy industry where earning power was closely related to workers' readiness to expose their bodies to hazardous conditions, the work culture generated around tunnel work was highly *machismo*, and carried over into characteristic forms of masculine sociability beyond the workplace centring on heavy drinking and smoking. Popular representations of the Irish construction worker have thus revered the 'tunnel tiger' as epitomising *machismo* virtues of strength, endurance, competitiveness, risk-taking and hard drinking.[93] Joe, however, avoids reference to his work experiences within the industry, precisely because the destructive effects of tunnel work upon his body constitute irrefutable evidence of his present inability to embody the manly ideals on which such an identity is based. This silence speaks not only of the physical toll exacted through years of punishing labour, of the constant bodily pain and loss of mobility; it implies too of the loss of a valued, deeply internalised self-image, leaving Joe with powerful feelings of inadequacy, loss and possibly guilt.

These anxieties exert a powerful influence on how Joe constructs his experiences in the interview. Joe's preferred narrative of material success enables him to reflect upon his life in England in a positive way: even if his years of work in the construction industry have cost him his health, he can derive satisfaction from the fact that this work has ultimately allowed for a good standard of living for him and his family, enabling him to fulfil the ideal of the breadwinner. However, as the product of a form of defensive splitting, this positive idealisation of the material rewards of work is concomitant with an attempt to diminish or deny the importance of work in itself to the self. This is narratively manifest, not only in Joe's avoidance of the issue of work in the interview, but in the implication that tunnel work was exploitative. Implicit in the phrase 'the money was good, the work was hard', this tendency towards the disavowal of work as exploitative emerged more fully in response to questions about the reception of Irish people in England:

Joe: I mean, in Birmingham there during the war like for instance, or after the war, there'd be digs advertised, no dogs or no Irish, yeah, the factory was in Trafford Park there, where all the big industry was in Trafford Park, which is down here in Manchester, the other side of Manchester, you'd see jobs advertised, outside, no Irish need apply.
Barry: This is in Manchester?
Joe: Yeah.
Barry: And what year would this be?
Joe: Arr, that's be going back now in the early 50s like, before my time, I've never seen anything like that, I have never no, I haven't, never, I've never seen it but ... the Irish here, they got, the jobs they got here. English people they wouldn't do it, do them, or they wouldn't be paid to do it ... they wouldn't be paid, the tunnel work that I worked in, I never seen any English men do it.[94]

Popular perceptions of Irish masculinity in post-war England continued to reflect the resilience of long-established stereotypes around Irish male roughness. One consequence of this was that migrants, in particular male migrants, often encountered hostility when securing lodgings, a point frequently noted in the diaries and memoirs of post-war migrants.[95] During the 1980s, in a context where the Troubles stimulated an intensification of anti-Irish hostility in England, a new generation of community activists operating at the edges of the established associational culture began to recover such discriminatory experiences as a means of substantiating claims about the historic status of the Irish as a disadvantaged and discriminated-against minority in Britain. Drawing heavily on forms of 'consciousness raising' and oral history, this process of recovery has helped solidify and publicise a powerful narrative of exclusion within the communal memory of the Irish in England, one that constructs the persistence of negative Irish stereotypes, Irish experiences within the labour and housing markets, high levels of Irish homelessness, alcoholism and mental health problems and the surveillance of Irish people under the Prevention of Terrorism Act, as linked elements of a shared experience of discrimination, disadvantage and exploitation.[96]

While Joe earlier insists that 'England has been good to me', as his narrative develops these tropes of exclusion and exploitation come to exert an increasing influence over his interpretation of his experiences.

Although Joe himself never saw the notorious 'no dogs, no Irish' signs, in his understanding they function as metonyms for a broad experience of Irish exclusion, one that includes the exploitation of Irish workers within the British labour market and, more specifically, the construction industry. Echoing the views of Donal Foley outlined above, Joe here presents Irish workers, himself included, as 'well-paid slaves', pressed into forms of work the native English refused to do.

By framing his experiences within this narrative, Joe is able to reinforce the strategy of defensive splitting deployed to negotiate the psychological effects of the injuries he sustained through his work as a tunnel-digger. By constructing the construction industry as exploitative, tunnel work becomes a deserving object of renunciation, enabling it to be split off without experiencing depressive emotions of loss or guilt. However, to reiterate Graham Dawson, manic defences always 'have reciprocal but unconscious consequences that impact back upon the self'. In implicitly denigrating the construction industry as exploitative, Joe constructs himself as the exploited, as a 'hard-working, well-paid slave'. In so constructing himself as a victim of the actions of others, Joe jeopardises the very sense of agency and achievement his idealisation of the material rewards of tunnel work is designed to protect from the depressive effects of his injuries. In short, the narrative of victimhood threatens to undermine the coherence of the preferred narrative of material success, leaving Joe with an understanding of his life from which he can derive little satisfaction, even if it allows him to make sense of his injuries in a way that absolves the self from blame and enables the gratification of aggressive impulses.

As such, additional ways are sought to preserve the valued image of migration success. Immediately after Joe's story about the exploitation of Irish labour he offers a distinctive response to the suggestion that Irish men were 'harder workers':

> Oh yeah, oh, by far, by far, great workers, great, great workers, great workers ... The people that worked in that tunnel work when I was working there, a lot of them like myself are crippled-up today, they worked terribly, terribly hard, but then, like I say, there was a lot of them worked hard and they spent their money, spent their money in the bar, I didn't, no, you know ... a lot of people, a lot, I'd say a lot of them a lot of them are well off like you know but there are a lot of them that spent their money really, really foolish, very, very foolish ...[97]

As well as the recovery of post-war migrants' experiences of popular hostility, the efforts of community activists to document the hidden history of Irish exclusion in England from the 1980s have uncovered the neglected experiences of a generation of Irish men who, having spent many years living the itinerant life of the labourer in England, have ultimately ended up homeless or living in sheltered accommodation, often with alcohol and mental health problems. Since then, charity workers, community activists and film-makers have narrated the experiences of these men as a tragic story of alienation, suffering and loss, most recently in the moving documentary *The Men of Arlington House*.[98] For Joe, however, who sits on the managerial board of a charity concerned with the welfare such men, this tragic story is reworked into a cautionary tale, enabling him to contrast the hamartia of these men with his own good sense. Although Joe agrees that Irish men were 'great workers', unlike Denis he does not take up this subject-position because, for him, it is tainted by the association with exploitation and injury: 'a lot of them like myself are crippled-up today'. Instead, Joe seeks to impose a moral distinction within the category of Irish workers on the basis of how prudently they exercised restraint in spaces of post-war consumption beyond the workplace. By implicitly constructing such men's downfall as retribution for their excessive lives, Joe is able to absolve his own actions from blame and re-establish a sense of agency, positioning his own restraint as responsible for his relative success. Through projecting his own anxieties onto the other, Joe is once again the protagonist in his own story, rather than a victim of circumstance.

The Irish round here

The injuries Joe has sustained through his work in the construction industry, and the way he seeks to negotiate anxieties associated with these injuries, also have important implications for how Joe frames a sense of belonging within the interview. Unsurprisingly, given the way 'England', 'work' and 'exploitation' are metonymically linked in Joe's narrative, 'England' does not constitute a site of belonging for him but is figured as a provider of goods and services. Although Joe 'enjoyed England' and 'England was good to me', it is never accorded the title of 'home'; in sharp contrast to Bill, this is exclusively reserved for the place left behind:

> To this day ... I'm still delighted to go back, to go back to, to Ireland, Ireland is still my home, I regard it as my home, though I live here and I'm happy here, but Ireland to me is home.[99]

Yet, although Joe continues to regard Ireland as his 'home', he has no plans to return there:

> Every Irish person you talk to, everyone had that dream, that you'd go back, you know, and I probably would of went back now, I probably would have went back when the boom was in Ireland, it started off ten

year ago, if I was fit and well, I would have, definitely would have gone home that time, yeah, I wouldn't not now, because the health service there is not as good as here ... if I take bad here, the hospital is five minutes away from here.[100]

Such was the severity of the injuries Joe sustained through working in construction that he has needed to undergo various operations to relieve the pain in his back and neck. In addition, Joe has had three heart attacks in the last ten years, one fairly recently. Given the fragility of Joe's health, he is thus heavily reliant on medical care, and as he explains, provision 'here' is better than what is available 'there'. Consequently, although Joe 'would have went back' some years ago, the condition of his health now makes this impractical. Thus, since securing the integrity of the self is also dependent on securing the integrity of the body, desire is not straightforward in Joe's narrative of belonging, even if the term 'home' is exclusively reserved for 'Ireland'.

In fact, Joe's designation of 'Ireland' as 'home' is not expressive of a desire to return, but of a deterritorialised sense of belonging related to an abstract idea of 'Ireland'. During the interview Joe reflected upon what he 'missed most' about Ireland:

[Y]ou know, you go to a neighbour's house at home ... that door was never locked, you just dipped the latch and walked in, you were welcome, never, never had that here, no, no, everyone, you know ... you could go visiting friends here, I do, go visiting friends, my mate's occasionally surely, alright, you know, but erm ... I wouldn't count it the same as Ireland but then, Ireland is that way now, you can't ... when I was growing up in Ireland, there never was a lock ... on our door, night or day ... never, the door was never locked, you never had to lock it, no ... people were ... there were, I'd say they were more neighbourly then.[101]

What Joe missed most about the rural Ireland of his childhood was its close-knittedness and neighbourliness. Although Joe goes visiting friends in England, he 'wouldn't count it the same as Ireland': walking into a house here uninvited would be regarded as an invasion of privacy. As Joe acknowledges, however, present-day Ireland, where the people lock their doors, is very different from the nostalgicised Ireland of his memories:

I never seen a television in my life in Ireland, at that time, nobody had them, simple as that ... little Bush radio ... we used to listen to the football on that on a Sunday ... and our house, it was a house that you'd call a [?] house like, and all the neighbours would be in, the house would be packed on a Sunday, football match ... the house would be packed, so it would, surely, but erm ... it was the best of the two ... to bring up kids, now I realise that ... at that time, now I'm not saying now, things are a little bit different, a little bit different now alright, but at that time, you could go out, you felt safe ... kids are not safe there now, there not safe here, well you know about that yourself ... kids are not safe here either ... it's changed in a lot of ways, I mean there was things ... there was things that happened at that time ... that we never knew about ... as children, I mean, there was abuse there with priests and all that goin' at that time, we, I know that now, I didn't know it then, [getting quieter] I didn't know it then like, I didn't know it then like you know, but ... I know it now ... there's ... when you listen to the news and everything that's gone on with Bertie ... Ahern, and all that, Charlie Haughey ... there was nothing ever before that happened that I knew of ... Haughey fiddled the country and he fiddled his, everybody, right, left and centre. Alright, it's not right to talk about the man, he's dead and gone, but eh, that was part of it like, Haughey brought that to light, the other man then, that brought the priests issue out, I don't know whether you'll remember him, well you will remember him, of course you'll remember him, was Bishop Casey ...[102]

Like England, southern Ireland has been subject to increasingly rapid economic and cultural change in the second half of the twentieth century. As well as rising affluence and the increasing commodification of culture, sex and corruption scandals involving political and religious elites have undermined the legitimacy of traditional sources of authority and punctured national myths about Irish moral superiority.[103] Viewed from the standpoint of a post-war migrant settled in England, such transformations have destabilised the pure, innocent Ireland of Joe's remembered past, signalling his cultural distancing from the present Ireland. When Joe designates Ireland 'home', it is this lost Ireland, idealised now in memory, which gives 'there' meaning as a site of belonging.

Crucially, like the narrative of Irish exclusion in England, the trope of 'Irish muscle' or the figure of the self-made man, this story of the loss of an idyllic past is shaped and sustained within the particular public of the Irish community in England. In Manchester, for example, community members have sought to reproduce this idealised place through their aestheticisation of the interior spaces of the local Irish centre, adorning its walls with images of untouched rural tranquillity and constructing a life-size installation of a thatched cottage in the main hall. As such, since the idealised vision of 'Ireland' invoked when Joe speaks of 'home' derives much of its meaning from the present context in which it is embedded, namely the particular public of the Irish community, it follows that Joe is actually expressing an identification with 'the Irish round here' as much as with the 'real' Ireland of today:

I always like to be involved in the Irish round here as well, and all that you know, I am the treasurer of Irish Community Care here as well, so I am so ... it keeps me ... very occupied at the moment like, so it does, it keeps me very, very occupied at the moment so it does.[104]

Since Joe was forced into retirement ten years ago, he has become increasingly involved with the activities of the local Irish community. As he points out repeatedly in the interview, he regularly attends functions at the centre, has acted in stage plays, is a member of the Federation of Irish Societies and, as he states here, sits on the managerial board of Irish Community Care, a local voluntary charity established in 1985 to cater to the special welfare needs of Irish people in the city. In one sense, highlighting his prominence within the local community represents a means by which Joe can secure a sense of status within the interview. In Bourdieu's sense of the term, if the construction industry represents a 'field' in which Bill has been able to accumulate distinct forms of social and cultural capital, the Irish community may also be viewed as a field in which Joe has been able to achieve a different sort of social distinction.

In the broader context of Joe's life in the last ten years, however, his increased participation in the activities of the local Irish community may also be seen as central to how he has come to terms with his deteriorating health and retirement, a process which in turn has shaped his sense of self in particular ways. If the Irish community represents a relational field, it is also a particular public which supplies a set of images in which Joe can invest to make sense of the events of his life. In this respect, his designation of Ireland as 'still my home' is psychically linked with his preferred narrative of work in England: in the same way that Joe's idealisation of the material rewards of work in England enables him to see his life 'here' as having been worthwhile, his idealisation of Ireland as 'home' represents a way of affirming the origins of the self, of securing its authenticity during a period of instability in its development. This does not intimate a desire for return to an Ireland in which those origins have been forgotten, but on the contrary, is dependent upon the recognition of those origins by others who have travelled the same migrant journeys, whose sense of the past is invested in a shared nostalgia.

Lives in re/construction: migrant memory and the functions of myth

The status of the Irish as a pool of cheap, flexible labour within the nineteenth-century British economy both troubled and pleased contemporaries. While the perception that Irish labourers undercut native workers fed into popular anti-Irish hostilities, resonating with fears over the cost of Irish pauperism and the uncivilising effect of the Irish upon native workers, employers and the state also recognised the value of the Irish in the context of rapid industrialisation.[105] If the *Report on the State of the Irish Poor* of 1836 designated the Irish 'a less civilised population', it recognised too that:

> We ought not ... to overlook the advantage of the demand for labour in England and Scotland being amply and adequately supplied, and at a cheap rate and at very short notice, by Irish; it is to be remembered that these Irish have been, and are, most efficient workmen; and they came in the hour of need, and that they afforded the chief part of the animal strength by which the great works of our manufacturing districts have been executed.[106]

Such ambivalence in relation to the Irish has strong echoes in the post-war period. Popular perceptions of Irish men continued to be informed by established stereotypes, yet in debates about the imposition of immigration controls the state would ultimately insist upon the shared history of British and Irish people, in part because of the value of 'unskilled', mobile Irish labour to the British economy during a period of intense reconstruction. In a real sense, particularly if one ignores the relative dispersal of the Irish within the post-war economy, Irish workers 'were hard-working, well-paid slaves, exactly what Britain wanted to rebuild their devastated country'.

There are, however, limits to any such emphasis on continuity. Most obviously, the dynamics of economic reconstruction in an era of full employment and rising demand were very different from those shaping employment during industrialisation, a difference expressed, not only in the said dispersal of the Irish within the post-war labour market, but in the growing influence of the Irish within the construction industry and, more generally, in rising standards of living and new patterns of popular consumption among workers in most sectors. Nor, moreover, should assumptions be made regarding the *meaning*, whether personal or collective, of Irish migrants' experiences within the labour market based on the fact of their commodification by British and Irish governments or their ambivalent positioning within British popular culture. While these issues were integral to the situation within which Irish migrant subjectivities were shaped, the oral histories, autobiographies and diaries examined in this chapter also reveal the specificity and diversity of the fantasies and anxieties engendered through migrants' negotiation of these circumstances. The construction industry was not only a place of suffering and exploitation, but an arena of masculine self-fashioning, its meanings defined by the ways in which migrants experienced and made sense of everyday work practices within a wider context of economic, social and cultural change.

These meanings form the basis of a powerful collective mythology of work in the construction industry. Close analysis of the interplay between personal and collective memory here shows how Irish experiences within the industry have been taken up by journalists, novelists, songwriters, community activists and historians who, having generalised and reshaped them in a variety of ways, have between them created a repository of popular images of the Irish construction worker in England. These memory practices underscore the collective significance of work within the industry as a formative aspect of post-war settlement, but they also evidence the evolution and variegation of communal memory, as different individuals and groups, engaged in diverse forms of discursive practice, have employed changing conventions of representation to reinscribe the meanings of work over time.

These processes of evolution and variegation intersect with personal memory production in complex ways. On the one hand, the internal differentiation of collective memory ensured the availability of a diverse repertoire of narrative forms on which individuals could draw to reconstruct their own experiences. A common theme throughout concerned the ways migrants negotiated multiple subject-positions as part of ongoing efforts to adapt collective myth to the particularities of their own circumstances, trajectories and present-day emotional needs. A chief function of collective myth at the level of personal memory thus concerned the possibilities it afforded for making sense of often difficult and dangerous working lives: through the adaption of collective tropes, migrants were able to reflect upon the migration journey as meaningful and worthwhile, in terms of shared criteria of evaluation offering a sense of social recognition for the life lived.

On the other hand, however, these efforts to validate the life lived were rarely straightforward: composing the migration journey as worthwhile presupposed the psychic renegotiation of past losses, conflicts and alternative destinies, involving multiple displacements, sublimations and 'rewritings'. The point here is not that investment in collective myth enabled migrants to repress the psychic consequences of their 'enslavement'; rather, the internal variegation of communal memory also evidences the operation of competing values within the discourse of Irish migrant identity in post-war England. Efforts to compose the migration journey as worthwhile embodied an attempt to interpret the particularities of past decisions, judgments and experiences in terms of competing ideals of masculine achievement, relating to notions of physical prowess and superior work ethic; technical aptitude and educational attainment; affluent consumption and economic advancement. Subjective change over the course of the migrant journey was a product of how migrants renegotiated the relationship between multiple images of self related to these ideals, in response to changing personal circumstances and wider shifts in the forms of collective memory itself.

Crucially, these internal conflicts exercised a powerful influence over issues of ethnicity and belonging within the narratives. While all the narratives were structured by an ongoing interplay between 'here' and 'there', the form of this articulation was different in each case. In part, this was because the dialogue between 'there' and 'here' was always mediated through other forms of intersubjective relation: migrants' creative interaction with the forms of communal and public memory embodied an effort to re/integrate parts of the self destabilised by the pressures, transformations and possibilities posed within multiple arenas of identity construction. The relationship between place, belonging and ethnic identification, and the ways this might change over the life course, was always contingent upon how subjectivities were formed in relation to a wider array of post-war discourses of the self, a notion we pursue further in the following chapter.

Notes

1. Parliamentary Papers, *Economic Survey for 1947*, Cmd 7046 (London, 1947).
2. K. Paul, 'A Case of Mistaken Identity: The Irish in Postwar Britain', *International Labour and Working-Class History* 49 (1996), 116–142.
3. P. Fitzgerald and B. Lambkin, *Migration in Irish History, 1607–2007* (London, 2008), 244–246.
4. J. A. Jackson, *The Irish in Britain* (London, 1963), 104.
5. For debates on post-war masculinity see L. King, *Family Men: Fatherhood and Masculinity in Britain, 1914–1960* (Oxford, 2015).
6. Images of the Irish as hard-drinking and prone to fighting were ubiquitous in British television series in the 1960s and 1970s. See, for example, *Till Death Us Do Part*, 'From Liverpool with Love' (BBC1, 18 July 1966) and *Fawlty Towers*, 'The Builders' (BBC1, 26 September 1975). For sociological and Catholic perspectives see M. Russell, 'The Irish Delinquent in England', *Studies: An Irish Quarterly Review* 53:210 (1964), 129–141; A. J. Sykes, 'Navvies: Their Work Attitudes', *Sociology* 3:1 (1969), 21–35 and 'Navvies: Their Social Relations', *Sociology* 3:2 (1969), 157–172; E. Hopkins, 'Irish Workers in England', *Christus Rex* 2:2 (1948), 17–24; T. Lane, 'The Irish in an English Parish', *The Furrow* 6:4 (1955), 211–214; G. Morley-Mower, 'Apostles or Lapsed?', *The Furrow* 9:4 (1958), 236–239.
7. Figures taken from tabulations in Jackson, *The Irish in Britain*, 198–199.
8. D. Foley, *Three Villages* (Dublin, 1977), 141.
9. E. Royle, *Modern Britain: A Social History 1750–1985* (London, 1989), 72–73, and J. Walvin, *Passage to Britain: Immigration in British History and Politics* (Harmondsworth, 1984), 59–60.
10. *The Irishmen: An Impression of Exile* (dir. Philip Donnellan, BBC, 1965).

11 'An Teach Irish Housing Association. A Profile' (1988), 2–4, AIB/ATHA/2/1. More recently, Jim Murphy's celebrated play *The Kings of Kilburn High Road* was staged in 2000 and was subsequently made into a film, screened in 2007. See *Kings* (dir. Tom Collins, Newgrange/Irish Film Board, 2007).
12 *The Men of Arlington* (dir. Enda Hughes, BBC1 Northern Ireland, 24 October 2011).
13 J. Kirk and C. Wall, *Work and Identity: Historical and Cultural Contexts* (Basingstoke, 2011), 10.
14 D. H. J. Morgan, *Discovering Men: Critical Studies on Men and Masculinity* (London, 1992), ch. 4.
15 D. Collinson and J. Hearn, '"Men" at "Work": Multiple Masculinities in Multiple Workplaces', in M. Mac an Ghaill (ed.), *Understanding Masculinities: Social Relations and Cultural Arenas* (London, 1996), 62–63.
16 L. Harte, *The Literature of the Irish in Britain: Autobiography and Memoir, 1725–2001* (Basingstoke, 2007), xxxiv.
17 Fitzgerald and Lambkin, *Migration in Irish History*, 66.
18 Denis Heaney (b. Kerry, 1927) PI/SA/7, 8.
19 Ibid., 12.
20 Ibid., 12–13.
21 L. Gilbert, 'Victory Festival', *Daily Mail*, 23 February 1945; J. Lee, 'A Tyre-Burst in Whitehall', *Evening News*, 29 September 1948; J. Lee, 'Mother Macree', *Evening News*, 19 November 1948.
22 Paul, 'A Case of Mistaken Identity', 119–120.
23 Home Office circular, 'Basis on Which Irish Labour Control is to be Continued after 31 March 1947', HO313/1330.
24 J. R. Short, *Housing in Britain: The Postwar Experience* (London, 1982), 42–44.
25 See L. W. Wood, *A Union to Build: The Story of UCATT* (London, 1979), 192–198 for a tabulation of average wage rises within the industry between 1951 and 1979.
26 Denis Heaney (b. Kerry, 1927) PI/SA/7, 14.
27 On the growth of 'company men' see U. Cowley, *The Men Who Built Britain: A History of the Irish Navvy* (Dublin, 2001), 181–183.
28 For example, J. B. Keane, *The Contractors* (Dublin, 1993); T. O' Grady and S. Pyke, *I Could Read the Sky* (London, 1997); D. MacAmhlaigh, *An Irish Navvy: The Diary of an Exile* (London, 1964); S. Ó Ciaráin, *Farewell to Mayo: An Emigrant's Memoirs of Ireland and Scotland* (Dublin, 1991); J. O'Donoghue, *In a Strange Land* (London, 1958); J. Phelan, *We Follow the Roads* (London, 1949); R. Power, *Apple on the Treetop* (Dublin, 1980); Patrick Campbell, *Tunnel Tigers* (Jersey City, NJ, 2000).
29 On the alleged individualism of the navvy see Sykes, 'Navvies: Their Work Attitudes', 21–35 and Sykes, 'Navvies: Their Social Relations', 157–172. More generally, see J. R. Colclough, *The Construction Industry of Great Britain* (London, 1965).
30 Denis Heaney (b. Kerry, 1927) PI/SA/7, 13.
31 Sykes, 'Navvies: Their Work Attitudes', 24; *Report of the Committee of Inquiry Under Prof. E. H. Phelps-Brown into Certain Matters Concerning Labour in Building and Civil Engineering*, Cmnd 3714-I (London, 1968), 40–44.

32 On the fluctuating character of work in the industry and its relation to government policy see Short, *Housing in Britain*, 91–94.
33 On 'the lump' and labour-only subcontracting see C. McGuire, L. Clarke and C. Wall, 'Battles on the Barbican: The Struggle for Trade Unionism in the British Building Industry, 1965–67', *History Workshop Journal* 75 (2013), 38–39.
34 For Marxian analyses of the exploitative nature of work in the industry see T. Austin, 'The Lump in the Construction Industry', in T. Nicholas (ed.), *Capital and Labour: A Marxist Primer* (London, 1980), 76–98, and more recently, E. Sutherland, 'Modes of Exploitation and Safety in the British Construction Industry', *Radical Statistics* 69 (1998), 34–52.
35 Wood, *A Union to Build*, 70–86; McGuire et al., 'Battles on the Barbican', 33–36.
36 O'Donoghue, *In a Strange Land*, 22.
37 MacAmhlaigh, *An Irish Navvy*, 29.
38 Sykes, 'Navvies: Their Work Attitudes', 28.
39 Sykes, 'Navvies: Their Social Relations', 160. See also Jackson, *The Irish in Britain*, 98.
40 Russell, 'The Irish Delinquent', 137–140.
41 S. Franklin, 'Sure, and I hope you're not tinking o' saying no to us, m'darlin', *Daily Mirror*, 2 May 1967, BCA/18222; D. Langton, 'Sure and the local pubs here'll be bearing the brunt of it, Paddy ..', *Sunday Mirror*, 10 December 1967, BCA/12466; G. Smith, 'That's the first break we've had since the breathanalyser', *Evening Standard*, 19 December 1967, BCA/12530; O. Lancaster, 'Sure, and how could Oi be ann immigrant, me not possessing a British passport', *Daily Express*, 26 February 1968, BCA/1299; JAK, 'Bloody foreigners', *Evening Standard*, 26 August 1969; BCA/16161.
42 Patrick J. Maguire, Fianna Fail TD for Monaghan, quoted in *Dáil Éireann Deb.*, CXLVIII, no. 3, 16 February 1955. For an extensive discussion of this mythology of superior fitness to work see C. Wills, *The Best Are Leaving: Emigration and Post-War Irish Culture* (Cambridge, 2015), ch. 1.
43 MacAmhlaigh, *An Irish Navvy*, 154.
44 Wills, *The Best are Leaving*, ch. 1.
45 Sykes, 'Navvies: Their Social Relations', 162
46 On the music-making cultures in post-war London and Birmingham see R. Hall, 'Irish Music and Dance in London, 1870–1970: A Socio-cultural History (DPhil thesis, University of Sussex, 1994), ch. 6, and A. Moran, 'Sites of Diaspora: The Irish Music of Birmingham' (PhD thesis, University of Cambridge, 2011).
47 Dominic Behan, 'McAlpine's Fusiliers' (Essex Music International, 1962).
48 *Irish Counties Journal*, December 1970, p. 3, AIB/ICA/Z/5/1.
49 The Irish Centre Welfare Office (Camden). Annual Report 1967, AIB/LIC/2/4.
50 Council for the Irish Centre, Camden. Twelfth Annual Report, 1966, AIB/LIC/AGM/1/3.
51 Constitution of the Council for the Irish Centre as Amended at the First Annual Meeting, 6 December 1961, AIB/LIC/AGM/1/25; *Irish Counties Journal*, December 1970, 5, AIB/ICA/Z/5/1.
52 For recent commemoration of Irish nurses see A. Guidera, 'The Irish Nurses Who Helped Build the NHS', *Irish Independent*, 22 July 2018; J. Shannon, 'The NHS and Its Irish Staff: 70 Years of Service', *Irish Times*, 2 July 2018.

53 Extract from the minutes of the founding members' meeting of the Irish Association Club, High Lane, Chorlton, 22 February 1985. Reproduced in A. Keegan and D. Claffey, *More Irish Manchester* (Stroud, 2006), 124–125.
54 Denis Heaney (b. Kerry, 1927) PI/SA/7, 14.
55 Ibid., 18.
56 Ibid., 21.
57 A. Offer, 'British Manual Workers: From Producers to Consumers, c. 1950–2000', *Contemporary British History* 22:4 (2008), 537–571.
58 B. Walter, 'Whiteness and Diasporic Irishness: Nation, Gender and Class', *Journal of Ethnic and Migration Studies* 37:9 (2011), 1302.
59 MacAmhlaigh, *An Irish Navvy*, 160.
60 Paul Fletcher, quoted in 'Top 100 and Financial Review 2000', *Construction News*, September 2000.
61 Denis Heaney (b. Kerry, 1927) PI/SA/7, 26–27.
62 Both the newspapers of the Irish in Britain and the English regional press regularly run features on Irish success in the construction industry, invariably telling the story of their protagonists through the 'rags-to-riches' form. For example, 'The Fortune Builders', *Irish Post*, 22 July 2000; 'Irish Building Millionaire Dies', *Irish Post*, 12 August 2000; 'Murphy's Law', *Evening Standard Magazine*, February 2004.
63 Keane, *The Contractors*, 6–7.
64 Ibid., 22.
65 Ibid., 124.
66 Ibid., 241.
67 Ibid., 251–52.
68 Bill Duffy (b. Roscommon, 1951) PI/SA/4, 1.
69 Ibid., 2.
70 Ibid., 5.
71 Ibid., 12.
72 Ibid., 13.
73 Ibid., 14.
74 Ibid.
75 Ibid.
76 Ibid., 15.
77 Ibid., 17.
78 McGuire et al., 'Battles on the Barbican', 37.
79 Bill Duffy (b. Roscommon, 1951) PI/SA/4, 27.
80 On post-war technocratic masculinities see M. Savage, 'Affluence and Social Change in the Making of Technocratic Middle-Class Identities: Britain, 1939–55', *Contemporary British History* 22:4 (2008), 457–476.
81 Bill Duffy (b. Roscommon, 1951) PI/SA/4, 6.
82 Ibid., 22.
83 Ibid., 26.
84 Ibid., 36.
85 Joe Doherty (b. Longford, 1944) PI/SA/3, 22.
86 Ibid., 1.
87 Ibid., 14.
88 Ibid., 13.
89 Ibid., 1.

90 Ibid., 6.
91 Ibid., 1.
92 Cowley, *The Men Who Built Britain*, 219–222.
93 See Campbell's *Tunnel Tigers* for an account of the everyday lives of tunnel-diggers in Scotland. See also, Sykes, 'Navvies: Their Social Relations', 162.
94 Joe Doherty (b. Longford, 1944) PI/SA/3, 14–15.
95 John B. Keane, for example, recalled that the many of the boarding houses on the street where he first lodged in Northampton in 1952 displayed the infamous 'No negroes, no Irish' signs, some with the additional italicised message: '*That means you, Paddy!*'. J. B. Keane, *Self-Portrait* (Cork, 1969), 42.
96 The report to receive the most coverage in the national press, in part because it was published by the Commission for Racial Equality, was M. J. Hickman and B. Walter, *Discrimination and the Irish Community in Britain: A Report of Research Undertaken for the Commission for Racial Equality* (London, 1997).
97 Joe Doherty (b. Longford, 1944) PI/SA/3, 15.
98 *The Men of Arlington*; see also *Prime Time: Ireland's Forgotten Generation* (RTE1, 22 December 2003) and *Arise, You Gallant Sweeneys!* (dir. Ian Nesbitt, Outside Films, 2010).
99 Joe Doherty (b. Longford, 1944) PI/SA/3, 8.
100 Ibid., 13.
101 Ibid., 14.
102 Ibid., 9.
103 See D. Ferriter, *The Transformation of Ireland: 1900–2000* (London, 2004), ch. 8, for a general account of recent social and political changes in Ireland.
104 Joe Doherty (b. Longford, 1944) PI/SA/3, 2.
105 For a survey of the contradictory attitudes expressed in response to Irish labour in Victorian Britain see D. M. MacRaild, *The Irish Diaspora in Britain, 1750–1939* (London, 2011), ch. 2.
106 Parliamentary Papers, *Report on the State of the Irish Poor* (London, 1836), xxiv–xxvii, quoted from R. Swift, 'The Historiography of the Irish in Nineteenth-Century Britain', in P. O'Sullivan (ed.), *The Irish World Wide: History, Heritage, Identity*, vol. 2: *The Irish in the New Communities* (London and New York, 1996), 61.

4

Falling away from the Church? Negotiating religious selfhoods in post-1945 England

Migrant subjectivity and discursive Catholicism

Writing in *The Furrow* in 1950, Fr Robert Culhane mused upon the uncertain implications of post-war change for England's Catholic population. Where this minority had long existed on the periphery of England's dominant Protestant culture, in the shifting religious atmosphere of the post-war world Catholics were no longer compelled to 'weather the storm of open bigotry'. On the other hand, however, the dissipation of the storm merely signalled the descent of 'an ever-thickening mist of religious indifference'. Under such conditions, pondered Culhane, would Irish 'boys and girls', then crossing to England in their thousands, be able to preserve their faith?

> How is the faith of the Irish Catholic immigrants affected by this climate? Does it show something of the weakness of the hothouse plant? In a word, have many of the Irish Catholics who have went to Britain in recent years denied to the Church the benefit of the faith of their childhood?[1]

For most of Culhane's contemporaries the signs were ominous. In the sizeable literature generated around the immigrant, the 'Irish boy and girl', raised in an atmosphere of intense piety at home, was habitually imagined to be 'falling away from the Church' in England, causing priests and Catholic social workers intense alarm.[2] For other contemporary observers, however, the picture was more complex. For those sociologists who registered the presence of the Irish immigrant, the Church appeared central to the Irish experience in post-war England, forming a vital institutional framework within which adjustment to urban life was negotiated.[3]

Similarly, within much of the autobiographical literature of the Irish in post-war England the Church, along with the pub, dancehall and Irish club, forms part of a network of overlapping social spaces where migrants negotiated the pleasures and deprivations of urban life. While the relative absence of sectarian hostility registers the diminishing importance of religion as a frontier of national belonging in this period, the contours of an urban, religiously inflected migrant consciousness were nevertheless shaped within these loci of adjustment. Donall MacAmhlaigh looked forward to Sunday Mass each week, for example, because it was a social occasion, after which the Irish in Northampton would congregate in the Irish club or a local pub:

> Holy Communion this morning, thank God. Sunday is the day we like best here in Northampton. All the Irish gather here in the Club after Mass – men, women and children. Tea is drunk, cards are played, work and sport discussed, mothers hold forth on the great things their children have done, friends and relations enquire about things at home from one another, Irish papers are sold and read, boys run around playing 'tig' and the accents of every county of Ireland can be heard in the place.[4]

On the other hand, the Church was also valued as a necessary restraining influence upon 'uncivilised' behaviour, the recurrence of which besmirched the respectability of the Irish in public view of their English counterparts:

> Murphy and I went off to Mass together. I was astonished at the sermon that was preached – all about the lads fighting in the pubs and dancehalls. The priest came out very strongly against them, saying they were nothing but ignorant beasts that let down their country and their Faith. There is no denying that this sort of thing is necessary for the devil has seized hold of enough Irishmen here in London.[5]

This chapter investigates the changing place of religion in migrants' lives in England and the 'discursive power' of Catholic ideals in shaping settlement experiences.[6] Focused on the experiences of two migrants who left Ireland in the 1940s and 1950s, the first section explores how ideals engendered through Catholic 'cultures of adjustment' were implicated in processes of emotional adaption, not only during the early post-arrival years, but over the longer life course.[7] While the maintenance of religious practice in England was not always easy, Catholic discourse offered a model of virtuous and socially respectable settlement in which migrants could recognise aspects of their own fears, ambitions and aspirations, and which supplied a moral framework in terms of which crucial decisions were taken and the significance of the settlement process evaluated. As well as a source of continuity with the past, with 'the simple faith' into which migrants had been inducted in Ireland, Catholic narratives of the self circulating within English Catholicism here absorbed the influence of wider post-war shifts in social and moral values, opening new possibilities for self-development and evaluation.[8]

The second section complicates this line of interpretation in a number of ways. The autobiographical literature of post-war settlement evidences the agency of the Church in shaping adjustment experiences, but it also registers a more critical attitude towards religious authority in England. In her *Memoirs of a Mayo Immigrant*, Margaret Lally recalled how, having left Mayo in 1964 a devout and pious Catholic, aged 15, her relationship to the Church was irreparably damaged following two deeply traumatic pregnancies. Following the first, which triggered a melanoma, Margaret was advised to avoid further childbirth, but, given her adherence to the Church's prohibition on contraception, she was pregnant with her second child within the year. This time, having refused an abortion, childbirth almost resulted in the death of both her son and herself. Margaret's gynaecologist now advised sterilisation, warning that next time she would not survive:

> About a month later, I went to see a Catholic priest to ask his permission to get sterilised. I told him my story and that I should not have carried my son because I had risked my life in doing so. I also told him about having had cancer, which was aggravated by my pregnancies. Well, he listened, and then answered, telling me that in the Catholic Church the belief is that while there is life to be born, let it be born. I said fine, but I would have to end my marriage as I could not take the risk of sleeping with my husband. He said that too was against the Catholic Church. So I asked him if he was telling me to sleep with my husband knowing that I would get pregnant, and that, in my mind, to do so was suicide. He said that wasn't the case, it was God's will. I asked him one final question – could I have his blessing and get sterilised? He said no, so I stood up to go but before I did, I asked him if it would be considered suicide if I jumped off the roof. He said that it would because I would be knowingly killing myself. I told him that the Catholic Church was trying to murder me with their rules and I walked away. As I got to the big oak doors at the end of the room, I told him what to do with his church and his rules. I had survived so much to see my children grow up, and there was no way I was going to let the church leave my children without their mother.[9]

From the nineteenth century, the Irish Catholic Church exercised an extraordinary influence over the making modern Irish society. Via its intervention in diverse areas of Irish life, from national politics to the family, the Church was able to propagate an intensely pious and culturally pervasive form of religiosity, characterised by devotional fervour, authoritarian church–laity relations and the permeation of a Catholic moral ethos throughout society.[10] From the 1960s, however, core elements of this culture have been progressively undermined. While this has been a relatively gradual process in Ireland, for the post-war emigrant generation settlement in England involved a more direct and extensive exposure to permissive leisure cultures, alternative discourses of sexual knowledge and emancipatory ideologies of gendered selfhood.[11] While some migrants refused the influence of these competing discourses, for others long-term settlement engendered a more reflexive perspective on the effects of religious authority, provoking complex reworkings of religious identification in their narratives of life in England.

Section two examines the impact of these transformations upon how two later migrants articulate the place of religion in shaping their own journeys of settlement. While the figure of the priest as symbol of moral authority and spiritual welfare remained ubiquitous within communal self-representations of Irish identity in England right up until the 1980s, since then accumulating revelations of clerical abuse relating back to the post-war decades have fundamentally destabilised this construction. This section explores how the transnational counter-memory of Church power engendered by these developments forms an important discursive prism through which subjects recall, interpret and justify their own changing relationship with religious norms, values and practices over the life course. Where earlier migrants endeavoured to reconcile their lived experiences in England with Catholic models of settlement, these later migrants mobilised the liberal critique of Church power to explain how excessive clerical control impeded the realisation of alternative ideals of self. Yet, while these narratives were related from a position of condemnation, the story of transition which they materialised did not manifest a linear trajectory of personal religious change, yielding the formation of a strictly 'secular' subject. As well as a story of transformation, this section also suggests how the renunciation of religious authority is an ambivalent process, involving the management of conflicting desires for autonomy from and conformity to deeply internalised religious prohibitions.

Fealty to faith and family: belief, belonging and discursive Catholicism

As the Catholic sociologist John Hickey observed in 1967, the social and economic reforms of the post-war decades offered many ordinary Catholics in England new 'opportunities for social mobility'.[12] Yet, while ordinary Catholic families may have embraced such opportunities, for many of the community's spiritual and intellectual leaders post-war improvements in living standards posed a complex social problem. Catholic literature produced during the period here emphasised the extent to which state intervention and expanding levels of popular consumption were unravelling England's moral fabric. Echoing broader conservative anxieties around the morally 'unsettled' nature of post-war society, Catholic clerics and intellectuals perceived the advent of welfarism and mass consumerism as morally corrosive forces which, by supplying the laity with alternative sources of ritual, identity and security, fundamentally undermined their attachment to the Church and conformity to religious ideals. The evidence for this was to be found, not only in the waning commitment to religious rituals and routines, but in the widespread valorisation of material acquisitiveness, consumer pleasure-seeking and individual self-fulfilment as popular objects of desire.[13]

Within this context, the mass arrival of Irish migrants, the majority young, single and from rural parishes in the west of Ireland, represented an uncertain asset. While the Irish influx embodied a 'vast potential of missionary strength', utilising this potential depended upon migrants' effective absorption into the English parish system.[14] Herein, while some migrants clung fast to 'the loyalties that meant so much at home', 'thousands of Irish exiles' quickly became 'caught up ... in the world of their fellows at work, of the people in the streets'.[15] The consequence for the Church was not only the 'lapsation' of migrants themselves, but the loss too of their religiously ignorant offspring, resulting in the overall dissipation of the Catholic population.[16]

In part, such concerns reflected anxieties around Irish migrants' close identification with problematised urban spaces. If the post-war expansion in public housing gradually transformed the domestic lives of the English working classes, for newly arrived migrants suburban domesticity was, initially at least, inaccessible.[17] Migrants, whether from Ireland, Europe or the New Commonwealth, could not apply for council housing until they had been resident in a local authority area for a prescribed number of years. And the comprehensive redevelopment of the urban cores of destination cities, piecemeal and protracted though it was, progressively reduced the stock of low-cost private rented accommodation over the period. Consequently, given the prevalence of discrimination within the wider rental market, many migrants gravitated towards, and became visibly concentrated in, so-called inner-urban 'twilight zones': streets of large, dilapidated Victorian terraces, situated on the periphery of the city's inner core, which had been purchased by migrant landlords and subdivided into multi-occupancy 'lodging houses'.

Set against the fantasy of white suburban domesticity, in the post-war English imagination such 'twilight zones' formed spaces of otherness, associated with socio-economic marginality and racial degeneration. Yet, for migrants forced to inhabit such districts the 'twilight zone' elicited a more nuanced gamut of reactions. While lodging-house rooms were themselves typically overcrowded, in crumbling repair and let at extortionate rates, the wards where they were located also evolved their own communal infrastructure of Irish pubs, clubs, cafes and dancehalls. When Richard Power first arrived in Birmingham in 1957, the 'digs' in which he would spend the next few months were initially encountered as squalid and congested. On his first night, he shared a grimy room with five other men, one within the same bed, and a carnivorous insect:

> It was hard to get to sleep that first night. I awoke again and again when I'd hear the footsteps of the lodgers going to work or returning home from work. The old man was snoring harshly, out of kilter with other nostrils, changing gear, then harmonising with them. I felt an insect sucking my blood under the shelter of the quilt, but I failed to locate it.[18]

Relatively quickly, however, Power found himself adapting, not only to the peculiar domestic rhythms of the lodging house, but to new routines of sociability structured around nightly trips to local pubs, dancehalls and other nearby leisure venues. Here, amidst crowds of similarly situated Irish migrants drawn from counties across Ireland, old friends were encountered and new contacts established, pints downed and information about work and lodgings exchanged. In all this, despite the deprivations of the lodging house, Power discerned an extension in the range of his personal freedoms:

> But this wasn't the end of my delights. I'd stretch out and light a cigarette. I'd have my agenda for the evening still to make out. I could go out, or to the picture or to a boxing match. Or I could wander down to the public house to look for interesting company. I'd lie back there, debating the pros and cons at my ease, and sometimes I wouldn't even go out at all.[19]

For Catholic observers, and indeed for the councils and committees of the emerging network of Irish associations, it was precisely these routines of sociability and consumption which compromised Irish religiosity in England. In part, this was a product of the degenerative effects of the 'twilight zone' itself: via the opportunities it offered for drinking and promiscuous sexual mixing, for unsavoury liaisons with 'undesirable companions', the immigrant quarter expanded the horizons of personal desire, engendering immoral habits that endangered migrants' souls and drew them away from the Church.[20] On the other hand, migrants' enthusiastic investment in these pleasures, noted repeatedly by observers, was also indicative of an intrinsic lack of resilience to the corrupting temptations of modern life.[21] If the immigrant quarter confronted migrants with a multitude of moral dangers, their capacity to navigate this environment was hampered by the behavioural consequences of a defective system of moral socialisation, itself a reflection of the untrammelled power of the Irish Church in an underdeveloped rural society.[22] Catholic constructions of the Irish migrant, particularly those formulated by English Catholic social scientists and the English hierarchy, thus inscribed the migrant experience within a wider discourse of social problematisation predicated on the identification of behavioural deviance from English societal norms.[23] Within this framing, stereotypical notions of Irish excess were implicitly mapped against an ideal conception of English civilisation, increasingly defined, in the morally conservative climate of the late 1940s and 1950s, in terms of innate English propensities for domestic order, personal responsibility and self-regulation. The consequences of migrants' defective socialisation were thus manifest in

> a lack of self-discipline and self-control, an underdeveloped sense of responsibility towards work-mates, employers and non-Catholics, a social-inferiority complex, a lack of articulateness about religion, a sense of ignorance about sex, and a view of clergy–laity relationships that polarizes at either complete acceptance of priestly authority in all matters, or equally complete rejection of any priestly authority.[24]

Undoubtedly, such observations picked out genuine problems of migrant adaption; certainly they motivated a remedial response. According to one recent assessment, in the absence of support from either the British or Irish state, Catholic migrant welfarism in England offered migrants a 'comforting and familiar voice' which endeavoured to 'bridge the void between the expectation and reality of emigration'.[25] At the same time, however, religious constructions of the 'deviant' migrant necessarily presupposed a conception of 'normal' settlement, elaborated in terms of those practices, behaviours and attitudes which secured migrants' faith and enabled them to 'make the grade in life'.[26] Above and beyond the immediate dangers of the urban reception area and the apparent deficiencies of migrants' moral training, discourses of migrant welfare here registered a concern with settlement as a long-term process, encompassing migrants' secure integration into parish life. Where some migrants were written off as 'poor material', 'inevitable failures' who 'would have been better advised not to emigrate in the first place', the waywardness of others reflected a perception of migration as temporary.[27] Such a perception, according to one authority, encouraged an existence of unfettered transience inimical to the formation of ties and steady habits:

> A type that is met with is the casual emigrant who spends a year or two in England and regards it as a vacation from religious practice. He was regular in attendance at Mass and the Sacraments in Ireland.

In England he stays away from both. When he returns to Ireland he begins to practise again.[28]

Consequently, for Irish community leaders, as well as for the priests and Catholic welfare workers who patronised and staffed their institutions, the problem of migrant deviancy would ultimately be resolved through 'putting down roots'; through the development of a 'fully integrated Irish community' which retained its 'basic cultural and spiritual background' while playing its full part 'in the social, economic and political life in this country'.[29] Central to this, and linking the concerns of community-builders with those of the Church, was the regulation of the migrant's domestic milieu: although, according to one Birmingham-based observer, 'there is a difficulty about the many thousands who live in lodgings and perhaps do not intend to stay here', those 'Irish who marry and settle down are easily incorporated into normal English Catholic life; for these there is no special problem'.[30] The construct of the deviant migrant was thus ultimately a foil for the counter-formation of a narrative of virtuous and socially respectable settlement, at the centre of which stood the twin institutions of Catholic marriage and the family. Successful marriage within the faith enabled the creation of a stable family environment in which the next generation of Catholics could be raised.[31] But it also enhanced the 'status and reputation' of the Irish community in England more generally, creating in the process an audience eager for images reflecting back their moral and social achievements. 'During the Sixties', claimed the *Irish Post*, the Irish in Britain 'underwent a major evolution', moving 'from traditional areas into the suburbs' and 'purchasing houses'. 'Today, therefore, one effortlessly comes upon thousands of settled Irish families with children going to school and a mild consciousness of that dichotomy in which one half of the family is most definitely Irish and the younger half not altogether sure as to their nationality'.[32]

This narrative of family-centred settlement supplied a set of evaluative ideals in terms of which Aileen interpreted the significance of her own experience of settlement in England after 1945. As we saw in Chapter 2, Aileen's experience of growing up on her family's small farm in Mayo between 1927 and 1945 had not been positive: as she recalled, she found the daily performance of unpaid farm labour arduous and exploitative, while her father, with whom she 'didn't get on', was 'an awful bully': 'he had a terrible temper. And he'd beat you unmercifully'.[33] As such, as Aileen reiterated throughout the interview, she 'was glad to leave home' for Doncaster in 1945 because she 'never saw any happiness in it'.

Nevertheless, if Aileen was 'glad' to leave home, it did not necessarily follow that she enjoyed her early years in England. Where many respondents who experienced difficult childhoods in Ireland tend to construct England as a space of liberation and self-fulfilment, Aileen's representations of her early encounters with English society emphasise simultaneously the difficulty of adjustment and the impossibility of return:

> I did find it strange when I came to England, and I think if I'd come from a happy home I think I would have gone home again, whatever would have happened. But I didn't. And I ... an unhappy home life is something you never forget.[34]

Aileen's sense of the strangeness of English society derived partly from her perception of the otherness of English customs and habits. As she recalls, when she first arrived she regarded the English as 'a different race altogether', and was struck by the 'more distant' forms of interpersonal interaction she encountered in the workplace.[35] As this implies, Aileen's sense of the strangeness of England also reflected a consciousness of her own otherness within her new and unfamiliar environment. Although Aileen enjoyed working in the various factories and hotels where she was employed in these years, and considered many of her colleagues and employers 'very nice people', she also recalled being regarded as something of a novelty:

> **Aileen:** Well I suppose I found it terribly strange. Yes. And ... you see people ... I suppose maybe I still speak with an Irish accent, I've never lost it. But I suppose then I was more Irish. And ... they'd come to listen to me. One man in particular. Would come to listen to me speak. Yeah. 'Cos he thought the Irish accent was, I suppose, funny maybe to him, I don't know. But he was a nice man.[36]

Similarly, although 'the Church' was and is 'very important' to Aileen, and she was determined to maintain her religion in England, she 'never got that involved' in parish life during her early years of settlement. This reflected the itinerant character of her working life during this period, as well as the fact that in some occupations, such as the hotel industry, working hours rendered religious observation difficult: 'I mean a lot of them (employers) wouldn't let you go to mass, on a Sunday.'[37] More generally, however, Aileen was discouraged from deeper immersion in parish life due to a sense of being an outsider:

> [I]t was very, very strange when I came here. I'll never forget the first Sunday I went to mass, and when I came out I didn't know a sinner ... and I looked round, I didn't know a sinner. And I thought, 'Oh, this is ... this is awful!' 'Cos at home, in the country, you knew everybody.[38]

Aileen's early years in England thus form a period of isolation and disorientation in her narrative; a phase in which she perceived herself a 'stranger' in an unfamiliar environment, and which she 'wouldn't like to live over again'.[39] As Aileen also states, however, over time she also 'got more used to the English way of life'.[40] Crucial in this adaption, and the critical turning point in her overall narrative of settlement, was the event of marriage. Aileen met her husband at a country hall dance in Mayo when she was 17 and, following her departure for England a year later, kept in touch with Sean via an ongoing exchange of letters. Two years later Sean migrated to England too, first to Bletchley in Buckinghamshire, then to Halifax, at which point Aileen moved to Bradford to be nearer to him. Then, in 1949 Sean and Aileen both moved to Manchester, where Aileen's sister was already living with her husband, and on 18 February 1950, they married at the Holy Name Church, Oxford Road. Thereafter, as Aileen states, 'we were married for 47 years. Very happy marriage. Marriage made in heaven.'[41]

One reason why marriage marks a turning point in Aileen's settlement narrative is because it is identified with a crucial transition in her residential history in England. Prior to getting married, this history had been characterised by a high degree of mobility and sharing, whether in hotel accommodation provided by her employers or boarding with her sister. Following marriage in 1950, however, Sean and Aileen rented their own one-bedroom flat together in Moss Side, then a dilapidated inner-urban district with a dense West Indian, Irish and Asian population. Following this, they moved to a larger house in the same area, but in 1954 'we came up here to Gorton', a working-class district located on the south-easterly edge of the city centre. Initially:

Aileen: When we came in here, it was just ... just temper on the walls, where ... You can see it upstairs now, where we're going to decorate. Where we took the paper off, 'twas just temper on the walls. And we came in here, 'twas rented at the time. But then we, we bought it, as sitting tenants.
Barry: Was that important, buying your house?
Aileen: Well it really was, because then it was your own, and then you could do what alterations you wanted, you know. 'Cos there was no ... no toilet inside, in the house, when we came here. My husband was the first one on this ... round here, that managed to get a toilet put in upstairs, yeah.[42]

For many migrants newly arrived after 1945, a common and recurrent problem concerned the poor quality of accommodation available in English towns and cities. Whether in rooms supplied by one's employer, multi-occupancy lodging houses in decaying twilight zones or makeshift caravans erected on building sites, the temporary, shared and rented forms of housing documented in migrants' testimonies were frequently associated with a catalogue of deprivations, from lack of privacy and poor food, to insecurity of tenure and extortionate rents. Given, however, the general shortage of housing in England up until the 1970s, coupled with the various barriers migrants faced in accessing newly constructed public housing, migrants' capacity to ascend from these sections of the housing market and realise the vaunted ideal of domestic affluence was heavily constrained. In this context, as Catholic advice literature explained, marriage opened the possibility of domestic improvement through the careful pooling of resources. While she only earned 'eighteen and six a week' on her own, saving together Aileen and Sean amassed £120 to 'set up home' in Gorton. This represented an advance in Sean and Aileen's social mobility, in that Gorton was a more 'respectable' residential area; but it also allowed them to mould their domestic environment in accordance with their own tastes and requirements, enhancing personal comfort and one's sense of autonomy: your house was now 'your own', as Aileen states, to do with as you please.

Additionally, however, homemaking was also integral to the development of family life. A second reason why marriage forms a turning point in Aileen's narrative concerns its close association with valued affective relationships. As Aileen recalled throughout the interview, her memories of Ireland were marred by her father's mistreatment of both herself and her mother: 'my mum was a lovely woman. But she was ... dictated to by my father.'[43] By contrast, Aileen's own husband features as a source of emotional self-fulfilment within her narrative: 'he was my life, I must say.'[44] Likewise, where Aileen depicts her own mother's experience of family life in terms of drudgery and subjugation, she portrays her own family as the 'best thing' to happen in her life:

Aileen: Well because we were, I don't know, I suppose because I was happy. Yeah. And I loved ... I loved having a family. Yeah, yeah. Yeah.
Barry: Do you think that's been the most important thing in your life?
Aileen: I do. Yeah. My marriage and, and ... my children.[45]

As noted above, a central aim of Catholic interventions into migrants' lives was to encourage marriage within the faith: this would facilitate migrants' adaption to their new environment, enabling new parish 'roots' to be planted, and over the longer term safeguard the intergenerational reproduction of the Catholic community. During the same period in which this intervention was enacted, however, Catholic understandings of marriage in England were themselves undergoing destabilisation and reconfiguration. While the late 1940s and 1950s are usually seen as a period of moral and religious conservatism in England, when fears around pre-marital sex, rising rates of divorce and new consumption habits provoked the reassertion of puritanical norms, Catholic discourses on marriage also reflected an increasing concern with the regulation of family relationships in accordance with shifting definitions of members' emotional and practical needs. As Alana Harris has shown, Catholic marriage guidance literature produced during the period portrayed family life as an arena of personal fulfilment and emotional enrichment, wherein individual members could expect to derive personal satisfactions and a powerful sense of purpose. Ideal constructions of the family promoted to the laity thus reflected the influence of wider post-war discourses on the virtues of 'companionate marriage', adapting the rhetoric of the Holy Family to incorporate notions of romantic love, domestic cooperation and familial intimacy.[46]

Husbands were still defined as the primary providers and ultimate moral arbiters within the family; but recalibrated conceptions of Catholic masculinity also encouraged men's increasing emotional immersion in family life, stressing the importance of fatherly care and devotion towards children, as well as love and adoration towards one's wife. And while Catholic models of the family continued to define womanhood in terms of domestic and maternal roles, the performance of these roles was elevated as a form of personal struggle and sacrifice. Mothers, as a reflection of the Virgin Mother, were the authors of the next generation of the Church, entitled to respect, deference and love for their supreme sacrifice.

For Aileen, the importance of these changing norms was that they publicly delegitimised the authoritarian and abusive familial relations she had endured growing up, opening in the process new space for the elaboration of alternative, more emotionally satisfying forms of married and family life. While the Church's insistence upon women's maternal obligations meant that Aileen did not return to work after the birth of her first daughter in 1954, an arrangement which ensured Sean 'had to work seven days a week', she was nevertheless 'quite happy to be at home when the children were young'. By contrast with her own experiences of family life in Ireland, Aileen spoke repeatedly with affection and pride about her own children's births, childhoods and achievements in life, reiterating how 'they are wonderful to me':

> I must only have been about 15, and I can remember my sister, my older sister, coming home telling us that somebody had twins and she called one of them Amy. And I said, 'Well, if ever I have a little girl I'm going to call her Amy', and I did. Yes. And my other daughter's Julie, and my son is John, yeah. Er ... I couldn't praise 'em enough, any of 'em, yes.[47]

Similarly, where Aileen's father is demonised as 'an awful bully' in her memories of Irish family life, her husband is idealised as a repository of the very opposite qualities:

We were 47 years married. Yeah. And he was ... so different to my father. He was such a kind, kind man, and he adored his children. Amy, she was the apple of his eye.[48]

Marriage was thus much more than a convenient refuge from isolation and dislocation; Aileen's husband in particular embodies in her narrative a longing for those things denied in her own childhood, of which her father deprived her growing up: love, affection, recognition, respect. Marriage thus signifies emotional repair and personal growth within Aileen's settlement narrative. In turn, given the seminal importance of this relationship in the development of the self, so there is a retrospective need to preserve it in celestial terms (a 'marriage made in heaven'), as a sacred object which validates the struggles of the younger self to make a better life in England, thus affirming the value of the life lived within the context of the inevitable losses of ageing.

In this latter respect, of negotiating the losses of ageing, this process of personal commemoration is further augmented by Aileen's continuing investment in religious practice:

Barry: How important has the church been over the course of your life in England?
Aileen: The church is very important to me. It is, yes. Well, we've been in this parish now, the Sacred Heart parish, for ... 48 ...? Yeah, 48 years. And, er, I still go to church every Sunday. And if there's mass during the week, if I can get there, I go to church. Oh, my church ... my church and my religion is important to me. Yeah.[49]

Following her marriage in 1950, Aileen still found it difficult to become 'involved' in parish life. While she continued to attend mass as often as possible, her local church in Moss Side, the Holy Name, was a 'massive church' where she found it difficult to establish personal relationships. On moving to Gorton, however, Aileen began to attend a new, much smaller church where she got to know the priests and congregation personally, and where she began to participate more fully in the wider life of the parish. Particularly once her children had left home, and following the death of her husband in 1996, Aileen began to devote an increasing amount of time to parish related events and activities:

I've been more involved with the Sacred Heart now, 'cos, er ... well we had one, going back now quite a few years, we had one lovely priest over here. I hope you'll meet Father O'Hara. He's, he's a Kerry man. And ... I did get very involved with him, now. I used to go over, and used to clean the church, and ... you know, do all this for him. 'Cos, of course, the children were bigger then. They were off my hands. And, I was ... And I think he's one of the nicest priests I have ever met. Very down to earth.[50]

Over the course of her adult life in England, Aileen's experiences of married and family life have supplied her with a powerful sense of identity and belonging. With the passing of her husband and dispersal of her children from the family home, however, these sources of selfhood are potentially destabilised. For Aileen, one response to this concerns becoming more 'involved' within alternative communities of belonging. As well as a source of social interaction, Aileen's parish community here represents a context where the values in terms of which she composes the ontological meaning of her life remain in circulation, supplying a sense of public recognition for the aims, struggles and achievements of the self. Consequently, just as it is important for Aileen to preserve an ideal image of married and family life within her personal recollections of settlement, so it is also important that current communities of belonging which support this preservation remain constant; change which endangers the salience of those values in terms of which the meaning of the past is reconstructed threatens the coherence and intelligibility of the present self:

Aileen: But, er ... religion has gone to pot.
Barry: Why do you think that's happened?
Aileen: I honestly don't know why it's happened. And I'm sure ... er, well I'm sure that the young priests, they must be very, er ... how shall I say it? They must find it very hard. 'Cos we have a young priest now over here, I think he's about 33. A lovely, young, English lad. But, erm ... I don't know. They must get very disheartened. Because he's made a ruling now ... er, that, er ... if you don't come to church for eight to twelve weeks before you have a baby christened, they make no exceptions, you won't get the child christened. And ... er, whether I'm right or whether I'm wrong, I think he's right. Erm ... Then he said he gets a knocking on his door, they have ... they want to get them into the Catholic school ... they've never been to church ... mass or meeting. So, I do think it's very disheartening for them. 'Cos he, he gave it off the altar last week, 'cos he must have had a lot of people aggravating him about, you know, wanting to get their child into school. They haven't ... maybe they've had the child christened, maybe not. They'll have them christened and that's the last you'll see of them then until ... they want them in the school. Which ... right ... rightly or wrongly, I don't think it's right. So he gave, er ... when he finished mass last week, he gave ... a talk about ... and he was making no exceptions for anybody. And ... he just happened to come into the hall to me afterwards and he says, 'Well, Aileen, what do you think about it?' And I said what I said this morning, I said, 'Well I think you were quite right.' I said, 'If every priest would do the same ...'
Barry: It might change things?

Aileen: It might change things. But I think ... all this here, they're living together now, and ... they don't get married, and they have children, and ... no, I don't agree with it at all.[51]

In a different way, these same values and ideals were implicated in the reconstruction and evaluation of Sean Hagan's experiences of settlement in England. Born in 1935, Sean grew up in rural Co. Offaly, the eldest son in a family of eight whose only source of income was his father's wages as a farm labourer. Thus, at the age of 12 Sean 'had to go out ... leave school and go out and work in the bogs' because 'we had to do six kids'. Thus began for Sean a nine-year period of work in physically strenuous and poorly paid jobs in support of his family. Within his account of this period leaving was depicted, not as a transitional moment, signifying self-fulfilment and personal ambition, but as an act of necessity, involving basic economic calculations:

> [L]ike I say, the work was scarce, and ... the money wasn't very good. And money was scarce, everything was scarce. And that's why I come to England. Otherwise I wouldn't have come.[52]

Structurally and thematically, Sean's settlement narrative shares much in common with this account of growing up in Ireland. When Sean arrived in England in 1956 he was immediately impressed by the ready availability of work: 'you didn't have to look for a job, walk right into a job ...'.[53] Sean immediately took a job in a cotton mill in Bolton, a job that was 'dirty' and 'busy' but much better paid 'than in Ireland', enabling Sean 'to send money home to my mother, every week'. After a mere six months, Sean met his wife and the couple were married soon afterwards. Although Sean emphasises that his wife was 'lovely' and the 'best thing' about 'coming to England', reflecting upon the brevity of their courtship he also considers that 'we got married too quick really I think':

> [Y]ou're more sensible as the years go on, aren't you. You know, I mi... might have had my own house ... and, and I say, well I got married ... after six months' courting I got married, and went in this rented house, instead I ... we should have ... pooled together and thought of buying it. We never thought that, we were only young then and ... we used to go out every night. Instead of saving and starting buying my own house. So that ... I didn't do, you know.[54]

After getting married Sean and his wife continued in the manner to which they had become accustomed, with Sean going to the pub and the Irish club and his wife to the bingo. After an unspecified length of time, however, Sean's wife 'got pregnant and she had to finish work'. Since the flat which Sean and his wife rented was cramped, and involved sharing bathroom and other facilities with other tenants, the birth of their first child underscored the importance of finding more suitable accommodation. As in Aileen's case, house purchase here formed the most realistic option, but without savings and with Sean now the sole wage-earner, amassing a deposit became more difficult. Consequently, when on a visit home Sean's parents offered to look after baby Margaret for a year, Sean and his wife agreed:

> 'Twas their first grandchild, and they said, 'Why'd you leave ... leave the ... leave ...', Margaret, she were called, 'why don't you leave Margaret with us, and go back and work together and ... and buy a house, and then when you come back next year, you can take her back with you?' And we agreed, you know. It was ... it upset us after, we should ... we made a mistake there. We left her, we left my eldest daughter with my mother and father in Ireland, and then we went back twelve months after, to bring her back. She wouldn't come back. She didn't want to ... she didn't want to come back.[55]

Margaret in fact never came back to live in England, and although as Sean states 'she's happy at home', leaving her there that first time remains Sean's main regret in life: 'we regretted it for the rest of our lives, me and my ... me and my wife'. Nor did leaving Margaret in Ireland enable, as intended, the purchasing of a home:

Sean: When we went home to bring her back, Margaret ... my wife was already expecting again. Which that was a mistake we made again.
Barry: Why?
Sean: Because we want ... we intend ... our intention was to come over, leave Margaret at home, come over and both of us work. And then buy a house of our own, you know. But we were only over here a couple of year ... er, a couple of months when I ... when she was expecting again. So that was a mistake, you know what I mean. We couldn't ... she had to finish work. And there was only the one wage then, coming in, and we had to pay the bills and that, and I couldn't afford to buy a house then.[56]

Sean and his wife had six more children, and after seven years in the cotton mill Sean took a job in the construction industry as a labourer. This work was 'heavy' and conditions on site were often 'terrible', but, as Sean emphasised, 'you put up with it, you had to put up with it, you know, you wanted the money, you had to put up with it, you know'. After 'about ten year', however, the work 'got too much, too ... heavy', and Sean took a job as a security guard at Rochdale College.[57] Although the pay on this job was only minimum wage, which meant that Sean 'used to have to do about 80 hours a week to make a wage'. Sean considered this his 'favourite' job. After seven to eight years in this job Sean retired.

By comparison with other male narratives in the sample, Sean's narrative of settlement can be seen as distinct in a number of important respects. Although Sean's work history forms an important strand of his settlement narrative, this history is not structured as a progressive narrative of migration success, whose function is to dramatise the achievements of the narrator. On the contrary, at the centre of Sean's settlement narrative is a story of regret and self-admonishment concerning past decisions on the use of financial resources and family planning. Where other male settlement narratives turn on the acquisition of forms of status, Sean's story, and his repeated use of phrases such as 'you had to', here tend to evoke the difficulties and struggles of raising a family on a low income.

Herein, where many male settlement narratives tend to background the roles of significant others within their lives, work and family interpenetrate as themes within Sean's account. Once married, Sean typically speaks from subject-positions which point to his enmeshment within the family. Thus work, for example, is not presented as an autonomous sphere in which one strives for personal success, but as a space in which one 'had to', as the sole provider, earn the wages necessary for family survival. In this way, the 'I' and 'you' tend to assimilate in Sean's account to the 'we', revealing an understanding of settlement as a joint rather than an individual struggle, shaped by a sense of duty and belonging to family, rather than a desire for individual recognition.

These features of Sean's narrative may be accounted for in a number of interrelated ways. Sean was the eldest son of a family for whom the struggle to survive through hard work in a hierarchical social world was a continuous, immutable fact of social existence. Without capital, except the value of his own labour, Sean's own possibilities for advancement within this context were extremely limited: having left school of necessity at the age of 12, the ensuing nine years of uninterrupted farm labour constituted firm evidence of the difficulty of improving one's standing in the world. This has contributed, it is suggested, to the generation of a narrative understanding of experience in which self and society remain static, whose central motif is struggle, where the goal is material survival rather than the achievement of 'significant selfhood'. And since social existence in England has been similarly defined by the performance of heavy, low-status labour in order to rear a large family on a single wage, so this narrative framework is easily adaptable to conceptualising the experiences of settlement. In this way economic position, as a dynamic which shapes Sean's experiences in similar ways on both sides of the Irish

Sea, forms a principle of subjective continuity in his account, despite the greater availability of steady employment in post-war England.

Additionally, however, the ways in which Sean makes social and personal sense of economic circumstances was also shaped by his investment in religious frameworks:

Sean: Oh yeah, church has always been important to me. I've always ... I've never missed church in my ... not that ... I haven't been forced to go, but I just go, automatically, you know.
Barry: Why was church so important whenever you were over here?
Sean: I don't know, it's just the way I was brought up, you know. My mother always made sure I went to mass on a Sunday ... First thing, get up out of bed and, on a Sunday morning, go to mass. Yeah and, and that stuck in my mind all the time. I've never missed mass.[58]

In common with Aileen, church remained an 'important' part of Sean's life following his arrival in England. As he explained, he always attended mass 'automatically' because 'it's just the way I was brought up'. Yet, if Sean and Aileen shared a similar commitment to maintaining their religious practice in England, Catholic efforts to regulate migrants' settlement trajectories also addressed male and female migrants in different ways, prescribing different forms of moral restraint related to their future roles within the family. While discourses on female settlement sought to caution young women against promiscuity and pre-marital sex, young male migrants were warned of the dangers of excessive consumption. According to one emigrant advice pamphlet, one of the most dangerous urban spaces was 'the public house', for

> there is no sight more degrading than drunken people, nothing is more likely to ruin home and family life than excess of drink. There have been far too many cases of drunkenness among Irish people in England and these have so often ended up in street fights which have been fully reported in English newspapers.[59]

As the pamphlet went on to explain, English materialism helped propagate these excesses. 'Many English people', it was claimed, 'seize any chance of making extra money' and if migrants did not exercise vigilance they too risked 'being caught up in this craze for money'. Not only did 'the people concerned become hard and materially-minded', their faith becoming 'weak' in the process, but 'the extra money you gain is often spent on gambling and drinking'. Instead, migrants should 'work hard for regular hours', earning 'sufficient to get what you need'.[60] Herein, in addition to supporting one's family back in Ireland, money should be channelled into preparations for the establishment of one's own family, specifically to enable house purchase:

Open a post-office savings bank book and put in it at least five to ten shillings a week, over and above what you send home to your family. This money will be a great help later on.[61]

These interlinked notions, of moral restraint, 'hard' work for 'sufficient' earnings and duty to family, were in turn echoed in wider narratives of English Catholic masculinity. While ideal masculinity underwent a degree of domestication after 1945, registered in the promotion of new expectations around marital reciprocity and greater emotional involvement in family life, Catholic manhood was still primarily assessed in terms of the realisation of the breadwinner ideal. Work here was not an avenue to career success, material riches or greater consumption, but a means of establishing and supporting the proper conduct of family life. Modelled on the figure of St Joseph, the motivations of the ideal Catholic man reflected a stoic and dogged resolve to provide for one's family, eschewing those worldly pleasures and distractions which threatened this fundamental object.

Such ideals are central to memory production within Sean's account. From one perspective, they are associated with psychic tensions within Sean's narrative: what Sean views as the main 'mistakes' and 'regrets' of the settlement experience (not saving, not buying a home, leaving Margaret in Ireland) represent failures of moral restraint and familial obligation, the emotional ramifications of which continue to affect Sean in the present:

> [T]he only thing I would … I'd have done differently was, I'd, I'd have my daughter, I'd have brought her up myself. Instead of leaving her … trying to make me own mother and father happy, you know? But I … I, I, slipped up, you know what I mean? I mean I'm happy, but … we were unhappy after, me and my wife. For leaving her over there, you know. We still loved her, you know, as our daughter, but … she always called us … we were the other mummy and daddy then. After twelve months, you know. 'Cos I … like it being the first grandchild, my mother and father had spoilt her you know. They thought the world of her you know, so.[62]

At these points, past experience is interpreted via a discourse of moral culpability, the operation of which registers an underlying contradiction within the Catholic model of virtuous settlement: while migrants were exhorted to establish stable family life in a respectable residence, the Church's prohibition on contraception and insistence on male providerism potentially compromised the realisation of this ideal by placing added financial pressure upon young families on relatively low wages. Sean, however, views the creation of such pressures as his responsibility, so that the hardships of the migration journey become effects of a personal failure to fulfil the role of 'breadwinner' in the prescribed way.

Overall, however, it is the steady and ultimately successful performance of this role which underpins the achievement of composure in Sean's narrative, enabling him to view past decisions as the 'mistakes' of a younger, less knowing self. If Sean made the 'wrong' choices when he first settled in England, frittering away his earnings on the temptations of the city, living the hard consequences of those choices over the long term has engendered wisdom, so that the very expression of regret signals the evolution of a more knowing subject. From this perspective, Sean's depiction of his experiences of work as something he 'put up with', as something he 'had to' endure, not only alludes to the heavy constraints upon Sean's life choices and the arduous character of this work, but underscores too his commitment and determination to ultimately do what he viewed as morally right. The younger self 'slipped up', but his mistakes are redeemable via the stoic and dogged performance of one's duty to provide.

Questioning 'the simple faith': contestation, counter-memory and the reworking of religious selfhoods

Sean's and Aileen's narratives exemplify one important trend within migrants' construction of religious selfhood in post-war England. Where Catholic observers at the time fretted over the apparent decline of migrant religiosity, Sean and Aileen present their experiences in terms of a myth of the pious generation. This is reflected, not only in Sean's and Aileen's unwavering commitment to the maintenance of devotional practice, but in the central importance ascribed to family life as a source of belonging and self-worth: a model of virtuous and respectable settlement, focused on the ideal of family, forms the main framework in terms of which the wider significance of migration is commemorated.

For other migrants, however, this mythology proved more problematic as a resource for self-reconstruction. Born in 1951, Bill grew up on his family's small farm in Roscommon, and recalled a rural childhood in which religion was a staple feature of everyday life. Due to his mother's insistence in particular, participation in mass and other forms of devotional ritual played a formative role in shaping the young self's experience of the world:

> The church, as far as your parents was ... my mother's, on my mother's side, was ... very important. [Sighs] To me it was, yes, it was a necessity, you had to go.[63]

When Bill migrated to Manchester in 1967, aged 16, these formative religious routines exercised a complex influence over his early settlement experiences. On the one hand, as a devout Catholic and Pioneer Bill's leisure routines in post-war England were initially tightly regulated by religious prescriptions: where mass attendance was woven into the basic fabric of Bill's narrative, forming a routine around which other events were narrated, pub-going was conspicuously absent from his account, reflecting Bill's determination to 'keep the pledge'. On the other hand, however, Bill arrived in England, not only devout, but determined to 'make a good living'. Following the example of other friends and family members who had 'done well for themselves', Bill set about building a successful career within the British construction industry, culminating in his appointment as a company director and the accumulation of a sizeable personal fortune.

These career ambitions impinged upon Bill's sense of religious selfhood in variable and mutating ways. When Bill elected to become a Pioneer during his teenage years, a chief motivation had been the destructive behaviour of his father: while his father had been a 'hard' and capable worker, his heavy drinking caused 'misery' for other family members and, at times, endangered the family's financial survival.[64] Consequently, given how alcohol consumption militated against the realisation of masculine imperatives in this context, so puritanical self-discipline was embraced by Bill early on in his life as part of his rejection of his father's unstable and anxiety-inducing masculinity. During the early phases of his work history, Bill's embrace of this code of self-restraint was consistent with, and a means of pursuing, personal success. The younger self's determination to 'make a living' was manifest, not only in dedication to learning his trade, but in the exercise of restraint over wider aspects of his life, from abstinence from alcohol to saving money for future investment in property and business opportunities.

As Bill ascended the career ladder, however, moving from 'the labour trench' to 'the boardroom', he also felt compelled to adapt to new social expectations. In addition to *making* money, within the professional circles in which he now moved he was also expected to know how to *enjoy* it:

> I came back and I saved the money, and then I was made up to a gangerman. And then, after a couple of years then, I didn't go down to Lincolnshire no more, because I was ... earning good money as a gangerman. I then became a foreman, after a number of years, and I can't remember how many years, and, er ... I was a foreman, and then I became a site agent, at twenty ... two, that's when I broke the pledge and started drinking, because that was the thing that was done then.[65]

More generally, as Bill's career progresses and his professional working life exerts ever-greater demands, the overall place of religion within his narrative is renegotiated. While Bill got married in 1975 and was able to buy a house immediately due to the high salary he was earning, new and greater work commitments increasingly took precedence over the performance of religious practice and involvement in domestic life:

> [T]he higher up you went, it was ... the diary controlled everything, 'Well I have to be there. I have to be in Birmingham. I have to be in ... Coventry, or London ... I have to be at board meeting and so-and-so, so-and-so.' She'd ring and say, 'Well can you be home?' 'Well I'm in Birmingham! It'll take me two hours!' You know, 'Well ... the kids has to ... go swimming', or something like that. I said, 'I can't!' And she had to put up with a lot, as far as that's concerned, because ... work ... you know, I've had a ... a good living, from ... what I've done, it paid everything, it ... you know ... when you came home you were knackered. You had the dinner, and [snores] gone in the ... chair. And she had to put up with that as well.[66]

In a different way, ever-deeper immersion in professional life also provoked critical reflection upon the role of the Church in limiting the younger self's personal development. As Bill's career progressed and he assumed new roles within his company, he was required to perform new tasks and learn new skills. Yet, while Bill enjoyed the challenges this involved, he also found the mastery of non-manual skills difficult due to the deficiencies of his National School education.[67] While the regular beatings he received from his teacher were here directly responsible for his early aversion to academic learning, for Bill ultimate culpability lay with the Church, whose control of local appointments and resources forced collective submission to clerical interests above the needs of ordinary people. One implication of this was a cruel and hypocritical stigmatisation of poverty:

> When you'd go to church on a Sunday, and ... the priest would read out the collections. You would have the, Tony McDaid was this teacher that I had, and 'Tony McDaid', er, 'ten shillings'. Erm, 'so-and-so, so-and-so, such a parish, five shillings. So-and-so, so-and-so, half a crown. So-and-so, so-and-so, sixpence. So-and-so, so-and-so, sixpence.' And he'd emphasise this 'sixpence', you know, it was ... soul-destroying this, as far as, 'cos that sixpence to them peoples was so important that I felt that, you know ... upset and ... you know, they didn't mind upsetting the people that didn't have any money. And that was something that I ... always objected to, you know, was that if people had ... gave sixpence, that's all they could afford. And they weren't working, they were paying in from a farm or selling chickens, or selling some pigs or selling something like that. They didn't have the money. And that sixpence was so important to them to give to the church. I think the church today is ... when you go to Rome, and I have been to Rome, and you

look at the gold and things that's in the churches in Rome, and ... the amount of money that has been collected through the years from poor people, if you like ... why isn't Rome doing more for the poor people of the world? The question you have to ask. Yes I go to church but ... there's some hypocrites in there.[68]

More generally, such techniques of shaming enshrined conformity as an imperative, proscribing personal autonomy, creating a mindless community of 'sheep':

The church controlled the school, a hundred per cent, the parish priest was the man in charge, and anything he said, you know, there was no such thing as saying, somebody saying, 'Ooh, we should do this.' As far as the church was concerned, it was go to mass on Sunday and ... do whatever you had to do, that other people did. And I think ... at that time, when I was brought up, was that, you know ... you did as Joe Bloggs did, and nobody went against the grain, as it were, 'I'm not going doing that. I'm not going to church, I'm not doing this.' We all followed like sheep.[69]

For Aileen and Sean, memories of the Church and church-going represented a source of personal continuity in their narratives of settlement in England. While Aileen felt that 'religion has gone to pot' in recent times, the implication was that the Church's traditional role and authority was natural and should be restored. Bill's memories, by contrast, invert this logic. Framing the disjunction between past and present as a positive difference, the Church of Bill's childhood is a cruel, self-serving and hypocritical institution, recognised as such from the distance of a more open and reflexive present. The traditional role and authority of the Church should not be restored; on the contrary, the changes which have beset the Church mark a liberation from its excesses.

In the wider context of the Irish community in England, such changes have gradually become visible within processes of public self-construction. As noted earlier, while the Church formed the main institutional framework for negotiating migrant problems in the 1940s and 1950s, over the period as a whole religious symbols and values have become less prevalent within public representations of Irish culture and ethnicity in England. Within the *Irish Post*, a key locus of such representations, this initially signalled waning appeal, reflecting the editors' concerns to reshape the content and tone of the publication in accordance with the wider marginalisation of religious influence within English popular culture. Hence, where priests and nuns were ubiquitous within the pages of the *Post* during its early years, as authors of moral advice columns, commentators on Irish life in Britain and photographed as organisers and attendees of social events, by the later 1970s religious influences were much less visible as the space allocated to sport, music, fashion and politics expanded.

More fundamentally, however, during the 1990s the Church's moral authority was actively and persistently challenged in the *Post*, due primarily to a rising tide of public scandals concerning priests' sexual conduct and institutional abuse relating back to the post-war decades. While the Bishop Casey scandal of May 1992 had a rather limited impact within the *Post*, during the same decade the letters pages of the paper became a key arena for the public transmission of personal narratives of sexual, physical and psychological abuse within institutions run by religious orders, many of which illuminated the connection between clerical abuse and migration to England. In an extended stream of personal remembrance relating to Industrial Schools and Magdalene Asylums readers were told, not only of systematic and sadistic abuse, but of the lives of suffering led by former pupils and inmates in English cities following their escape or release.[70] So prevalent, indeed, was this trajectory that a special helpline for victims resident in England was established in April 1998 following a public apology by the Christian Brothers, and between June and October the following year British-based victims gave testimony at a series of conferences in England, organised to supply evidence to the recently established Laffoy (Ryan) Commission to Inquire into Child Abuse.[71]

Thenceforth, this amplification of latent memories of clerical excess had a transformative effect upon how the post-war Irish Church was represented within the pages of the *Post*. While some contributors endeavoured to defend the Christian Brothers as Irish patriots, as the letters accumulated, with many detailing the horrific minutiae of routinised abuse over many years, the wider Church and post-war society as a whole came under attack.[72] As part of this broadening of the parameters of debate, the chain of association ran quickly from particular instances of abuse to general indictments of the morality of the post-independent social order. As journalist Ronan McGreevy claimed, while individual orders were certainly culpable, 'they could not have done what they did without the acquiescence of the Church, the state and Irish society generally'.[73] This failure to intervene, argued McGreevy, destroyed the moral credibility of the Irish Church, which, even as the evidence mounted, continued to evade responsibility, and it laid bare the servile complicity of the Irish state, which had feared giving offense to the hierarchy. Most disturbing, the silence of ordinary people signalled the confused morality of a mute population, itself brutalised into submission by a coercive religious regime.

However, while the revelations marked 'one of the most shameful episodes' in Irish history, evidencing a collective failure to protect the most vulnerable within post-war society, they also marked a turning point.⁷⁴ The mistreatment of the vulnerable served as a metaphor for the callousness of post-war society; but the act of the subjugated speaking truth against their erstwhile oppressors also served as a metaphor for the liberation of Irish society:

> The Irish people have changed. They reject the puritan ethos. They won't tolerate the big stick anymore. They want to see Christian tolerance at work, not only in the classroom, but everywhere in society.⁷⁵

This liberationist critique of post-war religious authority frames how Bill reconstructs his own memories of the Irish Church. More precisely, while Bill's own particular experiences do not mirror the confessional narratives of clerical abuse, the generalised subject-position which these revelations have generated, of individual subjection to a cruel, self-serving and morally hypocritical Church, is mobilised to negotiate points of psychic tension within Bill's ontological narrative of self. From one perspective, the notion of excessive Church power supplies a means of explaining and justifying the limitations of self-actualisation: although Bill's internalisation of Catholic puritanism helped foster habits of self-discipline which might be seen to have aided his advancement within the construction industry, positioning the Church as an impediment to self-development enables responsibility for self-perceived failures to be displaced way from the self. In this way, the denigration of excessive Church power becomes implicated in the preservation of Bill's preferred narrative of self-made migration success: Bill's overcoming of Church power to 'make it' in construction accentuates the scale of his achievement, while his verbal critique of this power, a narrative act of rebellion, differentiates him from the 'sheep' who 'followed' meekly, underscoring his autonomy, independence of mind and rationality.

From another perspective, however, Bill's denigration of the Church might also be read as a means of deflecting and containing a more fundamental internal conflict. While Bill was determined to 'make a good living' in England, his pursuit and realisation of this desire inevitably brought him into conflict with the moral puritanism so central to the formation of the younger self. In particular, the lifestyle and personal goals which Bill adopted conflicted with the Irish Church's sanctification of poverty and injunction to regulate base desires for material wealth:

> Many English people seize any chance of making extra money and there is a danger of Irish boys and girls in England being caught up in this craze for money, regardless of its effect on their lives ... the people concerned become hard and materially-minded and their faith becomes weak ... the extra money you gain is often spent on gambling and drinking, things which can do you much harm. Work hard for regular hours and earn sufficient to get what you need. You will be a better man or women for doing just that.⁷⁶

It is not coincidental, therefore, that Bill's antagonism towards the Church centres, not on the popular issues of sexual conduct, but on the morality of wealth. The function here of Bill's linked stories on parish collections and the opulence of Rome is less to dramatise the heroism of the migrant journey than to devalue the moral authority of the Church and its right to prescribe moral standards where the issue of materialism is concerned. Impugning the moral authority of the Church thus neutralises its capacity to judge and condemn the moral character of the self. In this way, it is suggested, an internal conflict of moral principle is projected outwards into the figure of the other: what Bill identifies as the Church's confused position on the morality of wealth is simultaneously an unconscious reflection of his own difficulty in reconciling two competing self-images; that of the businessman and the good Catholic.

Memories of the Church performed a similarly complex function in the final migration narrative addressed in this chapter. Born in 1940, Clare grew up in rural north Cork, the youngest in a family of two sisters and one brother, and recalled a childhood in which the everyday influence of the Church was pervasive:

> Well it ... As I say it was part of ... it was incorporated into the school so much that you ... the priest, there was a school, the church and the priest house, were all together, and the priest would often ... pop in to see us, and we all had to jump up, you know, in reverence, and we were always told we had to go to church on the way to school and, and on the way home, you had to go in and say a prayer, and it was just part of the culture, you know.[77]

In accordance with the Church's views on the aims of settlement in England, when Clare elected to migrate to London in 1957, aged 17, marriage quickly superseded work as the focus of her narrative. Although Clare had undergone specialist secretarial training in Ireland and soon found employment with Lloyd's bank in the City, within a month of arriving she had met her future husband Sean at the Shamrock Ballroom, an Irish dancehall in Elephant and Castle. Within 20 months Clare and Sean were married, at St Mary's, Clapham Common, and within two years following this Clare gave birth to the first of three children.[78] This, as in Aileen's account, marked a transitional moment in Clare's life history: motherhood coincided with her departure from the labour market, leaving Sean as the sole 'breadwinner' within the newly established family.

Yet, while marriage and motherhood formed important events within Clare's narrative, their significance was not defined in terms of conventional notions of Catholic femininity. If Clare's memories of courtship represented a period of autonomy and self-discovery in her account, her wedding day was associated with compulsion, miscommunication and financial loss, setting the couple back in their plans to purchase a house:

> We had saved up a deposit for a house, and then we couldn't ... we had to spend it on the wedding. 'Cos I always remember, 38 people at the wedding, that was all we could have, and at that time you had to get married before 12 because there was no mass after midday in the Catholic church in those days. So then you'd have the wedding breakfast, as ... as opposed to, you know ... And, and I remember we had it in a pub, in Kennington, the Horns Tavern had a function room upstairs, and we had ... the music was, I think, record player, things like that. And then you had to provide the drinks, and you had to provide tea then in the afternoon. And we actually, 'twas like we spent all our money in there ourselves, and we had a honeymoon in the Isle of Wight, we went away at 5 o'clock that day, somebody took us, and ... We always said ... Sean said, 'If we were getting married again', he said, 'no way would we go away that day!' We left them all there, you know, celebrating the rest of the day, and also we had an arrangement with the pub ... Sean had an extension 'til 12, for people to enjoy themselves, and there was an arrangement that any drink that was left over, that they would take back, but at the end of the day apparently, my brother was, he was in the army, he was doing his national service at the time, and he'd only just come out, and he was saying, 'Look! Look at all this beer, all this stuff that's left!' He said this, you know, 'They've paid for all this, we'll take it back so' ... [laughs] So they took it all back to somebody's house, and had another pi ... So when we come back, we had another bill for all this drink, but they didn't know this arrangement was made, you know, it was just ... just something we laugh about really, I think, you know ... So then we had to kind of start all over again ... saving for a deposit for a house.[79]

In important respects, this memory of the strains and impositions of her wedding day prefigure and condense Clare's feelings about marriage and family life as a whole. Although Clare and Sean's wedding had decimated their savings, within two years they had recuperated the losses, and in 1960 they purchased their first house in Kent, moving later to Surrey. However, with Sean commuting to London daily for work Clare was left 'at home all day with the children', and, lacking a support network, Clare became 'awfully homesick'. In response, in order to be closer to family members, they decided to return to Ireland:

> Well we were in Kent, and we moved up to Surrey to be nearer London, 'cos Sean was commuting, and 'twas getting ... was a very bad service down to north Kent, and it was always ... there were lots of strikes and, leaves on the line, and snow and all that ... [Sighs] But I was awfully homesick, and I was at home all day with the children, 'cos I was no longer working, and ... and he used to be away from early morning 'til late in the evening, you know, it was ... I was so homesick, and I just wanted to go back to Ireland so much. So he applied for some jobs, and

there weren't many jobs in the sixties, so he got a job with the plant hire people, and he went to Dublin for an interview, and he got the job, he could have had either in Dublin, or in Cork, so we plumped for Cork 'cos my parents lived in at the time. So, we sold the house and … lock, stock and barrel, moved all our furniture, everything, and went off back to Ireland.[80]

Return migration, however, did not resolve Clare's sense of dissatisfaction with married life. Although resettlement enabled greater accessibility to 'the beach and country', achieving an affluent in lifestyle in 1970s Cork proved difficult. As Clare recalled, even though Sean was able to secure reasonably well-paid employment, house purchase was expensive: having put down a deposit for a newbuild in Bishopstown, they were forced to take out a bridging loan to finance the completion of the property as the contractors raised the initial asking price at successive stages of the building process. Even then, after three years Clare and Sean were still renting, with completion still some way off. To make matters worse, Sean and Clare were also confronted with accumulating health care bills as Sean's wage disqualified them from state assistance:

And then, as I say, my daughter is a very bad asthmatic, and she … she really started with her asthma there. And I used to have the doctor in just so often, and it was … I used to be, as I say, I used to pay, the doctor used to be something like one pound ten shillings, which was like … when your average wage would have been about seven pounds then … I was, I could cope with that, but I used to be frightened then to take the prescription to the chemist, 'cos I thought, 'How much will that be?' That could have been as much as four pounds … And all this was kind of, eating at us …[81]

In addition to these financial anxieties, resettlement in Ireland also provoked Clare to reflect upon the limitations of her roles, as mother and wife, within her family. At school, Clare had been 'quite bright' and prior to giving birth to her first child had secured an interesting job with a publishing firm in London. A year after returning to Ireland, Clare's desire for a career of her own was reignited after she applied for and was offered a position at the *Cork Examiner*. This, as Clare explained, would have strengthened the family's financial position, as well as being a 'prestigious job' that might have led into a professional journalism role. Sean, however, 'didn't want to know':

At one stage I applied for a job at the *Cork Examiner*, it was unheard of women to work in there … And I wrote to the *Cor* … *Cork Examiner*, and … 'Cos I, I was … before I finished work I, in … I was in a publishing company in London, and I quite enjoyed it, and honestly, if I had my life over again, if I had opportunities, that is what I would love to have been, as a journalist, I realise that now. But ... so I kind of wrote in and said I'd done this, I'd done that, is there any ... And then this guy, I don't know if you know the Crosby group of newspapers, they own the *Irish Post* and all those, they own the ... they own the *Examiner* paper, in Cork and ... so, so I went in for an interview, and there was real old ... old family concerned in the Crosby group of newspapers, and this old guy upstairs, he was one of the Crosby family, so he had a job that, 'twas like six in the evening 'til two in the morning, er ... the copy typers really, and you'd be there, and the reporters'd be out and about at night and they'd 'phone in, and you'd take their stories for the paper. And, he said, to six 'til two, but we'll provide a taxi home for you, you know at two in the morning, and he said, 'Can you really do this with three children?' I said, 'Yeah!' 'Cos I thought, that would be ideal, to get home and still be up with them, but 'twas getting Sean home at six o' clock, and he didn't want to know, as you know, women didn't work, and ... and Sean liked calling for his pint on the way home. So he would never guarantee that he'd be home in time for me to get down to work, and, and if I'd persevered, you know, in those days, you know I thought, 'God, I could have got somebody in to sit for a couple of hours until he came home', because it would have ... it was just to bridge the gap to get us to stay in Ireland, and have an income. And when I think of it today, Barry, that would have been ... that would have ended up in a very partic... a very prestigious job there, I ... was really kind of narked about that.[82]

While Aileen's early years in England were represented as a period of otherness and isolation in her narrative, marriage and maternity marked an emotional upswing in her overall account of settlement. For Clare, by contrast, marriage and family life are associated with regret and thwarted desires, provoking retrospective speculation on possible alternative histories of the self. Thus, where financial strain evidences the achievements of the self in Aileen's account, for Clare it signifies her and Sean's failure to realise the promise of affluent domesticity. And where Aileen sought to consecrate marriage and motherhood as sources of personal self-fulfilment, for Clare the compulsory performance of these roles signified a limiting of the self, associated with unrealised ambitions for personal development via a professional career.

In turn, just as marriage and family life are signified in divergent ways in Aileen's and Clare's narratives, so too is the place of religion. Where Aileen's narrative emphasised the enduring importance of Catholic discourses of femininity as a framework for self-evaluation, Clare's narrative registers an explicit turning against the Church and its claims to authority. Within this transitional narrative of religious selfhood, the

Church is identified as an agent of patriarchal control, responsible for the thwarting of Clare's personal ambitions and aspirations:

Barry: And, through this period, both before you tried to go back, and then even when you came back, was the Church still important?
Clare: No. I blame the Church for a lot of, like, there was just kind of, brought us up so very, very narrow minded and I ...we hadn't the freedom. There was no kind of ...there was no advice on sexuality or anything like that, and everything was taboo, and when we came to England so green, and so naïve, you could be very, very vulnerable, and ... and that's a very, very dangerous thing. I mean we were never told anything of the facts of life, or anything, you know, we were so innocent. And that annoys me when I look back, I mean I envy people today who can live together or whatever ... before they get married, because like, we ... I was only 19 when I got married, Sean was 24 ... he was five years older ... And I, basically, if we were living together, we wouldn't have got married so soon or anything you know. And we had an awful lot of rough periods in our marriage, you know. We didn't get on a lot. Because, you know, he used to go drinking after work, or he'd go with his mates, and the woman's place was in the house, and all this kind of thing ... and that annoys me about the Church, you know, 'cos that was always the man's you know ... you've got to obey, you know, yeah. Yeah. And that's what you learned, you know ... And as I say, as I get older, I thought I'd be getting more devout, but I'm not, and ... I go to mass when I feel like it and I ... none of my children go to church anymore, so ... And none of my friends' children that I know of, very few of them go to church anymore. So, there's something wrong, you know.[83]

Although Clare and Aileen both saw marriage and the establishment of a family as a core object of the migration journey, the expectations in terms of which they evaluated married and family life were significantly different. For Clare, who arrived in England some 12 years after Aileen, marriage was both a vehicle for achieving a certain socio-economic status and a relationship within which she expected to be supported in the pursuit of individual forms of self-development, outside of and beyond her roles as wife and mother. However, while such conceptions of femininity were increasingly prevalent within English popular culture during this period, Sean's enforcement of asymmetrical gender relations within the marriage relationship impeded both the family's achievement of affluence and Clare's pursuit of a career. For Clare, these unrealised possibilities were inextricably related to the self-negating effects of Catholic doctrine. The Church's prohibition on 'living in sin' encouraged her and Sean to get married too quickly, before they really knew each other or what they wanted from married life; and thereafter, the patriarchal requirement to 'obey' one's husband destabilised her and Sean's married relationship, creating a legacy of personal regret.

For Clare, therefore, over the course of the migration journey the Church has become an object of antagonism, reconditioning her commitment to religious practice as a voluntary, rather than an automatic, routine of everyday life. As in Bill's account, a liberal critique of Church power is mobilised to illuminate the religious repression of personal desire, and to explain and allocate blame for the mistakes of the younger self. This strategy of memory, termed 'uchronic' by Portelli, manages the sense of disappointment flowing from past failures through holding out the possibility of an alternative trajectory had the self been the agent of its own destiny.[84]

Yet, while Clare regrets the influence the Church exercised over her decision-making in the past and rejects the authority of the Church to define these aspects of her life in the present, it does not follow that the formative impact of 'the puritan ethos' is thereby negated. While Clare portrays religious norms as a source of exploitation and subjugation, in other parts of her narrative these same norms continue to organise evaluations self and other, past and present. While the Church's endorsement of women's 'place within the home' thwarted her own desires for personal satisfaction, Clare's representation of femininity in her narrative often reflected normative conceptions of the 'good' and 'bad' mother:

> I had this friend and her mother ... I always remember we used to say, 'Go over to the post office, go over and see if the wire has come', and we'd go, 'Has the wire come yet?' 'No, no it hasn't come yet.' So when there was a wire come, it meant she could change it ... and she'd have money, you know, for the week ... As I said, this particular mother, I wouldn't say she was a particularly good mother, 'cos she never seemed to get up to get the kids to school or anything, they made ... they did it themselves, but she used to buy this big box of chocolates, that's what sticks in my mind. And she'd sit there and gorge, and she'd just give us the ones she didn't like, the hard ones, you know.[85]

And while affluence was a central aim of her own migration journey, Clare regarded 'materialism' as a deleterious force within contemporary Irish society, set in contrast with the more authentic frugal comforts of the 1940s and 1950s:

> That seems to have changed a lot of ... in Ireland, the visiting seems to have stopped, the heart seems to have gone out of Ireland, with the young people. But I put it all down to too much materialism, and that. And they have these big houses now, these great big kitchens, but the hospitality isn't there. I mean, you'd be hard, you know, to even get a cup of tea from some of them when you go in. That old, innate hospitality isn't there.[86]

The revelations around clerical abuse have ventilated a powerful critique of Church power within the collective imaginary of the Irish in England. However, to the extent that this liberalising narrative equates 'the rejection of the puritan ethos' with the emergence of an autonomous subject standing outside the workings of religious power, it obscures how subjection to religious prohibitions was generative of the Irish Catholic subject as a divided formation, structured by an ambivalent relation to religious authority. Internalised religious prohibitions could be experienced as a source of repression and self-reproach, generating, in the context of settlement, a desire to diminish and split off religious identifications. And undoubtedly, for migrants like Clare and Bill, whose narratives register a clear conflict between religious norms and other forms of identification, the liberalising critique of Church power has strengthened and legitimised this impulse to rebel against internalised religious authority. At the same time, however, wholesale renunciation of this identification is also likely to be an ontologically destabilising act, feeding into rather than resolving Clare's sense of loss and regret, and producing in turn a countervailing desire to preserve aspects of one's disavowed religious identity. This integrative impulse is manifest in the tendency to imaginatively segregate positive and negative aspects of Irish Catholic culture, enabling the retention and narrative deployment of the former as positive attributes of the self and marks of social distinction.

These dynamics produce a distinctive ambivalence at the level of memory production. On the one hand, Catholic Ireland is remembered through tropes of restriction, repression and hypocrisy. This narrative explains the failure to realise various ambitions in England as a legacy of Catholic control, while also accentuating the achievements of the self in having overcome these impediments. On the other hand, Catholic Ireland is also remembered through tropes of moral purity, authenticity and communal reciprocity, embodying a cultural apex from which contemporary Ireland has since degenerated. This nostalgic form of memory, which screens out the problematic role of the Church while idealising metonymically associated aspects of Catholic culture, expresses a need to preserve an affirmative image of one's origins as compensation for the losses of migration. Perhaps more fundamentally, it is also a mechanism of collective belonging, expressing a need to recognise one's personal experiences as part of a larger, more meaningful whole:

> I mean, we ... when we get together in the kitchen downstairs, we have a laugh because we talk about ... we talk about, in the winter, having coats on the bed, you know when it was very cold. Because, people didn't have all these extras and there was ... you know, and ... we were all, we can kind of all identify. There's a few odd people who say, 'Oh!

We never did this!' and 'We had this, and we had that', you know, but it isn't true, 'cos we were all ... it ... there was a lot more heart there, and everybody had ... nobody was very well off, and ... and there was a lot of bartering, and helping each other out and, you know, if you needed a cup of sugar, or whatever, two eggs, you'd borrow, you know. And all that's gone, you know ... the heart has d... has gone out of Ireland, that's the way I see it. And, I get very disappointed when I go back really. Yeah.[87]

Deconstructing the pious generation: memory, myth and religious change

In her nostalgic memoir *Me and Mine. A Warm-Hearted Memoir of a London Irish Family*, Anna May Mangan recalls the attributes and possessions her impoverished relatives carried with them from Ireland to London in the 1950s. Alongside 'hopeful hearts', a deficient education and a 'heavyweight work ethic', Mangan's relatives cherished an imperturbable religious faith which, suffusing even the most mundane aspects of everyday life, fortified them against adversity. When her father's cousin Lizzine arrived in London her first residence was St Mary's Hospital, having injured herself jumping from the platform of a moving bus. During her recuperation, staff and patients at the hospital learned the reason for her good fortune:

> Always a glass-half-full sort of girl, Lizzine regularly told staff and other patients that it was St Christopher who had protected her from death overseas and in thanks and praise she held her medal of the Saint aloft using her unbroken right arm during all her waking hours. St Christopher, Patron Saint of Travellers, hadn't been working alone. She believed it was he and St Drogo, Patron Saint of Broken Bones, who had teamed up to arrange her recovery, under the directorship of St Anthony, Patron Saint of Miracles.[88]

The oral narratives examined in this chapter deconstruct the workings of this myth of piety to reveal the profound ambivalences at it centre. From one perspective, they can be read as substantiating the central role played by religion in the lives of the post-war generation, revealing in the process the enduring importance of the myth in shaping understandings of migrant selfhood. While contemporary observers lamented how Irish migrants were 'falling away from the Church', the testimonies of Sean and Aileen complicate any simple equation between settlement and secularisation. Not only did Sean and Aileen depart an Ireland where the Catholic Church exercised a powerful cultural hegemony; puritanical Christian values were also central to the definition of public morality within English culture until the late 1950s, despite the alarmist rhetoric of Irish prelates.

Within this context, the model of virtuous settlement promulgated by the Church resonated simultaneously with Irish Catholic and popular English cultural norms: while migrants were warned against the moral dangers of 'pagan' England, successful settlement was defined in terms of the realisation of stable family life and suburban domesticity, a framework consistent with both popular conceptions of social respectability and Catholic regulatory imperatives. What Sean's and Aileen's narratives illustrate is the capacity of this discourse to address, in a coherent and flexible way, different and potentially contradictory emotional needs and desires at different points in the settlement process. Catholic models of the self supplied a vehicle for the articulation of the cultural origins of the self, *and* a means by which the self could be reshaped in accordance with wider societal norms, enabling cultural adaption and investment in alternative ideals. They thus formed a source of psychic stability *and* a mechanism of subjective reworking, and at the tail end of the migrant journey offered a culturally intelligible framework in terms of which the actions of the younger self could be positively reconstructed and assessed. For these reasons, Sean and Aileen presented their religious convictions as invariable and undisturbed by the settlement process, emphasising continuity between past and present versions of the religious self while backgrounding subtle adaptions in their interpretation of religious values around marriage and family life.

Nevertheless, while Catholicism formed a vital source of identity for migrants such as Sean and Aileen, the extent to which Catholic discourse could assimilate the shifting norms of an increasingly affluent and permissive society was also limited. Catholic regulatory imperatives were broadly consistent with the valorisation of marriage and family life within post-war society, but particular injunctions and prohibitions produced contradictory implications. If migrants were urged to marry and purchase a home in order to escape the moral dangers of the 'twilight zone', prohibitions against contraception and working motherhood placed strain upon family economies, impeding house purchase and the realisation of expanding consumerist imperatives. If men were expected to devote themselves to providing for their families, their status dependent upon success in the labour market, they were also expected to regard the pursuit of affluence and the consumer pleasures it enabled as forms of sin. Perhaps most obviously, while Catholic discourses on the family elevated and revered women as wives and mothers, promising personal self-fulfilment through these roles, the ideal Catholic woman remained officially subject to patriarchal control within marriage at a time when popular understandings of gender relations increasingly stressed the needs and entitlements of the individual.

For Sean and Aileen, these tensions did not provoke questions about the legitimacy of religious authority over the self. Instead, while the self-limiting effects of religious prohibitions were intimated in their accounts, both positioned themselves as responsible for managing the challenges and demands of the migration process within the moral rules set by the Church. Thus, to the extent such tensions formed principles of plot development, it was their endurance that contributed to the overall meaning of settlement as a personal achievement. For Bill and Clare, by contrast, who left Ireland at a time when Catholic hegemony was increasingly contested and arrived in England at the beginning of a sexual revolution, tensions between religious norms and competing ideals of the self formed key points of antagonism within their accounts of life in England. Where Sean and Aileen emphasised conformity to a model of virtuous settlement promulgated in the 1940s and 1950s, Bill and Clare recalled how excessive clerical control constrained personal development. In so doing, Bill and Clare were not merely venting anger; they located themselves as personal subjects of a more generalised critique of Church power, relating a story of personal transformation in which a more autonomous, assertive and self-aware version of self was constructed against the demonised figure of a cruel, self-serving and hypocritical Church.

Nevertheless, despite this performative aspect of Bill's and Clare's memory stories, the reworking of religious identification this implies was not straightforward. Bill's and Clare's narratives certainly register a transition in religious selfhood, but they also manifest the continuation of a conflictual internal dialogue between internalised religious prohibitions and other parts of the self. The outcome of settlement for Bill and Clare is not 'secularisation', but the formation of more ambivalent forms of religious identification, the articulation of which impinges upon other aspects of memory production, inhibiting the imposition of a stable closure upon the significance of settlement. As regards practice and belief itself, the outworking of this tension has motivated a 'privatisation' of religious selfhood – the rejection of the Church's given right to define the terms of morality and the adaption of personal belief to accommodate the personal circumstances of settlement in England and the emotional need to preserve personal achievements from Church devaluation. Clare and Bill have thus not 'fallen away' from the Church, but they have fundamentally reinterpreted their relationship to it, resulting in the circumscription of the role of religion in their lives, but also in an unresolved legacy of conflicting emotions.

Hence the fundamental ambivalence of nostalgic commemoration. The myth of piety which organises commemorative representations of the religiosity of the post-war generation expresses a sense of pride in collective origins and a hallowed image of moral respectability. Nevertheless, as a record of change, nostalgia also registers the otherness of the past.

While Irish achievements in business, music and cultural heritage continue to be celebrated as indices of mobility, integration and identity, piety has receded to the background of contemporary representations of Irishness in England. Insinuated in the gentle irony of Anna May Mangan's depiction of Lizzine's obscure convictions, it is increasingly visible as a relic of the post-war settlement milieu, ephemera of a lost innocence, rather than a present reality. Nostalgia expresses longing for the past; but it also discloses its disavowal.

Notes

1. R. Culhane, 'Irish Catholics in Britain', *The Furrow* 1:8 (1950), 387.
2. E. Hopkins, 'Irish Workers in England', *Christus Rex* 2:2 (1948), 17–24; T. Lane, 'The Irish in an English Parish', *The Furrow* 6:4 (1955), 211–214; G. Morley-Mower, 'Apostles or Lapsed?', *The Furrow* 9:4 (1958), 236–239.
3. J. A. Jackson, *The Irish in Britain* (London, 1963), ch. 4; J. Rex and R. Moore, *Race, Community and Conflict: A Study of Sparkbrook* (London, 1967), 151.
4. D. MacAmhlaigh, *An Irish Navvy: The Diary of an Exile* (London, 1964), 40.
5. Ibid., 67.
6. On the concept of 'discursive power' see C. Brown, *The Death of Christian Britain: Understanding Secularisation, 1800–2000* (Cambridge, 2001), Introduction.
7. E. Delaney, *The Irish in Post-War Britain* (Oxford, 2007), 128.
8. A. Harris, *Faith in the Family: A Lived Religious History of English Catholicism 1945–82* (Manchester, 2013), ch. 4. See also C. Langhamer, *The English in Love: The Intimate Story of an Emotional Revolution* (Oxford, 2013), and Judy Giles, *The Parlour and the Suburb. Domestic Identities, Class, Femininity and Modernity* (Oxford, 2004).
9. M. Lally, *Memoirs of a Mayo Immigrant* (Aberdeenshire, 2006), 90–91.
10. T. Inglis, *Moral Monopoly: The Catholic Church in Modern Irish Society* (Dublin, 1987), chs 5–8; J. Whyte, *Church and State in Modern Ireland, 1923–1970* (Dublin, 1971).
11. On change in the Irish context, see L. Fuller, *Irish Catholicism since 1950. The Undoing of a Culture* (Dublin, 2002), esp. chs 3–6; B. Girvin, 'Church, State and Society in Ireland since 1960', *Eire-Ireland* 43:1 (2008), 74–98, and B. Girvin, 'Contraception, Moral Panic and Social Change in Ireland, 1969–79', *Irish Political Studies* 23:4 (2008), 555–576. For the English debates see Brown, *The Death of Christian Britain*; J. Morris, 'The Strange Death of Christian Britain: Another Look at the Secularization Debate', *Historical Journal* 46:4 (2003), 963–976; D. Nash, 'Reconnecting Religion with Social and Cultural History: Secularization's Failure as a Master Narrative', *Cultural and Social History* 1:3 (2002), 302–325.
12. J. Hickey, *Urban Catholics: Urban Catholicism in England and Wales from 1829 to the Present Day* (London, 1967), 160.
13. J. Keating, 'Faith and Community Threatened? Roman Catholic Responses to the Welfare State, Materialism and Social Mobility, 1945–62', *Twentieth Century British History* 9:1 (1998), 86–108.

14 E. Hopkins, 'Comment: Irish Catholics in England', *The Furrow* 1:8 (1950), 403.
15 Editor, 'The Exiled Irish', *Blackfriars*, March 1951, 50.
16 L. Sheil, 'Marriage and the Leakage', *The Furrow* 9:8 (1958), 522–529.
17 Rex and Moore, *Race, Community and Conflict*, ch. 1.
18 R. Power, *Apple on the Treetop* (Dublin, 1958), 168.
19 Ibid., 188.
20 'Irish Warned of "Dangers"', *Observer*, 5 June 1955; A. P. Boland, 'A London Parish', *The Furrow* 9:4 (1958), 239–242; T. Lane, 'Comment: The Irish in England', *The Furrow* 5:4 (1954), 229; Hopkins, 'Comment: Irish Catholics in England', 398–399, 400.
21 Culhane, 'Irish Catholics in Britain', 389–390; S. M. O Nuallain, 'Change of Outlook in Ireland', *The Furrow* 9:4 (1958), 255–260.
22 M. Prendergast, 'The Family That Isn't', *Christus Rex* 14:2 (1960), 94–95; R. Hauser, 'Hypothesis of Preliminary Action Research for the Irish Problem', report for Centre for Group Studies (London, 1963), Dublin Diocesan Archives, Dublin, AB8/B/XIX/17g.
23 These ideas were also discernible within the local press in major destination cities. See J. Moran, *Irish Birmingham: A History* (Liverpool, 2010), 173–175.
24 A. E. C. W. Spencer, *Arrangements for the Integration of Irish Immigrants in England and Wales* (Dublin, 2012 (1954)), 22.
25 P. Kennedy, *Welcoming the Stranger: Irish Migrant Welfare in Britain since 1957* (Dublin, 2015), vii.
26 The Council of the Irish Centre, Camden, Eighteenth Annual Report, 1972, 1, AIB/LIC/AGM/1/6
27 Culhane, 'Irish Catholics in Britain', 388; Eugene Bodkin, 'Irish Catholics in England: Comment', *The Furrow* 1:8 (1950), 213–215; Irish Centre Welfare Office, Annual Report, 1967, 1, AIB/LIC/Z/4
28 Culhane, 'Irish Catholics in Britain', 390.
29 'One Year Old Today', *Irish Post*, 13 February 1971.
30 G. Hodgson, 'Comment: The Irish in Britain', *The Furrow* 5:4 (1954), 227.
31 Catholic Truth Society of Ireland, *A Catholic Handbook for Irish Men and Women Going to England* (Dublin, 1953), 22.
32 'The Irish in Changing West London', *Irish Post*, 20 February 1971.
33 Aileen Walsh (b. Mayo, 1929) PI/SA/10, 5.
34 Ibid.
35 Ibid., 16.
36 Ibid., 15.
37 Ibid., 13.
38 Ibid., 4.
39 Ibid., 18.
40 Ibid., 22.
41 Ibid., 4.
42 Ibid., 15.
43 Ibid., 2.
44 Ibid., 11.
45 Ibid., 25.
46 Harris, *Faith in the Family*, ch. 4.
47 Ibid., 15.

48 Ibid., 8.
49 Ibid., 11.
50 Ibid., 18.
51 Ibid., 25.
52 Sean Hagan (b. Dublin, 1935) PI/SA/6, 4.
53 Ibid., 5.
54 Ibid., 7.
55 Ibid., 9.
56 Ibid., 10.
57 Ibid., 14.
58 Ibid., 17.
59 CTS, *A Catholic Handbook*, 9.
60 Ibid., 10.
61 Ibid., 11.
62 Sean Hagan (b. Dublin, 1935) PI/SA/6, 22.
63 Bill Duffy (b. Roscommon, 1951) PI/SA/4, 2.
64 Ibid.
65 Ibid., 13–14.
66 Ibid., 26–27.
67 Ibid., 17.
68 Ibid., 3–4.
69 Ibid., 3.
70 'Letters: Terrible Beatings', *Irish Post*, 22 February 1992; 'Letters: Terrible Memories of the 'School for Slaves', *Irish Post*, 21 March 1992; 'Letters: Absence of Legal Aid', *Irish Post*, 11 April 1992; 'Letters: Whipping Left Scars That Will Never Heal', *Irish Post*, 25 April 1992.
71 'Breaking the Silence', *Irish Post*, 25 May 1998; 'Calls Flood in from Victims of Abuse', *Irish Post*, 3 October 1998; M. Doyle, 'Artane Abused Seek Justice', *Irish Post*, 29 May 1999; 'Comment: Help for Artane Boys is at Hand', *Irish Post*, 29 May 1999; R. McGreevy, 'Day of Awful Revelations', *Irish Post*, 12 June 1999; R. McGreevy, 'Survivors Share Child Abuse Pain', *Irish Post*, 12 June 1999.
72 F. Dolan, 'The Walk to Gethsemane', *Irish Post*, 4 April 1998; S. Roberts, 'Another Side to the Story', *Irish Post*, 4 April 1998; Annie O., 'Don't Single Them Out', *Irish Post*, 11 July 1998; V. Marne, 'Time to Stop Whinging', *Irish Post*, 24 October 1998; T. Mahon, 'Fashion to Bash Clergy', *Irish Post*, 31 October 1998; 'The Debt We Owe Christian Brothers', *Irish Post*, 31 October 1998.
73 R. McGreevy, 'Is Sorry Enough?', *Irish Post*, 10 October 1998.
74 R. McGreevy, 'Atonement', *Irish Post*, 22 May 1999
75 J. Doheny, 'Catholic Church Must Adapt and Change with the Times', *Irish Post*, 8 August 1998
76 CTS, *A Catholic Handbook*, 10.
77 Bill Duffy (b. Roscommon, 1951) PI/SA/4, 4.
78 Clare Cullen (b. Cork, 1940) PI/SA/1, 1–7.
79 Ibid., 15.
80 Ibid., 16.
81 Ibid., 17.

82 Ibid., 17–18.
83 Ibid., 18.
84 A. Portelli, *The Death of Luigi Trastulli and Other Stories: Form and Meaning in Oral History* (New York, 1991), ch. 6.
85 Clare Cullen (b. Cork, 1940) PI/SA/1, 9.
86 Ibid., 19.
87 Ibid., 20.
88 A. M. Mangan, *Me and Mine: A Warm-Hearted Memoir of a London Irish Family* (London, 2011), 6–7.

5

Nothing but the same old story? Otherness, belonging and the processes of migrant memory

Foreign and familiar: the politics of Irish migrant reception in post-war England

Whatever the material hardships of the settlement process, Irish migrants arriving in England between 1945 and 1968 encountered a culture where 'the Irish Question' was no longer central to public debate, and where colour had largely replaced religion as the dominant criterion of national belonging. If the pathologisation of Irish propensities formed a key means of stabilising identities in Victorian Britain, the unsettling effects of rapid change in post-war society returned in the spectre of an alternative other: journalists, politicians and social scientists speculating on the post-war 'immigration problem' often appeared to assume that the Irish were indistinguishable from the 'ordinary' working class, exercised as they were by the unassimilable difference of the 'coloured immigrant'. Hence, despite Ireland's formal departure from the Commonwealth in 1949, Irish entry to Britain was not restricted under the 1962 Commonwealth Immigrants Act.[1] And in the expanding sociological literature on 'race relations' the Irish did not feature as a group requiring remedial attention because, it was claimed, they were 'largely accepted', their 'full participation' in the 'Welfare State' wholly 'unquestioned'.[2]

Yet, if the Irish were now figured as 'the same' within certain fields of discourse, such processes appeared contingent upon the othering of the 'coloured immigrant', against whom the Irish migrant's 'sameness' was partially produced. One implication of this was that Irish 'sameness' in post-war England was predicated on the maintenance of hierarchical difference between categories of migrant, engendering an incentive for Irish migrants to project their whiteness as a means of locating themselves as 'ordinary' citizens.³ Such a process afforded one means by which Irish migrants could fashion 'insider' belongings in post-war England, facilitating their disappearance into the English working class. From another perspective, however, the contingency of Irish 'sameness' upon the arrival of other migrants also alludes to its inherent instability: although the otherness of the Irish was less visible within political and sociological discourses, within the emerging framework of British multiculturalism the very designation of the Irish as 'the same' appeared to enact a denial of their claims to difference.

As Mo Moulton has suggested, this kind of denial reflected a fundamental ambivalence in how Irishness was regarded in twentieth-century England, stemming from the unresolved legacies of Anglo-Irish history. As earlier noted, while the Anglo-Irish Treaty effected a political settlement of the 'Irish Question', the continued presence of Irish people and cultures within English society after 1921 necessitated a complex process of accommodation and disavowal. In effect, because Irishness was inextricably woven 'into the very fabric English life', so its meanings had to be 'civilised' via a process of cultural splitting which rendered Irish political identities 'foreign' while domesticating Irish culture as an object for popular consumption. In this way, the symbolic threat which Irishness potentially posed to hegemonic narratives of British unity, democracy and stability was transformed rather than expelled, enabling accommodation and enjoyment: 'the Irish Question was removed from the volatile realm of politics and reassigned to the rich interwar landscape of domestic and associational life, where Irishness could be safely reinterpreted as an enthusiasm, a heritage, or a leisure activity, rather than a public identity for which men and women would be prepared to die'.⁴

After 1945, this ambivalence continued to structure popular perceptions of the Irish. Where the historical debate on the reception of the Irish often treats difference as a binary category, the reality was more complex: English discourses on Ireland and Irishness operated inclusions and exclusions simultaneously, vacillating between perspectives at different moments, in response to changing circumstances.⁵ Particularly relative to 'coloured' migrants, the Irish were familiar and desirable. This was registered, not only in the granting of rights to the Irish not afforded other migrants, but in the prominence assigned Irishness within the civic calendar of English cities and, more generally, the pervasive idealisation of Ireland's landscape, culture and inherently 'friendly' people within post-war popular culture. According to the *Manchester Guardian*, for example 'the biggest attraction of Ireland to the visitor is the Irish people. This is not just a generalisation. It is a fact confirmed, over and over again.'⁶

On the other hand, England's 'enjoyment' of Ireland's mystique remained dependent upon cultural forgetting. Where issues pertaining to the constitutional relationship between Britain and Ireland arose, this mechanism of disavowal came under pressure, and the latent anxieties underlying English constructions manifested themselves in a range of defensive attitudes that reasserted English-Irish difference. This was evident in popular reactions to wartime neutrality, Ireland's departure from the Commonwealth, and the 1962 Commonwealth Immigration Act, all of which reminded the public how 'distressful' Ireland was.[7] But it was, unsurprisingly, most apparent during the Troubles, when Irishness returned within English consciousness as a markedly 'foreign' identity, associated once again with 'the volatile realm of politics'. Against the backdrop of Britain's controversial military intervention in Northern Ireland and the Republican bombing campaign in England, the gentle mockery of post-war representations gave way to a more aggressive stereotypical discourse, signalling the re-emergence of Irishness as a threat within the collective imaginary of English society.[8]

This chapter explores the enduring importance of the British–Irish political relationship as a context for the shaping of cultural identities in post-1945 English society. Focusing on the memory of a single ethnically-charged event, namely the 1996 bombing of the Manchester Arndale, it presents a case study of the ways three migrants negotiate problems of self-positioning and identification created by the advent of the Troubles. It does so, not only to recover a submerged local history of ethnic tension, but to investigate more generally how the tensions generated by the conflict impacted upon migrants' sense of national and ethnic selfhood. The event of the bomb here serves as a lens through which to illuminate the wider workings of Irish communal memory of the Troubles, including its dynamic relation to English societal narratives on the conflict, and the complex articulation of personal memories of the period.

Attending to these dynamics, the chapter explores how the ambivalence of English discourse was mirrored in the internal divisions of Irish communal memory, and how individuals' personal histories of adaption over the life course conditioned how these divisions were incorporated into the self. Personal memories of the bomb were thus not unmediated recollections of the event or its aftermath, but embodied attempts to negotiate this complex discursive landscape in order to manage or resolve the contradictions of identification the Troubles dramatised for post-war migrants. As such, they shine a light upon the Troubles as a significant identity problem for the Irish in post-war England, revealing of both the limitations of whiteness and the importance of the conflict in stimulating reflection upon questions of belonging.

3 Michael Cummings, 'Begorrah – can't have you fearful English living with us ... and mind you do nothing to prevent us from living with you fearful English', *Sunday Express*, 16 November 1961, BCA/MC1019. The cartoon refers to public debate on the likely exclusion of the Irish from proposed restrictions on immigration.

Memory, myth and emotional adaption: reconstructing memories of the 1996 Manchester bomb

At a quarter past eleven in the morning, on Saturday 15 June 1996, the PIRA exploded a 3,000-lb bomb in Manchester, the second largest bomb on the British mainland since the Second World War. Contained within a white transit van parked on Corporation Street, only yards from the Arndale shopping centre in the city's main retail district, the bomb caused extensive damage to the city centre and injured over 200 civilians, most of whom had been struck by falling glass and debris. Within the hour, over 81 ambulances, dispatched from Greater Manchester, West Yorkshire, Lancashire and Merseyside, would arrive to a scene of smoke and rubble to treat the wounded and traumatised.[9]

For many British journalists writing in the national press, the bomb's chief significance lay in its tactical function within the 'end-game' politics then being played out between the political actors who would eventually sign the 1998 Good Friday Agreement.[10] The bomb's relation to this context, plus the fact that no deaths had resulted, partially explain the relatively constrained response of the national press, which on the whole eschewed the rhetoric of outrage that frequently saturated the post-attack coverage of such incidents in the 1970s and 1980s. At the local level, however, the bomb was figured as 'a chilling reminder of the IRA's capacity for evil', and provided local journalists, civic leaders and politicians with an opportunity to summon local memory of the 'blitz'.[11] Titles and subheadings in five local papers proclaimed the event a shared experience of 'horror', 'terror' and 'tragedy', inflicted by 'evil' and 'cowardly' bombers upon 'innocent' and 'vulnerable' civilians.[12] Yet, while Mancunians were 'shell-shocked', they would also 'battle through this difficult time as they have before.'[13] Leonard Rose, chairman of the Jewish Social and Cultural Society, wrote to Lord Mayor Derek Shaw to express his confidence that 'the spirit which saw us through the darkest days of the Blitz will once again prevail.'[14] As reported in the *Manchester Evening Times*, the Lord Mayor agreed:

> The lion-hearted spirit of the people of Manchester is well-known through-out the country and we will not be defeated by these repeated terrorist attacks. If a lion is wounded it comes back stronger and I fully expect that attitude from our people ... their resilience and pluck was inevitable. Everyone was in shock but there was a determination about them – we are known for our guts.[15]

The position of the city's large Irish population in relation to the civic 'we' constructed through this reportage was ambiguous. In keeping with conventions established since partition, official representations of the Troubles after 1968 were heavily conditioned by the need to limit the conflict's impact upon domestic British society and politics.[16] Instead of mobilising popular support for a national 'war', therefore, official narratives tended to frame Britain's intervention as a 'peace-keeping' operation, in which Britain performed a disinterested 'third party' role. Yet, if political elites sought to depoliticise the conflict, this was only necessary in the first place because of the ways coverage of its development undermined British self-perceptions, creating popular dissatisfaction and periodic calls for withdrawal. Particularly following the deployment of British troops in 1969, British public opinion has expressed outrage at the loss of soldiers' lives, incredulity at repeated charges of army brutality and frustration at the legal regulations constraining soldiers' capacity to escalate military force.[17] In this context, popular representations of the conflict, particularly within the tabloid media, crystallised a narrative in which the vulnerable, bewildered and unfairly maligned British Tommy struggled against an evil and unscrupulous terrorist adversary, the incomprehensibility of whom was figured through historic tropes of Irish irrationality, treachery and proclivity towards violence.[18]

Popular responses to the PIRA's bombing campaign in England reflected these tensions in an analogous way. Where this campaign was intended to force partition onto the political agenda in England, from the early 1970s British political elites endeavoured to mute the import of Republican attacks by defining bombers as 'terrorists': as unrepresentative fanatics whose violence was exceptional rather than expressive of antagonistic national interests.[19] In this way, public officials sought to displace the meaning of bombs from the semantic field of 'war' into that of 'criminal justice', deflecting domestic pressure for retaliatory violence. However, while the state's overall management of the conflict ultimately constrained the impact of the PIRA's campaign, the detonation of Republican bombs unavoidably incited ethnic hostility within English cities, partially as a consequence of the human costs of attacks, but also as a result of the ways counter-terrorism practices came to target Irish people as a 'suspect community', potentially harbouring terrorists.[20] In effect, while the rhetoric of 'terrorism' was intended to isolate bombers as unrepresentative fanatics, 'Irishness' and 'terrorism' simply became synonymous within post-attack reactions, the elision pre-structured by the established equation of Irishness with violence and treachery within English cultural memory.[21]

Popular responses to the Manchester bomb likewise registered the effects of these processes. While the Lord Mayor's office received numerous letters from the public protesting the 'innocence' of the wider Irish community, on the day of the attack an article in the *Manchester*

When Irish eyes are smiling

4 Les Gibbard, 'When Irish eyes are smiling', *Guardian*, 9 March 1973, BCA/03673. The cartoon refers to the PIRA car bomb in Whitehall, London, on 8 March 1973, killing one and injuring 238 others.

Evening News reported that 'police believe the IRA has a number of units in mainland Britain.'[22] By Monday the location of the internal threat had seemingly become more precise. In a page-two article entitled 'Why Manchester?', the text tacitly sets up an association between '50,000 Irish-born people in Manchester' and 'the bombers' evil message of terror'. According to the second paragraph:

> As anti-terrorist forensic experts pieced together fragments of the lorry bomb in the hunt for clues, fears mounted that a local active IRA cell could be capable of carrying out further attacks.[23]

Such implications, which the *Manchester Evening News* evolved in the ensuing months into a serialised story about the 'hunt' for men with 'Irish accents', facilitated a process whereby local anger incited by the bomb was displaced onto the local Irish community in the form of a suspicious gaze. On the evening following the bomb, the Irish Heritage Centre at Cheetham Hill would receive several abusive phone calls, one warning 'Watch out, you murdering Irish bastards, you are going to get it tonight!'[24] In Middleton that night ten men walked into and violently vandalised a local Irish bar in full view of staff and customers.[25]

This atmosphere of hostility and suspicion was recalled in a distinct way in the migration narrative of Sean, who was living in Rochdale, a northern suburb of Greater Manchester, at the time of the bomb. Born in 1935, Sean grew up in Co. Offaly before migrating to Bolton in 1956, aged 21. Upon arrival, Sean immediately found work in a cotton mill, and soon after met his Clare-born wife at a local Irish club, marrying her within the year at a local Catholic church. Sean would spend the next 20 years working and raising his family of four children in the town, before moving to Rochdale in 1976. This coincided with a spell of employment as a labourer for Wimpey's building contractors, before Sean secured work as a night-time security guard at Rochdale College, where he was employed at the time of the bomb in 1996.

In his account of these aspects of his experiences in England, Sean did not recall tension with English people. On the contrary, he stressed how friendly English people had been when he first took up employment in Bolton, explaining that most of his friends, both inside and outside of work, had been English at that time:

> Oh, they were all very friendly, you know, they were all very sociable and that. Yeah, I didn't have, find any fault with any of them. And they were all English people. All of them. You only got the odd Irish man amongst ... about 40 English people, and ... you got on great with them! All my friends were English, when I was in Bolton. Yeah.[26]

Despite this, however, with the commencement of the PIRA's bombing campaign in the early 1970s, Sean began to feel 'awkward' in public spaces 'every time anything happened ... because they were all talking about it, you know?'[27] Most prominent in Sean's memories of this period was the aftermath of the Manchester bomb, which was recalled as a period of particular tension:

Sean: My local pub in Rochdale, I walked into it. I used to call for a pint on my way home from work. And they used to all salute you when you come in. 'Hiya, hiya Sean', or ... And this day, when that bomb went off (excuse me) I went into the pub for a pint again. There was a big hush. When I opened my mouth for ... to ask for my pint. They were ... and they wasn't waiting for you. They used to have it ready. When they see me coming through the door they used to pump the pint. Waiting until I opened my mouth and then as soon as they heard my accent, there was a big hush.
Barry: What did that make you feel like?

Sean: I, I were embarrassed. I stopped going in. For a couple of months, yeah. I stopped going in the pub. I felt very embarrassed. It was shocking, that, I didn't agree with that bombing there, in ... It wasn't nice, was it? Not nice for the people that were living here, you know.
Barry: And do you go back to the pub now?
Sean: Oh, they were ... well it's closed down now. I used ... oh I did, I went back to it, eventually, when everything calmed down. But ... on that ... I remember that, I'll never forget that. When that happened. I, I felt very embarrassed. Even embarrassed in work, when, when I went to work. All my mates, workmates are English and that. And you were one, the Irish man, there was just you ...[28]

The first thing to note about this story is that certain details conflict with other parts of Sean's life history. In this memory, the pub scene occurs after Sean has finished work, on Saturday, 15 June 1996. As Sean recalled in the section of his narrative concerning work, however, in 1996 he was working as a security guard at Rochdale College, where he typically worked seven night shifts a week, between the hours of 4 p.m. and 6.30 a.m. Calling for a drink after work was thus unlikely to have been a regular practice during this phase of Sean's work history. Further, Sean mentions feeling 'embarrassed' among his 'workmates' who 'were all English'. However, as Sean earlier explained, he usually worked alone during his time as a night security guard.[29] Such inconsistencies, it is suggested, here point to a process of unconscious reworking, whereby salient details of earlier incidents have been incorporated into the memory of the Manchester bomb, which thereby comes to stand for more than the event itself.

It is important here to note that the 1996 bomb was not in fact the first attack by republicans in the Manchester area. While London formed the main focus of the PIRA's campaign in England, between 1974 and 1992 Manchester was subject to eight separate attacks, while nearby Warrington was subject to two in 1992 alone. These attacks resulted in some 15 deaths with many more injured, and, as reported in the local press, created suspicions around Irish people living in the Greater Manchester area.[30] This was perhaps most pronounced in the mid-1970s, when a PIRA bomb-making factory was discovered by police in Fallowfield, resulting in four local Irish people receiving medium term prison sentences for conspiracy to cause explosions in February 1975.[31]

Sean's composite memory of the Manchester bomb therefore alludes to a longer history of local tensions during the Troubles in Britain. At the same time, however, it also points to the workings of an Irish communal memory of the Troubles, in interaction with processes of personal identity. As noted earlier, a central claim of scholars of the Irish in Britain is that there has been a public silence in Britain concerning the experiences of the Irish, and that Irish migrants, in particular those who arrived during the post-war years, have adopted a 'low public profile' about their identity due to overwhelming pressures to incorporate themselves within the terms of white Britishness. Within this narrative, the period of the Troubles is often presented as exemplary given the repressive effects of the 1974 Prevention of Terrorism Act and the hostility displayed towards Irish people within the wider press and media. In fact, however, while the Irish were certainly imagined as a 'suspect community' during the period, from the early 1980s onwards this positioning of the 'Irish community' incited the production of a communal counter-narrative, the central message of which underscored the victimisation of Irish people. Driven by a flowering of community activism, an important outcome of this development was the pushing of the problem of anti-Irish discrimination onto local authority agendas and, as the period progressed, an enhanced public profile for 'the Irish community in Britain' as an 'ethnic minority'. In the 1990s in particular, a number of publicly funded research reports, such as *Discrimination and the Irish Community in Britain: A Report of Research Undertaken for the Commission for Racial Equality*, made the national headlines, their publication coinciding with ongoing debates around institutional racism and British justice sparked by the release of the Guildford Four in 1989 and the Birmingham Six in 1991. The importance of such reports here is that they collected personal narratives of discrimination shaped at the level of the local and particular, and made them available to a national audience in generalised form, generating a degree of public sympathy for the idea that Irish people in Britain had suffered unfairly as a result of popular suspicions aroused by the Troubles.

In terms of the reconstruction of personal experience following the Manchester bomb, these processes have made available a subject-position from which individuals such as Sean can relate and receive recognition for their own personal experiences of hostility. In the process, reconstruction is shaped in accordance with the form of the generalised image, such that fragments of experience relating to temporally distinct but paradigmatically associated events crystallise into a memory that is factually inconsistent but 'autobiographically true'.[32] This 'autobiographical truth' in turn provides access to what the bomb, and the Troubles more generally, mean to Sean personally. Sean's story of the 'big hush', set in the communal space of the pub, relates an experience of coming 'under suspicion', of social stigmatisation, in a place where he was usually warmly received, inducing a feeling of 'embarrassment'. As well as awkward self-consciousness, the term is also suggestive here of the emotion of shame; of an unsettling awareness of a discrepancy between how Sean wanted and expected others to see him, and how they did so in reality following the bomb. If the story of the 'big hush' constructs an analogy for the way in which the Troubles rendered Sean's Irishness an object of suspicion, the term 'embarrassment' intimates how this gaze has been internalised, producing a desire to hide oneself away from familiar places. As such, the term articulates conflict within a dual sense of belonging: Sean recognises himself as 'Irish' and how this identifies him with the actions of the bombers, but he identifies too with the community of his local pub where he has socialised with English neighbours, workmates and friends for many years. Because the bomb represented an attack on this community, so it is remembered by Sean as an event which placed an unwanted strain on valued personal relationships, the importance of which signify his emotional adaption to life in England.

Sean works to resolve this conflict in two interrelated ways:

Sean: It was just very awkward. They just stared at you, you know. Was not nice. Not a nice thing to happen. That's why it was lovely and peaceful there up to a few weeks ago, wasn't it? They're starting again. Very embarrassing, that, again, innit. And a couple ... for a few hooligans, you know. Because it's united now, in the last few years, now. It's been great the last 12 year. It's been great over there. Let's hope ... let's hope it settles down again. You know, we don't like this bl... this bombing, it's shocking. Not doing anything for us. Not doing any good for ... for the Irish people is it?[33]

On 7 March 2009, two weeks prior to my interview with Sean, dissident Republicans in Northern Ireland shot and killed two British soldiers stationed at Massereene army base in Co. Antrim, the first political murders in the province since the 1997 ceasefire.[34] Sean's identification of 'a few hooligans' as the cause of the problem 'over there' constitutes a tactic by which, at a number of points during the discussion, he endeavoured to differentiate himself from the views and actions of 'extreme' Republicanism. As he earlier states in relation to the Manchester bomb, Sean 'didn't agree with that bombing there': 'I think it's pointless, what they are doing, myself.' Sean prefers to focus on what he sees as the progress that has been made towards 'peace' in Northern Ireland. If harmony could be maintained 'over there', Sean seems to be saying, a closure could be imposed 'over here' and the tensions of the past allowed to fade: 'let's hope ... let's hope it settles down again. You know, we don't like this ...this bombing, it's shocking.'

In constructing himself as a member of a local Irish community opposed to 'this bombing', Sean here locates a subject-position which opens the possibility of realignment between the categories 'Mancunian' and 'Irish' through positing a shared experience of victimisation in opposition to the perpetrators of the bomb. As suggested above, the British discourse on the Troubles was not in fact a unitary formation, but internally divided between a virulent discourse of revenge and renunciation, and a more self-critical liberal framework. Originating in the 1930s, but apparent within the liberal and leftwing press throughout the post-war decades, this tradition of representation conceived 'Ulster' as an affront to British democratic traditions, portraying the Unionist regime as an effective 'dictatorship' governing through the use of emergency powers and systematic discrimination against the Catholic minority.[35] Within this view, the conflict in Northern Ireland was not a simple product of Irish irrationality, but rooted in failures of democratic governance, including British governments' sustained neglect of political developments in the province since 1921.[36]

In turn, if the Troubles reflected a failure of British democracy, so the targeting of England's Irish minority in the wake of terrorist atrocities represented a further corruption of British liberal standards, with dangerous ramifications for domestic politics in England. The distinction between 'terrorism' and British democracy on which the official response to bombs was predicated here left open the possibility of a counter-representation which, portraying the PIRA as unrepresentative of the whole, split the object of suspicion into innocent and guilty elements. The Birmingham pub bombings of November 1974, for example, provoked calls for a 'counter-attack', but leading politicians on the whole sought to limit the public appetite for retaliation.[37] According to Roy Jenkins, Labour Home Secretary and MP for Birmingham Stechford at the time, it was vital that the nation remain 'rational and calm' in order to 'prevent any spread into this island' of 'conditions such as, unfortunately, have persisted in Northern Ireland for some time'. To that end, it was crucial that the 'innocence' of the majority of Irish people should be made 'clear':

> I have represented for nearly 25 years the city of Birmingham, which has a large Irish community of about 100,000. During the whole of that period relations have been excellent between that community and the native-born population. It would be a tragedy if these relations were damaged by what has been done by a tiny minority. It is of great importance that we should recognise how utterly alien and repugnant to the overwhelming majority of the Irish is what is being done by a few totally unrepresentative fringe figures of their community. How

important it is that it should be made overwhelmingly clear that they offer no shelter to those who commit these crimes, and how important it is, too, that the community in this country does not allow its understandable feelings to be expressed in hostility or vengeance towards innocent Irish people here. If that were to take place the damage would be still greater and the victory for the extremists and the terrorists would also be great.[38]

Following the Manchester bomb local politicians and journalists made use of these moral distinctions to defend the reputation of the Irish community. If some local reactions insinuated the treachery of the Irish, other public figures, some of Irish extraction, sought to uphold the community's 'innocence'. Following the pub attack in Middleton the chairman of the Middleton Township Committee, Henry West, condemned the attacks as 'sick': 'It is tarring the whole Irish population with the abomination done by a tiny minority.'[39] According to an article in the *Manchester Evening News* on the Tuesday after the bomb, which asked 'Why Us?':

> It is a question which puzzles those of Irish descent who live and work here just as much as those who are proud to call themselves native Mancunians. They are deeply embarrassed to be associated by birth with such cowardly, callous scum.[40]

This construction of local Irish 'embarrassment' established the basic parameters within which local Irish community leaders sought to dispel popular suspicions concerning Irish people. Michael Reilly, chairman of the Irish Association Social Club in Chorlton, wrote to the Lord Mayor to wish 'the British government success in finding and bringing to justice those responsible' for the bomb. The Association's members, 'an integral part of the community for over forty years', had always striven 'towards friendship and integration with the people of Manchester', and sought now to 'totally disassociate themselves from the uncivilised, cowardly minority who have brought feelings of shame to the Irish nation, with their unjustifiable, unwarranted destruction of your beautiful city.'[41] Similarly, in the local press Michael Forde, chairman of the Irish World Heritage Centre at Cheetham Hill and vice-chair of the Federation of Irish Societies, emphasised that 'Irish people' regarded Manchester as 'their city', 'reflected in the contributions they make to their city in all sorts of ways'. As such, 'this horror, that has been done in the name of the Irish people, has sickened the Irish people everywhere, not least in Manchester':

> I thought that all this futile misery of guns and bombs was behind us. We Irish are not just gutted by what the IRA did. We are horrified, saddened and angry. We believed that after 25 years of being in the

front line we could all live together in peace. Whenever a bomb has gone off, the Irish people have gone under suspicion. And it is so unfair.[42]

With its central themes of unfair victimisation, shared anger towards the PIRA, community ties, and the desire for 'peace', Michael Forde's response to local hostility following the bomb echoed that of many other community representatives called upon to speak following attacks in the past.[43] Formulated within the conservative space of 'official' associational culture, and expressive of a 'respectable' code of Irishness associated with aspirational settlement in England during the post-war decades, this narrative protests the innocence of an unfairly suspected Irish community, presented as integrated within British society, and seeks reparation with that society through the disavowal of PIRA violence and the idealisation of peace. For Sean, who settled in England in 1952, this narrative provides a framework within which he seeks to construct a personal memory of the bomb that facilitates negotiation of the conflict of belonging the event dramatises for him. Through projecting culpability onto an unrepresentative band of 'hooligans', Sean endeavours to restore coherence between how he would like his local community to perceive him and how he imagines they perceive him in actuality, enabling 'embarrassment' to dissipate and Sean to belong unproblematically to the Irish community in Rochdale and his local community of friends, neighbours and workmates.

In the process, however, the politics associated with this identity conflict at the institutional level are rendered invisible in Sean's narrative. Because the community narrative through which Sean constructs his experiences works defensively to split off the historical and political context in which Republican strategy was formulated, so it could be seen as supportive of the regulatory function of the suspicious gaze, providing a subject-position which discourages the public expression of support for nationalist goals. In this respect, the personal memories of my second respondent were distinct from those of Sean. Joe, a retired construction worker, migrated from a small farming background in Longford to Birmingham in 1962, aged 17, before moving to Manchester in 1965. Unlike the majority of respondents in the sample, who usually waited until asked about their experiences of the Troubles, Joe zoned in on Anglo-Irish political history early on in the interview. During the course of a discussion about memories of school, occurring some four minutes after the beginning of the interview, Joe recalled that one of his teachers at technical school, attended between 1956 and 1959, was 'Rory Brady':[44]

> It was the norm then that you went to technical school for a couple o'years ... my teacher, believe it or not, at the time ... was a well-known man, you've probably will have heard of him, Rory Brady?[45]

As Joe went on to explain, 'Rory Brady', a 'brilliant teacher', was 'one of the Republicans ... he's President of Sinn Fein at the moment'. Joe 'was in school the day he was taken out of it', that is 'he was virtually lifted for being a member of an illegal organisation'. At the time, Joe 'didn't understand why', however:

> When we started you know getting a bit of sense, y'know, started to learn what politics was about, we found out then.[46]

These stories appropriate the chance intersection between the biographies of the Republican leader, whose political credentials were unknown to the young Joe, and the young self as evidence of a shared lineage.[47] However, the appeal to nationalist credentials upon which this strategy relies involves the assumption that both interviewer and interviewee share the same national political frame of reference. This assumption, apparent in Joe's supposition that I 'probably will have heard of him', has been arrived at as a result of my own Northern Irish accent, which is here interpreted as a signifier of a shared national political identity, triggering and shaping Joe's recollection of childhood in relation to nationalist themes.

This dynamic, in interaction with a particular code of Irish masculinity, has implications for how Joe remembers the Manchester bomb:

Barry: How did you feel walking round Manchester as an Irish person after that?

Joe: Well ... [very long pause, sigh] ... how did I feel? I felt bad that it had happened here in Manchester, I did feel bad about it, but then ... you have to realise, I had to realise then, that ... [pause] ... there's peace now, thank God, touch wood, in Northern Ireland ... but at that time there wasn't peace, ... [pause] ... and the ... Catholic population in Ireland, at that time and for years beforehand, never got fair play, that's the way I look at that, from that point of view I have to speak, honestly what I feel, I mean I'll give you a couple of incidents ... on it ... [pause] ... Catholic people in Ireland, Northern Ireland, like I have to say, I have, I have my wife here and I have three sons right, if we were living in Northern Ireland at that time, four people in the house would be entitled to vote, but there was only one person allowed to vote, one person had, carried the vote ... if you had the Protestant people next door, there could be four people living in that house; them four people had a vote. That was the way it was.[48] I had a cousin?, did have a cousin living in Armagh in Northern Ireland, and at that time she was living, blocks of houses each side of the street, but she was living on the righthand side of the street, the last house on the righthand side of the street, the rest of the houses all down that side were Protestant

right, when she walked out her door she had to walk across the road, she couldn't walk down the footpath, that is my feeling on it you know. It's brought, alright, a lot of bad things happened surely, and a lot of people lost their lives in it, people that shouldn't have, both Protestant and Catholic, but, it had to be to bring peace, it was the only way, it was the only way forward, for to see peace, I mean, there's people that's against this what's gone on like now with the settlement that's gone on there now, but I'm not; I'm happy for to see peace, that's all, you know, that I would say like, but I mean, that's been goin' on for 300 years, you know, I'm sure you know a bit about the history of it anyway?
Barry: I know a wee bit ... about ...
Joe: I would say you do alright, you know, what part are you from yourself?
Barry: Ah, Cookstown, in Co. Tyrone.
Joe: You'll know, you'll know about it ...[49]

Where Sean's main memory of the Manchester bomb takes as its spatial referent the communal setting of a local pub, Joe here frames his response within an institutional mode of discourse, using the question as an opportunity to articulate an ideological position on British–Irish relations, in effect to offer a nationalist justification for the bomb. Thus, where Sean tells of the anxieties he experienced through becoming the object of a suspicious gaze, Joe reads a question about 'feelings' as an invitation to express political 'feelings'. In offering a justification for those feelings that potentially conflicts with the efforts of the authorities in Britain to proscribe support for Irish Republicanism during the Troubles, Joe may be viewed as contesting dominant British narratives on the conflict, which criminalised Republican violence as 'terrorism'.

In the 1970s and 1980s, publicly suggesting that PIRA violence in Britain served a valid political purpose rendered one suspect in the panoptical eye of the British state. For this reason, 'official' representatives of the 'Irish community', figures who often had substantial business interests in Britain, routinely sought to disassociate the 'community' from the activities of militant Republicanism. It did not automatically follow, however, that Republican and anti-imperial narratives were inaudible within wider British society. In addition to single-issue groups such as Troops Out, which saw Northern Ireland as a 'sectarian state based on Protestant privilege', the radicalisation of Irish activism that occurred in cities such as London, Manchester and Birmingham from the 1980s onwards was driven by groups which linked 'anti-Irish racism' with Britain's 'imperialist' agenda in the region.[50] For the Irish in Britain Representation Group (IBRG), for example, established in the wake of the 1981 hunger strikes, 'the primary function of the PTA [Prevention of Terrorism Act] was to silence and politically neutralise the Irish community in Britain' with the result 'that every Irish person was deemed suspect and guilty'.[51] As such, 'anti-Irish racism has resulted from a history of colonisation and a policy of stripping Ireland of its resources and culture',[52] entailing that 'the lives of Irish people living in Britain are underscored and structured by Britain's relationship to Ireland'.[53] In turn, therefore, the 'struggle' for 'freedom' in 'Ireland' necessarily overlaps with the 'struggle' for identity and self-empowerment in Britain.

> Our primary task is to liberate our own community, to build up, to agitate, to organise, to campaign, to educate, to finally see our community free from oppression. But we realise we can never be free whilst our sisters and brothers remain oppressed in the north of Ireland.[54]

The activism of the IBRG played an important role in forcing official acknowledgement of the discrimination faced by Irish people during the period of the Troubles, and the terms of its discourse echo through the literature on Irish identity and disadvantage that emerged into public space in the 1990s. More importantly here, however, the militant narrative of Irish identity which such groups circulated offered an alternative framework in which migrants like Joe could situate their own experiences of the period. In this regard, encouraged by the intersubjective dynamic obtaining, a strategy of self-composure is discernible within this part of Joe's account whereby he perceives the interview as a 'safe' space in which to express a marginal perspective on the Troubles, and as providing an audience from which he can derive a sense of recognition for the version of self projected.

Nevertheless, the composure achieved through this process is not without its ambivalences. On the one hand, Joe's justification of PIRA tactics implicitly constructs the PIRA as heroic defenders of justice; as men prepared to use violence against oppressive forces to secure entitlements to equality and freedom. In thus defending the PIRA, so Joe, who deploys techniques of exposition and formal argument to authorise his voice, also becomes a heroic defender of justice. These stories and the way they are told here enact a gendered project of self-fashioning, expressive of an identification with ideals embodied in romantic portrayals of the Irish Republican soldier. Yet the image of masculine certainty here projected is complicated by the deep pauses that punctuate the beginning of the response. These pauses, together with the admission that he 'felt bad that it had happened here', hint at an underlying complexity of emotions and attachments, backgrounded through Joe's attempt to construct his memories of the bomb at the institutional level of discourse. Here, an aversion to emotional display appears to shape Joe's narrative strategy: if the militant discourse taken up permits access to a heroic version of masculinity, the concomitant focus on the abstract and general permits a backgrounding of anxieties that might otherwise disrupt the image of masculine certainty Joe wishes to project.

Other responses made by Joe provide a deeper understanding of the emotional processes that threaten this image:

> Well it was, it was ... it was a hard time for the Irish people like, I can't say, like, that ... that I ever encountered anything bad, they said to me about it, but, you see here in Manchester we're lucky, the community, I'm involved like in the Irish community in a lot of ways and we've a great relationship with Manchester town hall, the night of the bombing here all the councillors from Manchester town hall, they came up to the Centre, you know ...[55]

As Joe here suggests, the 'Irish community' in Manchester views itself as having 'a great relationship with Manchester town hall'. Many local councillors come from Irish families and, as Joe recalls, only hours after the Manchester bomb the Irish centre at Cheetham Hill received a visit from local councillors, including Richard Leese, then leader of the city council, to offer support.[56] In recalling this memory through the collective 'we', however, Joe shifts to a different subject-position, inviting recognition of a different form of masculine status. If in the previous extract Joe seeks to identify himself with a heroic image of politicised Irish masculinity, here and elsewhere in his narrative he identifies himself with 'the Irish people in Manchester', and more specifically, with 'Irish community' leadership and 'the councillors from Manchester town hall'.

Joe's effort to identify himself as a local community leader here refers us back to the details of his settlement touched upon in Chapter 3. In his narrative as a whole Joe sought to construct his settlement in England as a story of personal success and achievement. In the first instance, this had to do with how his earnings as a tunnel-digger within the construction industry had afforded him a degree of affluence, enabling him to buy a house and raise a family in Manchester. In later years, however, the heavy nature of the work Joe performed to secure this material success has taken its toll on his body, such that he is 'crippled-up today'.[57] In the interview, in the face of the threat these facts posed to the image of masculine achievement Joe wished to project, Joe sought to bolster his preferred migration success story through reference to what he viewed as his prominent position within the local Irish community, whose official institutions he appears to have become increasingly involved with following his retirement, but also by denigrating aspects of Britishness, which he implicitly viewed as responsible for his 'crippled-up' bodily state. Joe's work experiences in England have thus engendered a certain antipathy towards British institutions which have sanctioned his exploitation as a labourer, but also an emotional investment in the public of the local Irish community, this being a space where he can affirm a sense of personal distinction and belonging.

The Manchester bomb brings the different impulses and identifications engendered through these work experiences into conflict. The reason why, as Joe states above, he 'felt bad that it had happened here' was because the Manchester bomb brings into sharp focus a conflict between his ideological sympathy for the PIRA's cause and a counterposed sense of belonging to 'the Irish people in Manchester', a construction which incorporates both 'Irish' and 'Manchester'. Not only, as we have seen, did public figures and Irish community leaders portray the Irish community as victims of the PIRA's tactics after the bomb, but when the IBRG invited a Sinn Fein councillor to speak at a pre-election meeting in the city less than a year after the attack, local councillors expressed condemnation, constructing Sinn Fein as representatives of the PIRA.[58] Among them was council leader Richard Leese, who took particular offence over the IBRG's refusal to include the Manchester bomb on the agenda for discussion at the meeting:

> Any visit by a Sinn Fein representative should be on the basis they apologise for the attack on the people of Manchester that took place and a pledge that no attack will ever take place again ... To come to the city and not even mention the attack is outrageous and a slur on all people, including those of Irish origin.[59]

The version of self Joe wishes to project through his narrative thus depends upon the performance of two roles ideologically opposed within public discourse: the determined Irish republican, and the local community leader who is well integrated into local circuits of civic power. In contrast to Sean or public representatives of the IBRG, Joe cannot negotiate this tension through a strategy of projective disavowal, shifting the anxiety generated onto another object, without destabilising other parts of the self. If the PIRA are disavowed as culpable, Joe's self-image as an 'Irishman' within the interview is destabilised; if, by contrast, the British authorities are positioned in this role, the sense of status and belonging Joe derives from his 'great relationship' with 'Manchester town hall' comes under threat. Joe's strategy for negotiating the conflict in the interview thus involves an attempt to diminish its seriousness while creating an emotional distance between the event of the bomb and his personal feelings and experiences. Thus, the bomb 'was a hard time for the Irish people' but 'I can't say, like, that ... that I ever encountered anything bad'.

As it turns out, this claim was not wholly accurate. Later, in a separate discussion about how Irish people were received in England more generally, Joe suddenly remembers that the police came to his house to investigate a possible link with terrorist activities one Christmas morning, a monitoring practice many Irish people in Britain were subject to during the period of the Troubles:

Barry: Was there any trouble with the police over here ever or anything like that?

Joe: I have never any trouble with them, they came here once, oh Christ aye, they did yeah, they came here once.

Barry: What was that about?

Joe: They came here because somebody they had, they had a report that I had some guns in the house, I said, went to the door, 'Can we come in', course you can, what's it about? He said 'Do you have guns in the house?' It had just come Christmas time you know, 'Jesus!', I said, 'there's a rake of guns', I said, 'here, surely to Christ there is, come in to the front room to you see them', and the kids, 'all flaming kids' stuff!' I said, 'there's no guns in this house', you know, they never even searched.

Barry: And why do you think they came?

Joe: I don't know, I think mebbe some … somebody could have, with me being Irish, someone could have just reported me, they never said, they just said they had a report … so, I says to them, like, at the door, before I let them in, well I says, lads, I said, I hope, I said, that you can substantiate what you're saying, because, I said, there's no guns here, I invited them in … the kids playtoys …

Barry: How did you feel about that, about them comin' round after Christmas?

Joe: Well, I didn't feel … I didn't feel great about it, but then I thought to myself, well, I had nothin' to hide, and then … it come into my mind, that they were doing' their job, they got a report.[60]

Joe's recollection of this experience of coming under suspicion contrasts sharply with how Sean remembers encountering hostility in his local pub after the Manchester bomb. For Sean, the bomb and the Troubles more generally constituted events in relation to which he actively expressed a sense of victimisation. Such feelings were inextricably linked to an active process of memory whereby distinct experiences blurred into a general, collective memory of the Troubles as a period of being under suspicion. By contrast, Joe has not only kept distinct events separate in his memory; he also appears to have actively forgotten events where he was the direct target of a suspicious gaze. The memory Joe here recounts concerning the police appears to emerge spontaneously, as if the question about the police uncovers an experience that has been layered over with other, preferred memories of the period.

In keeping with the interpretation developed above, one explanation for the forgetting of such experiences within Joe's narrative is that they potentially undermine the versions of self he wishes to project within the interview. On the one hand, the irresistible invasion of the state's surveillance apparatus into the private space of the home on Christmas morning, in full view of family, negates Joe's status within that context: Joe is no longer master in his own home. On the other, the police's visit to Joe's house, occurring in full view of neighbours on Christmas Day, potentially criminalises Joe in the eyes of the community. This calls into question his proclaimed 'great relationship' with Manchester town hall, and with it the self-image of migration success this 'great relationship' serves to protect from the emasculating effects of the injuries Joe sustained within the construction industry. As an experience which undermines different parts of the self simultaneously, Joe's visit from the police is thus a difficult memory.

This underpins the initial forgetting of the event, but also the form of the memory when it is recounted. Hence Joe's use of irony in telling a story whose central feature is a wry incongruity between 'guns' and 'children's toys', a narrative strategy that creates emotional distance through diminishing the seriousness of the intrusion while enabling Joe to present himself as unperturbed and in control of the situation. Similarly, when Joe is invited to describe his feelings an understated acknowledgement that 'I didn't feel great about it' is quickly rationalised away in terms of a masculine imperative that, by framing the incident within the semantic field of work, permits empathy with the 'lads': 'they were doing their job'. In these instances, as in Joe's memories of the Troubles more generally, conflicting identifications based on gender, belonging and the interview relation intersect to encourage a strategy of emotional management that centres on deflection and aversion in order to preserve an impermeable image of self.

In the narrative of my third respondent, the memory produced as a result of such interactions takes a different form again. Born in 1941, Kate migrated from Sligo to Manchester in 1961 to take up work as a general nurse in Manchester Infirmary, and like Sean recalled highly positive memories of interactions with English people during this early phase of settlement. Remembering how she used to go dancing with English men she was a young nurse in Stockport Infirmary, Kate recalled how 'I found them very ... funny. We always used to have great laughs':[61]

> They did, they loved to be with the Irish. Er, they all ... 'When are we going? When are we going again to the dance? When are we going to meet your friends? When are we ... er ...', you know, and all that. But the ... I liked it, I did like the English, and I do, and I've worked with a lot of English people.[62]

The onset of the Troubles, by which time Kate was married with twins, marked a change in this relation of mutual affection, however:

> Ooh ... I used to ... I used to try and calm down my ... my accent. Or say, don't tell ... you know, tell them ... Now the Jews were alright. It

was the English. They hate ... especially, when we lived in Park Hill Avenue there was a woman across the road. There was two families. One was English, and one was Irish. They were from Donegal. And, so the Irish ones were alright, but this ... and the Irish ones had a son. And he was over in Aberdeen. You know, over in there where England had their their base. He was over there and he was in the English army. And the other woman, she was Scotch, and her son was in the army. And he was sent to Northern Ireland. Oh! Well I had to keep my door shut. Oh dear. And I used to say to Pat, 'Don't say a word when you're going out! Jump into the van and go! Because', I said ... because I knew him. He'd, he'd eff her off and all that type of thing. Oh and I used to ... and ... she used to come over, you know when the Troubles started? The Troubles started, she used to ... she'd come over. And she'd say to me ... she'd say, 'If my son ... If them IRA or so-and-so's', she said, 'touch a hair on my son's head', she said, 'I'll be over here for you.' Oh! Oh, well I ... and I ... well, we had to keep our mouths shut. I couldn't ... I couldn't speak much, because people then knew I was Irish.[63]

Reproducing many of the features of Sean's memory, Kate here recalls an experience of 'coming under suspicion', of having 'to keep our mouths shut' in order to conceal verbal signifiers of Irishness. As a result, just as Sean had to avoid his local pub, Kate had to 'keep my door shut', suggesting how for both the tensions generated through the Troubles worked to separate them from communal spaces where English and Irish routinely mixed. Where Kate's memory differs from Sean's is in its spatial referent: where Sean's memories of 'coming under suspicion' referred to the masculine space of the pub, Kate 'shuts her door' on her local neighbourhood, solidifying the boundary separating the interior of the home from the communal space of the neighbourhood. Where Sean recalls estrangement from a communal space of leisure and sociability, Kate thus recalls being penned within her home, encircled by the hostile gaze of neighbours as her husband exits the scene.

As Kate went on explain, such neighbourhood hostilities tended to increase 'specially when there was a bomb'. Following the Manchester bomb in particular, Kate feared for the physical safety of her children 'because they might attack them':

You know, oh God, Manchester. Oh ... oh ... had to hide me, and the kids, I had to keep them in, and I had to keep them, keep their mouth shut, and not say anything, you know. Because they might attack them. In the ... you know, they were, er, Irish, of Irish parents you see.[64]

This memory contains two factual inaccuracies, revealing, as in Sean's case, the effects of a memory process whereby collective constructions of the Irish suspectee appear to have reshaped personal experience in particular ways. Firstly, given that Kate's children were born and raised in Manchester, and so would have had English accents, it does not make literal sense for Kate to have kept her children's 'mouth shut' following the bomb. Secondly, as the bomb was in 1996, all her children would have been adults at the time; some, possibly all, may not even have been living at home. The suggestion, as in Sean's case, is that earlier, emotionally significant experiences of 'coming under suspicion', when Kate's children were young and under her daily care, have come to define her memory of the Troubles as a whole. Facilitated by the circulation of generalised images of Irish victimisation within the public space from the 1990s, this process has encouraged the forgetting of the specificity of individual events, such that all instances of 'coming under suspicion' associated with the memory frame of the Troubles blur, in effect, into the one definitive experience.

This renders specific details of Kate's memory of the Manchester bomb factually suspect, but it also permits insight into what the Troubles, as a key period/event within her experiences of settlement in England, means to her. In this respect, one of the ways Kate's congealed memory of the Troubles differs from that of Sean concerns how her embodied experience of 'coming under suspicion' has been shaped by discourses of femininity which identify women with maternity and domesticity. Kate's memory of the Manchester bomb thus recalls her within the home, in the role of protective mother, worrying about the safety of her children and taking steps to preserve it. This suggests how the effects of hostility were experienced relationally for Kate, as affecting emotionally significant others within an inter-subjective sense of self, but also how such occasions, or the recollection of such occasions, could provide opportunities to realise idealised images of the 'good mother'.

A second important way in which Kate's memories differed from Sean's concerns their relation with institutional modes of discourse. As we explore further Kate's memories of the Manchester bomb, an important difference emerged in relation to her presentation of the PIRA:

Barry: What happened after that?
Kate: Well they kept at … they kept going about it, you know, 'Oh the Irish!', you know, 'You're so-and-so's', and all that. 'And the IRA are, so you could belong to the IRA, and you could be helping the IRA, and you could be doing this, You could be doing that, and you could be doing …' And I … and I said, 'Look, I …', I said, 'I am not … I'm as against it as you are.' I said, 'I don't like it any more than you do. But', I said, 'the way the IRA are sucking at it, is the English people are over there, in our … co… in our pla… in our Ireland.'[65]

Kate here recalls how she sought to distance herself from the aims and activities of the PIRA in the face of prevalent suspicions, protesting that

'I'm as against it as you are'. In constructing a subject-position inhabitable by both accuser and accused in opposition to the PIRA's violence, such a formulation replicates the strategy of disassociation deployed by community leaders and Sean. However, this effort to collapse differences between 'English' and 'Irish' in relation to the PIRA is immediately complicated by Kate's effort to explain 'the way the IRA are sucking at it' which, by reintroducing history, re-establishes the opposition between 'English people' and 'our Ireland'. Here, after finally locating the term that best expresses her understanding, Kate manages to verbalise a resistance to the accusatory voice interrogating the self in the historical present. The memory thus unmutes a sense of sympathy for the PIRA's political aims, revealing in the process how Kate's understanding of the Troubles at the level of institutional politics is framed in traditional nationalist terms: the phrase 'our Ireland' constructs the conflict as a territorial competition between 'the English people' and the Irish; the state of Northern Ireland or the role of the majority population within that state do not figure.

However, as Kate's vacillations, from condemnation of the PIRA to recognition of its aims, suggests, her habitation of this subject-position was not steadily fixed. A little further on, as Kate pondered the issue of 'peace' and the ceasefire, the reasons for this ambivalence became clearer:

> You know, if the peace has got a chance. I was so pleased about that. About the way ... but I think what do you call thems are very, very clever men. Gerry Adams. And I think he speaks so well. And I've watched him on telly, and no matter who tries to fluster him, or cajole him, or anything, and he sits there, and he's ... so good, and he speaks so well, I think, 'God, he's an educated man'. Er, but I didn't believe in what they were doing. But ... but then there was this programme on the radio saying they're going to pull the troops out. And I, I'm thinking to myself, 'Well that's good'. I mean we d... if that got peace, and er, peace is to have a chance, well why not take them out? And this is what they're doing. They're killing. And I think that's awful. That really is. I really do ... And I was so pleased that they did, Gerry Adams, and Martin McGuinness and all the others came out, and did ... condoned [condemned] what they had done. You know, they said, well, 'We ... we don't belie... we don't want it, and we don't ... it's not us'. But it's part of them, isn't it? But I think there's probably be, always be somebody won't want peace.[66]

Revealing a new dimension to the effects of gender in her account, in Kate's story Gerry Adams appears as an object of projective idealisation, a father figure embodying traits of wisdom, composure and determination. Such idealisation not only evokes a sense of national pride, but helps fortify Kate against personal feelings of powerlessness. 'But', as

Kate reiterates, 'I didn't believe in what they were doing' because 'they're killing'. If in the previous extract the self is envisioned in conflicted dialogue with an accusatory 'they', struggling to justify itself in the glare of a suspicious gaze, it is now caught up in a related conversation about the moral acceptability of political violence, one that complicates Kate's identification with the image of empowered Irishness projected by Gerry Adams. The opposing positions taken up by Kate in the previous extract here appear to be underpinned by tension between a gendered form of identification with an empowering symbol of militant Irishness and the internalised prescriptions of a moral code that prohibits 'killing'.

Kate, who is a devout Catholic, attempts to resolve this tension through investment in the idea of 'peace': she was 'so pleased' when Sinn Fein agreed to 'take the troops out' and 'condemned what they had done' because this potentially enables a backgrounding of their problematic association with violence. In the last instance, however, Kate is unsure about whether these events deliver complete redemption, whether the PIRA can ever be rehabilitated as permissible objects of admiration. Rather, what 'they had done' remains 'part of them'. Investment in 'peace' thus ultimately produces an uncertain closure: 'I think there's probably be, always be somebody won't want peace.'

Nothing but the same old story? Rethinking the Troubles and 'Irish identity' in England

> It is only by understanding the ambivalence and the antagonism of the desire of the Other that we can avoid the increasingly facile adoption of the notion of the homogenised Other.[67]

While migrants tended to recall the post-war decades in positive terms, stressing friendships with English people as the norm, all remembered the Troubles as a period of increased tension, when Irish people came 'under suspicion'. Yet, if the Troubles was remembered collectively as a period of heightened tensions, these tensions were inscribed differently at the level of personal memory production. For Sean, 'coming under suspicion' was remembered in terms of 'embarrassment' and exclusions from familiar local spaces, which constituted important sites of belonging within his narrative. The Troubles thus disrupted a hybrid sense of belonging that incorporated identifications with a particular conservative Catholic Irishness and local community spaces where the majority population was English. The conservative narrative through which Sean understood his experiences provided a means of negotiating this conflict through the way it projected responsibility for divisive events onto the perpetrators of the bomb. Making use of this formulation, Sean sought to disassociate his own Irish identity from the violence of the PIRA, creating the possibility of a realignment between the categories 'English' and 'Irish' through the construction of a shared subject-position of victimisation. An effect of the internalisation of this understanding, which anxiously disavowed comprehension of the PIRA's motivations, however, was that talk of politics was tightly circumscribed: the narrative inculcated a kind of taboo concerning the PIRA, producing a particular kind of silence within Sean's account.

Joe's narrative did not evidence the effects of this particular taboo, in part because he recalled his experiences through two competing constructions simultaneously. By taking up at different points the subject-position provided by a more militant, nationalistic discourse on the Troubles, Joe was able to locate his experiences within a broader political and historical framework, creating possibilities for the contestation of the muting effects of wider English discourses. However, the splitting of 'Irish' and 'English' upon which this performance of self was premised tended to be destabilised at precisely the points where dualities of belonging were tacitly or explicitly recognised. Where Sean's narrative is orientated towards the restoration of harmony between multiple objects of belonging, Joe's sense of belonging is potentially more sharply split, in part because the code of Irishness expressed through the militant narrative is constituted through opposition to ideas of Britishness. This tends to resonate with the splitting effects of anti-Irish stereotypes, entailing that multiple belongings become oppositional and mutually exclusive rather than reconcilable. Hence the more decentred character of Joe's narrative, as he shifts back and forth, to and from discursively split subject-positions without ultimately arriving at a point of closure.

Kate's memory of the bomb both shared features with and differed from Sean's and Joe's narratives. In common with Sean, Kate recalled the aftermath of the bomb as a period when her Irishness rendered her an object of suspicion, creating tensions between English and Irish people in contrast with earlier experiences. In contrast with Sean, but in common with Joe, Kate negotiated this suspicious gaze in two different ways simultaneously, disavowing the PIRA's tactics one moment, rationalising them the next through reference to a nationalist understanding of the conflict in Northern Ireland. Where Kate's narrative diverges most clearly on these different points of commonality with Sean's and Joe's accounts is in relation to the effects of gender. While both Sean and Kate recall the bomb as an experience of coming under suspicion, in Kate's case she is envisioned as enclosed within her home, in the role of protective mother, worrying about the safety of her children and taking steps to preserve it. In this respect, Kate's narrative is suggestive of how the very form and themes of one's experience of being othered could be affected by the way gender regulates one's position within social space, shaping affective relationships with significant others.

Taken together, close analysis of these narratives permits four general observations regarding the significance of the Troubles for understanding Irish experiences in post-war England. Most obviously, all three narratives reveal how the Troubles, or remembrance of the Troubles, brought different parts of the self into contradiction. Memories of the period do not occasion unsettling emotions merely because they recall experiences of hostility and discrimination; rather, the composure of these experiences is complicated by the need to reconcile contradictory forms of belonging, reflecting the ambivalent position of the Irish in post-war society. Migrant recollections of the period are never unmediated representations of lived experience, but embody *performances* of identity, as part of which the past is actively reconstructed and interpreted in order to manage, transform or resolve the contradictions of identification dramatised by the Troubles. This function of memory renders oral narrative a rich source for analysing the subjective impact of the Troubles upon migrants and how they adapt emotionally, but it also cautions against literal readings of personal histories of the period.

Secondly, where there has been a tendency to view migrants as an undifferentiated collective, by activists as well as the state, a historical perspective evidences how interpretations of the Troubles are shaped through the prism of longer personal histories of settlement. The kind of identity conflict the Troubles posed for individuals, and the way they sought to resolve these conflicts through interpretation of the past, depended upon the accretion of a sense of self over the life course, rooted in the particularities of individual settlement trajectories and their personal emotional legacies. As in other contexts, the issue of Irish belongings in England was inseparable from the routine forms of psychic adaption to the migration process: the event of the Troubles further demonstrates how the dialogue between 'here' and 'there' is always mediated by other forms of identification, themselves the outcome of the self's negotiation of conflicts within the everyday contexts of work and family, church and neighbourhood.

Thirdly, attention to the specificity of individual interpretations also reveals how the reconstruction of experience is constantly mediated through an available repertoire of cultural narratives, the formation and circulation of which is inextricably shaped by the wider politics of the Troubles in England. Attention to this politics indicates the limitations of a model of discourse that conceives English responses during the period solely in terms of repression and negation. The point is not that English discourse comprised occasional chinks of visibility, where the truth of Irish victimhood shone through, but that the forms of communal memory through which Irish migrants interpret the Troubles were dynamically *produced* in relation to the complex workings of English discourse. The repressive model here obscures, not only how the Troubles was generative of Irish discourses of identity, but how the ambivalence of English discourse was mirrored in the internal fracturing of Irish communal memory. Irish communal memory of the Troubles thus registers, not uniformity, but the articulation of competing conceptions of ethnicity within the post-war imaginary of the Irish in England: one forged through the lived experience of post-war settlement and shaped by post-war discourses of Irish neo-revivalism, Catholicism, domesticity and affluence, the other associated with second-generation militancy, Northern Republicanism and official conceptions of British multiculturalism.

It follows from this that institutional discourses on 'discrimination', 'invisibility' and 'suspicion' must themselves be understood as shaped and produced within the context of the Troubles, and as forming part of the repertoire of discursive forms available to individuals for self-construction. Tropes such as 'discrimination', 'invisibility' and 'suspicion' do not merely describe Irish people's experience; they are implicated in its construction, creating both silences and spaces from which to speak. In turn, it further follows that the meanings of 'discrimination' have a contingent and relational dimension: the meaning of experiences of othering changes in relation to shifts in collective consciousness of those experiences, as contemporary events reshape communal memories of different phases of settlement. In order to assess the subjective impact of racial discourse it is necessary, therefore, to situate personal understandings of othering within the context of wider shifts in cultural memory, the forms of which shape interpretations of difference, retrospectively and in the present.

Finally, what all these processes – the variegation of communal memory, the differential impact of diverse trajectories of settlement and the plural character of belongings – collectively indicate is the wider complexity of the position of the Irish in post-war England. A case study of the Irish challenges complacent assumptions concerning the homogeneity of 'whiteness' in post-1945 England, revealing not only the historical contingency and internal differentiation of 'whiteness', but the ways in which Irish activists participated in the making of British multiculturalism within the context of the Troubles. Ironically, however, the very emphasis on discrimination and disadvantage this entailed has tended to underplay the complexity of English responses to Irishness and the full spectrum of possibilities for identification this enabled. What these narratives suggest is that, in order to understand how 'whiteness' was experienced from an Irish standpoint, it is necessary to take seriously the major shifts in British identity over the twentieth century, alongside the ambivalent continuities of English perceptions; to consider, that is, the historically changing and individually specific ways discourses of otherness and sameness were implicated *simultaneously* in the production of white Irish subjectivities.

Notes

1. K. Paul, *Whitewashing Britain: Race and Citizenship in the Postwar Era* (New York, 1997), 107–109.
2. E. J. B. Rose et al., *Colour and Citizenship: A Report on British Race Relations* (Oxford, 1969), 19.
3. Brenda Grady (b. Galway, 1927) PI/SA/5, 16.
4. M. Moulton, *Ireland and the Irish in Interwar England* (Cambridge, 2014), 4.
5. Recent interventions include J. Bailkin, *The Afterlife of Empire* (Berkeley, CA, 2012), ch. 6; J. Corbally, 'The Jarring Irish: Postwar Immigration to the Heart of Empire', *Radical History Review* 104 (2009), 103–125; E. Delaney, *The Irish in Post-War Britain* (Oxford, 2007); M. Hickman, 'Reconstructing and Deconstructing "Race": British Political Discourses about the Irish in Britain', *Ethnic and Racial Studies* 21:2 (1998), 296–299; Paul, *Whitewashing Britain*, 107–109; R. Weight, *Patriots: National Identity in Britain 1940–2000* (London, 2002), 141–149.
6. 'The Irish – a Friendly People', *Manchester Guardian*, 16 January 1958; 'Gossip along the Irish Border is not about Guns', *Manchester Guardian*, 19 October 1959; 'Eire Fairy', *Daily Mail*, 15 October 1946; 'Ireland's Castles', *Picture Post*, 8 April 1950; 'Sixty-Six Acres of Stout', *Picture Post*, 22 August 1953.
7. 'Ireland Puts the Clock Back Twenty Years', *Daily Mail*, 16 February 1949.
8. On the longer history of Irish stereotypes in modern Britain see L. P. Curtis, *Apes and Angels: The Irishman in Victorian Caricature* (Washington, DC, 1997); M. de Nie, *The Eternal Paddy: Irish Identity and the British Press, 1798–1882* (Madison, WI, 2004); R. Foster, *Paddy and Mr Punch: Connections in Irish and English History* (London, 1995).
9. 'Anatomy of a Bomb', *Manchester Evening News*, 17 June 1996.
10. D. Sharrock, 'In the Mind of the IRA, a Ceasefire May Represent not a Goal but a Tactical Option', *Guardian*, 17 June 1996; 'What the Papers Say', *Evening Standard*, 17 June 1996; M. Bentham, 'Sinn Fein are Shunned in Wake of the Blast', *Sun*, 17 June 1996; C. Reiss, 'Major Vows: Fight for Peace Goes On', *Evening Standard*, 17 June 1996; W. Rees-Mogg, 'Exploding Their Own Strategy', *The Times*, 17 June 1996.
11. 'Anatomy of a Bomb'.
12. Words from titles and sub-headings in the *Manchester Evening News, Wigan Observer, Stockport Express, Moston Express* and *Middleton and North Manchester Guardian* during the two weeks following the bomb.
13. John Major, Prime Minister, to Derek Shaw, Lord Mayor of Manchester, 21 June 1996, Greater Manchester County Record Office (hereafter GMCRO), GB127.M480/62168 Box 23.
14. Leonard Rose, chairman of Club Thursday, the Jewish Social and Cultural Society, to Derek Shaw, Lord Mayor of Manchester, 18 June 1996, GMCRO, GB127.M480/62168 Box 23.
15. Quoted in 'Beware the Wounded Lion', *Manchester Evening News*, 17 June 1996.
16. D. G. Boyce, *The Irish Question and British Politics 1868–1996* (London, 1996), 9, ch. 4.

17 P. Dixon, '"A Real Stirring in the Nation": Military Families, British Public Opinion, and Withdrawal from Northern Ireland', in G. Dawson, J. Dover and S. Hopkins (eds), *The Northern Ireland Troubles in Britain: Impacts, Engagements, Legacies and Memories* (Manchester, 2017), 41–56.
18 See, for example, P. Rigby, 'I wonder if they knew how many times we've felt like doing the same', *Sun*, 18 July 1972, BCA/22866; P. Rigby, 'Is that the freedom they are fighting for?', *Sun*, 12 March 1971, BCA/19885; Emmwood, 'Stand up all those in favour of sterner measures', *Daily Mail*, 10 August 1971, BCA/ MW2785; JAK, 'With our luck this one probably is Jack Lynch!', *Evening Standard*, 20 August 1971, BCA/20971; Cummings, 'If only the British Army will get out, the IRA will undertake the new political shape of Ireland', *Sunday Express*, 6 February 1972, BCA/21955; Mac, "'S'alright chaps, no more grilling – we're just going to let you de-fuse your own bombs instead', *Daily Mail*, 4 March 1972, BCA/22116.
19 On the broad aims of the PIRA campaign see R. English, *Armed Struggle: The History of the IRA* (London, 2003), ch. 4; G. McGladdery, *The Provisional IRA in England: The Bombing Campaign 1973–1997* (Dublin, 2006), ch. 2. As regards the Manchester bomb, this attack also had more specific tactical objectives, namely to highlight and contest Sinn Fein's exclusion from official talks (203).
20 The most detailed survey of the operation of the PTA remains P. Hillyard, *Suspect Community: People's Experience of the Prevention of Terrorism Acts in Britain* (London, 1993).
21 See, for example, P. Rigby, 'Shure, an' it's time we started showing the British what sort of people we really are!', *Sun*, 1 November 1971, BCA/21346; Emmwood, 'I'm beginning to get suspicious ...', *Daily Mail*, 5 December 1972, BCA/ MW2935; B. Cookson (no caption), *Evening News*, 9 March 1973, BCA/24072.
22 For example, Desmond Lawless to Lord Mayor, 15 June 1996; Mary White to Lord Mayor, 16 June 1996; Tom Campion to Lord Mayor, 19 June 1996, GMCRO, GB127.M480/62168 Box 23. 'MPs Fury as Peace Hopes Dim', *Manchester Evening News*, 15 June 1996.
23 'Why Manchester?', *Manchester Evening News*, 17 June 1996.
24 A. Grimes, 'IRA "Bombed Their Own"', *Manchester Evening News*, 20 June 1996.
25 'Terror Backlash', *Middleton and North Manchester Guardian*, 20 June 1996; '"Sick" Attack on Irish Pub', *Moston Express*, 20 June 1996.
26 Sean Hagan (b. Dublin, 1935) PI/SA/6, 13.
27 Ibid., 32.
28 Ibid., 34.
29 Ibid., 16–17.
30 'Special Edition: Bridge Street Bombing', *Warrington Guardian*, 22 March 1993.
31 'Context: A Quest for Real Peace', *Manchester Evening News*, 13 June 2006.
32 A. Portelli, 'What Makes Oral History Different?', in R. Perks and A. Thomson (eds), *The Oral History Reader*, 2nd edn (London, 2006), 45
33 Sean Hagan (b. Dublin, 1935) PI/SA/6, 34.

34 Details from BBC report, 'Two Soldiers Killed in Northern Ireland', 9 March 2.
35 This narrative crystallised in particular in reactions to the 1936 report of the National Council for Civil Liberties on the Special Powers Act. See *The Special Powers Acts of Northern Ireland: Report of a Commission of Inquiry* (London, 1936), Hull History Centre (hereafter HHC), U DCL/100/4. For the post-war replenishment of this narrative see, for example, G. Bing, *John Bull's Other Island. A Tribune Pamphlet* (London, 1950), HHC, U DCL/55/2, and 'Ulster: The Bomb on our Doorstep', *Daily Herald*, 3 July 1953.
36 See, for example, N. Mansbridge, 'The crooked pillar', *Punch*, 16 October 1968, BCA/14063. This line of interpretation was most prevalent in the *Guardian*, *New Statesman* and *The Times*.
37 Enoch Powell, *Hansard* Deb., 22 November 1974, vol. 881, col. 1677; Ronald Bell, *Hansard* Deb., 22 November 1974, col. 1682.
38 Home Secretary, Roy Jenkins, *Hansard* Deb., 22 November 1974, vol. 881, col. 1673
39 *Moston Express*, 20 June 1996.
40 *Manchester Evening News*, 18 June 1996.
41 Michael Reilly, Chair of the Irish Association Social Club, Chorlton, to Lord Mayor Derek Shaw, 7 July 1996, GMCRO, GB127.M480/62168 Box 23.
42 M. Forde, quoted in, 'IRA "Bombed Their Own"', *Manchester Evening News*, 20 June 1996.
43 'Disapproval', *Irish Post*, 9 February 1974; 'Guildford', *Irish Post*, 12 October 1974; 'Birmingham', *Irish Post*, 30 November 1974.
44 Rory Brady, or Ruairi O Bradaigh, is a prominent Irish republican.
45 Joe Doherty (b. Longford, 1944) PI/SA/3, 2.
46 Ibid., 3.
47 O'Brady, however, taught in Roscommon, not Longford, and was arrested in Cavan. See Robert W. White, *Ruairi O Bradaigh: The Life and Politics of an Irish Revolutionary* (Bloomington, IN, 2006).
48 Although the Unionist regime did engage in gerrymandering of local electoral boundaries, religious discrimination did not in fact exist with respect to the franchise. See J. Whyte, 'How Much Discrimination Was There under the Unionist Regime, 1921–68?', in T. Gallagher and J. O'Connell (eds), *Contemporary Irish Studies* (Manchester, 1983), 1–36.
49 Joe Doherty (b. Longford, 1944) PI/SA/3, 5.
50 *Tom Tom*, November 1975, BCC, Acc/MS 1611/F/7/3/4/1.
51 *An Pobal Eirthe (The Risen People)*, no. 3, February 1989, 5. On the emergence of the IBRG see 'An Excuse for Postponing Effective Action', *Irish Post*, 1 August 1981; 'Now's the Time for Action', *Irish Post*, 5 September 1981; 'In Search of a Political Voice', *Irish Post*, 14 November 1981; 'Irish Must Look to Themselves for Help', *Irish Post*, 14 November 1981.
52 'IBRG Policy on Anti-Irish Racism', *Pobal Eirthe (The Risen People)*, no. 3, February 1989, 4.
53 IBRG, 'Policy Statement on Northern Ireland' (Birmingham, 20 September, 1986), BCC, Acc/MS 1611/F/3.
54 *An Pobal Eirthe (The Risen People)*, no. 3, February 1989, 4.
55 Joe Doherty (b. Longford, 1944) PI/SA/3, 5.

56 C. Elliott, 'Manchester's Irish Brush Off the Verbal Backlash but Feel the Sorrow', *Guardian*, 17 June 1996.
57 Joe Doherty (b. Longford, 1944) PI/SA/3, 15.
58 'Sinn Fein to Address Public Meeting in Manchester', *Manchester Evening News*, 10 April 1997.
59 Quoted in 'Council Chief Condemns Decision to Invite Sinn Fein Councillor to Manchester', *Manchester Evening News*, 11 April 1997.
60 Joe Doherty (b. Longford, 1944) PI/SA/3, 12.
61 Kate Daly (b. Sligo, 1941) PI/SA/2, 36.
62 Ibid., 37.
63 Ibid., 69–70.
64 Ibid., 1.
65 Ibid., 71.
66 Ibid., 72–73.
67 H. Bhabha, *The Location of Culture* (London, 1994), 52.

Conclusion: Myth, memory and minority history

As Mary Midgely reminds us, myths are neither 'lies' nor 'detached stories'. They are, rather, 'imaginative patterns, networks of powerful symbols that suggest particular ways of interpreting the world'.[1] Precisely because of this power, the rhetoric of myth contributes to the enactment of social and cultural boundaries. As Raphael Samuel and Paul Thompson observed of national myths:

> National myths and the sense of national identity which they help build ... raise fundamental questions of just who belongs and who does not. Time and again, in rallying solidarity they also exclude, and persecute the excluded.[2]

The 'ethnic turn' within recent scholarship on the Irish in Britain advances the interrogation of exclusionary myths of British national identity in important ways, contributing to the reimagining of Britain as a multicultural nation. Where the dominance of the imperial/colonial model within British migration studies has tended to reinforce the myth of pre-1945 British cultural homogeneity, scholarship on the Irish in post-war Britain alludes to the continuities of a much longer history of 'multicultural racism'. In so doing, this scholarship broadens understanding of the varieties of British racism, and in the process forces recognition of the silences of the colour paradigm and how these are implicated, not only in the exclusion of white–other experiences, but in the consolidation of wider fantasies of British homogeneity.

Clearly, the need for such recognition remains urgent in contemporary Britain. Since the research for this book began the British people have voted, following a polarising referendum debate, to leave the EU. While the factors which motivated this are complex and varied, racist and xenophobic attitudes were and are integral to the popular consensus established around Britain's perceived need to 'take back control' from outsiders and recover its rightful place in the world. During the long, torturous debate, commentators and the public alike seemed unaware of the parallels with defining moments in recent British immigration history, such as the 1905 Aliens Act or the 1962 Commonwealth Immigrants Act, when the hostile reception of pre-EU waves of migration motivated legislation to restrict inward movement and sharpen national borders. As in these instances, commentators seemed unable or unwilling to expose the mechanisms by which race is mobilised politically in British society. So effective, indeed, were these mechanisms that other factors militating against 'social cohesion', such as long-run deindustrialisation, the erosion of citizenship and the impact of austerity, barely registered as pertinent questions, while prominent Remain supporters appeared incapable of refuting anti-immigration rhetoric, offering migrants' 'contribution' to the NHS and utility to the British economy as counter-arguments within a debate based fundamentally on the question of belonging.

These developments reveal starkly the consequences of a refusal to acknowledge the longer history of racism and xenophobia within British society. As Wendy Ugolini has recently reiterated, a society in denial about the agency of such attitudes in its past is unlikely to recognise their agency in the present.[3] Simultaneously, however, such developments also underscore the need for historical reflexivity concerning the production and processes of 'identity' more generally. Above and beyond the refusal to acknowledge uncomfortable histories, ongoing debates over 'social cohesion' and Britain's post-imperial destiny persistently register a powerful impulse to return to an idealised 'time before'; to recover, as 'protection against various postmodern assaults on the coherence and integrity of the self', an innate and immemorial Britishness conceived as the historical outcome of 'native' social, cultural and political traditions.[4] What such appeals misunderstand or ignore, however, is the fundamental *contingency* of identity formations. As Tony Kushner has argued, politicians and civil servants 'struggling to deal with the complexity of identities' routinely fail to recognise that:

> Englishness or Britishness is imaginary and that it has often been defined, often ambivalently, against the 'other'. The 'self' has been constantly constructed and reconstructed in the form of external national rivals ... through internal minorities ... or a combination of both.[5]

The appeal to an innate and immemorial Britishness is not only forgetful about persecution in the past; it also rests upon a fantasy of continuity and self-sameness over time. How national identity has been constructed differently under different historical conditions is thus screened out of popular consciousness, together with the processes of competition and contestation necessarily involved. In turn, because identity is not conceived as an outcome of historical conditions in the first place, so contemporary 'crises' of identity are not graspable as the outcome of long-run historical processes, the effects of which serve to transform or dissolve the enabling conditions of earlier formations. In the absence of this historical perspective, identity is more easily reified as a 'thing' which must be defended or preserved, a logic which conceives difference as absolute and equates change in the present with a 'loss' of self.

One implication is that appeals to restore 'traditional' values engage in a kind of inverse anachronism, seeking to impose fantasies of identity constructed in the past upon contemporary circumstances formed by fundamentally different historical processes. More fundamentally, myths of continuity and self-sameness over time obscure the fact that societies are engaged in an ongoing process of reformulating identities, fostering a view of change as exceptional and destructive and producing a tendency to read the visible effects of long-run change in the present as causes. From this perspective, the perpetuation of exclusionary processes depends, not only on the denial of persecution in the past, but on refusal of the complexities of *identity construction* over time.

Crucially, however, if such complexity is to be fully recognised these arguments must be applied across the board; not only at the level of national myth, but also at the level of minority histories. The 'invisibility' paradigm contests the exclusions of British national mythology, but it might itself be regarded as a locus of myth; a vector of 'identity history' concerned with the production and dissemination of a 'useable past'.[6] As John Tosh has argued, while 'identity history' has 'helped sustain a vibrant politics of diversity in Britain', increasing the 'pride and confidence of previously marginalised groups', it also tends to underplay the 'moral complexity of the past' because 'so often a single emotional response is demanded'.[7] Above all, identity history

> trades on a spurious identity between 'them' and 'us': 'we' are all signed up to the same struggle, all looking forward to its successful resolution. Ancestors are recruited to a contemporary agenda, whereas *their* identities would be much more faithfully captured by registering the yawning difference between our circumstances and theirs ... Ethnic identity is in reality an indefinite process of movement and mediation, without fixity. Essentialising one's relation to people in the past robs them of their potential to bring today's assumptions and priorities into question.[8]

Minority history, conceived as recovery or commemoration, presents a challenge to the homogenising tendencies inherent in national myth.

At its most incisive, it forces confrontation with submerged histories of persecution, unsettling complacent assumptions about the intrinsic fairness and beneficence of the 'British people'. To the extent, however, that such histories elide the totality of migrant subjectivities, masking the processes by which minority identities are produced and reformulated over time, they potentially consolidate wider tendencies towards reification and ethnic absolutism, affirming the equation of difference/change with loss/absence. Minority and majority identities are interpreted alike through a lens of permanency, possessing historically fixed constituents which obscure the dilemmas of identity formation in the past and the possibilities of difference in the present.

This book has applied Popular Memory Theory to the case of the Irish in an effort to shift attention from reified collectivities towards 'the always unpredictable mechanisms of identification'.[9] Herein, attention to the shifting relationship between cultural myth, the psychology of personal memory and the embodied experience of everyday life demonstrates the inadequacy of a unitary narrative, whether of assimilation or exclusion, as a means of grasping the complexity of the post-1945 Irish migrant experience. Where memory is often regarded as a mechanism of antagonism within the longer history of British–Irish relations, the processes of migrant memory in post-war England illuminate a complex narrative ecology, reflecting the extent to which post-war England formed a hospitable and dynamic discursive environment in which English perceptions and migrant self-understandings shaped each other in diverse and historically changing ways. Memory production registered the enduring importance of the British–Irish political relationship as a context in which British and Irish identities were shaped, but memory did not take the form of a struggle against national forgetting and disavowal, where minority and dominant narratives were locked in a relation of contest and opposition. Instead, the ambivalence of long-run processes of English cultural accommodation, by which migrants were confronted with competing designations under changing historical conditions, contributed to the articulation of multiple and contradictory stories about identity, belonging and difference.

These stories did not resolve themselves into a coherent discourse of Irish identity; rather, they existed in dynamic tension, offering competing ways of interpreting English–Irish relations and the significance of the post-war settlement experience. What the processes of migrant memory here evidence is the complex agency of a dialogic process of self-construction, by which differently situated individuals draw upon and contribute to collective formulations as a means of negotiating the pressures and possibilities of the migration journey. From one angle, these interactions demonstrate how understandings of ethnic selfhood were constantly mediated through wider processes of cultural production and social interaction: the values and ideals manifest in both communal myth and personal narratives of settlement registered the seminal importance of wider post-war social, cultural and economic transformations, in Ireland as well as England, in forming the outlook, aspirations and anxieties of post-war migrants. The workings of migrant memory thus illuminate post-war migration as an important vector of socio-cultural *reciprocity* and *hybridisation* within the development of the British–Irish relationship after 1945.

From another angle, however, all these processes were themselves powerfully structured by the dynamics of emotional adaption: how migrants interacted with available myths was underpinned by ongoing efforts to manage the emotional consequences of migration. Since these consequences were rooted in the particularity of lived relationships and the circumstances of important life events, so they were highly *specific*: individual strategies of memory 'composure', by which migrants endeavoured to reconcile conflictual versions of experience, evolved from distinctive configurations of psychic conflict, differentiating how migrants evaluated the outcomes of settlement and invested in wider narratives of identity and belonging. Since, however, these processes of integration co-articulated with tendencies towards psychic splitting, so composure of the emotional consequences of migration also produced migrant subjectivity as an *internally divided* formation. Migrants' life histories negotiated a tension between personal experience and the norms embedded within public narratives of identity; but these negotiations were themselves refracted through ongoing efforts to compose unresolved tensions between past and present, 'there' and 'here', with the result that 'identity' involved constant vacillation between competing desires, attachments and images of self. Subjective adaption was thus open-ended and incomplete: personal understandings of belonging were intrinsically *ambivalent* and *unstable*, oscillating and evolving over the life course in response to the changing demands of different phases of the settlement process and wider shifts in the configuration of popular memory.

Approached through the lens of Popular Memory Theory, the processes of migrant memory thus form a useful resource for analysing the production, reformation and diversification of migrant subjectivities under changing historical conditions. These processes illuminate how migrant identities are constructed through the negotiation and adaption of historically constituted discourses of race and ethnicity, class and gender, within the societies migrants have left as well as those in which they settle. And they deepen understanding of the dynamic interrelationship between the individual, culture and historical process, revealing layers of complexity in the migrant experience frequently concealed by group-based ontologies and generalising accounts of ethnic relations. In so bringing the 'unpredictable mechanisms of identification' into

Conclusion 225

sharp focus, a critical history of migrant memory thus supplies tools for rethinking the basis of 'identity' and for exploring alternative ontologies. 'Identity' may then serve, less as an ideal or fixed boundary, than as a prism in which we recognise our shared complexity, where we grasp the possibilities of our ever-changing horizons.

Notes

1 M. Midgley, *The Myths We Live By* (London, 2004), 1.
2 R. Samuel and P. Thompson (eds), *The Myths We Live By* (London, 1990), 18–19.
3 W. Ugolini, 'Weaving the Italian Experience into the British Immigration Narrative', in J. Craig-Norton, C. Hoffman and T. Kushner (eds), *Migrant Britain: Histories and Historiographies. Essays in Honour of Colin Holmes* (London, 2018), 123.
4 P. Gilroy, *Postcolonial Melancholia* (New York, 2005), 6.
5 T. Kushner, 'Colin Holmes and the Development of Migrant and Anti-Migrant Historiography', in Craig-Norton et al., *Migrant Britain*, 26.
6 J. Tosh, *Why History Matters* (Basingstoke, 2008), 12.
7 Ibid., 14.
8 Ibid., 15.
9 Gilroy, *Postcolonial Melancholia*, xv.

Appendix: Interviews

All 26 interviews were conducted and transcribed between 2008 and 2017. From this wider sample a core sample of ten interviews (sample A) was then selected for in-depth analysis. Note that pseudonyms are used in sample A interviews.

Project interviews sample A (core sample)

Clare Cullen

Born: 1940, grew up in north Cork
Parents: Mother, housewife; Father, sergeant in Civic Guards
Education: National School until 14, secretarial college
Migration: London 1957, Kent 1960, Cork 196?, Oldham 197?
Post-migration work: Bank
Marriage: 1959, three children
Interview: 04/03/09
Reference: Clare Cullen (b. Cork, 1940) PI/SA/1

Kate Daly

Born: 1941, grew up Co. Sligo
Parents: Mother, housewife; Father, farmer and quarry owner
Education: National School until 14, convent in Roscommon
Migration: Dublin 1959, Manchester 1961
Pre-migration work: Children's nurse
Post-migration work: General nurse, factory line operative, care worker
Marriage: 1964, four children

Interview: 25/03/12
Reference: Kate Daly (b. Sligo, 1941) PI/SA/2

Joe Doherty

Born: 1944, grew up Co. Longford
Parents: Mother, housewife; Father, farmer and thatcher
Education: National School until 14, then local vocational school until 16.
Migration: Birmingham 1962, Manchester 1964
Pre-migration work: Turf cutting
Post-migration work: Factory operative, construction industry
Marriage: 1969, four children
Interview: 27/04/08
Reference: Joe Doherty (b. Longford, 1944) PI/SA/3

Bill Duffy

Born: 1951, grew up Co. Roscommon
Parents: Mother, housewife; Father, farmer
Education: National School until 13
Migration: Manchester 1967
Post-migration work: Construction industry (labourer, site manager, executive)
Marriage: 1975, three children
Interview: 13/03/12
Reference: Bill Duffy (b. Roscommon, 1951) PI/SA/4

Brenda Grady

Born: 1927, grew up Co. Galway
Parents: Mother, housewife; Father, farmer
Education: National School until 14
Migration: Lymme1946, Manchester 1947
Pre-migration work: Domestic servant
Post-migration work: Domestic servant, receptionist, housewife, dinner-lady
Marriage: 1949, six children
Interview: 14/04/08
Reference: Brenda Grady (b. Galway, 1927) PI/SA/5

Sean Hagan

Born: 1935, grew up Co. Offaly

Parents: Mother, housewife; Father, rural labourer
Education: National School until 12
Migration: Bolton 1956
Pre-migration work: Turf cutting, beet picking, road worker, Irish army
Post-migration work: Cotton mill (warehouse), construction (labourer), night watchman
Marriage: 1957, six children
Interview: 18/02/09
Reference: Sean Hagan (b. Dublin, 1935) PI/SA/6

Denis Heaney

Born: 1927, grew up Co. Kerry
Parents: Mother, housewife; Father, farmer
Education: National School until 14
Migration: London 1948, various locations in the south-east 1948–1956, Leigh 1956, Stockport 1958, Manchester 1993
Pre-migration work: Turf cutting
Post-migration work: Foundry, construction (labourer, subcontractor)
Marriage: 1952, two children
Interview: 20/03/10
Reference: Denis Heaney (b. Kerry, 1927) PI/SA/7

Rosie Long

Born: 1938, grew up in Cork City
Parents: Mother, orderly at mental asylum, orderly at school for the blind; Father, left family
Education: Girls convent until 14
Migration: London 1954, Oldham 1966
Pre-migration work: Hospital orderly, orderly at school for the blind
Post-migration work: Domestic servant, food server, care worker
Marriage: 1960, two children, plus four children from a second relationship
Interview: 11/02/09
Reference: Rosie Long (b. Cork, 1938) PI/SA/8

Paul Quinn

Born: 1938, grew up in Galway
Parents: Mother, housewife; Father, farmer
Education: National School until 13
Migration: Manchester 1962, London 1970
Pre-migration work: Farm labourer, building

Post-migration work: Construction industry
Marriage: 1975, three children
Interview: 27/05/13
Reference: Paul Quinn (b. Galway, 1938) PI/SA/9

Aileen Walsh

Born: 1927, grew up in Mayo
Parents: Mother, housewife; Father, farmer
Education: National School until 14
Migration: Doncaster 1945, Bradford 1947, Manchester 1949
Pre-migration work: Domestic
Post-migration work: Hotel maid, factory operative, waitress
Marriage: 1950, three children
Interview: 20/7/2012
Reference: Aileen Walsh (b. Mayo, 1929) PI/SA/10

Project interviews sample B (wider sample)

James Devlin (b. Kerry, 1940), interview 02/02/2010, PI/SB/1
Tony McCabe (b. Cork, 1938), interview 22/03/2009, PI/SB/2
Terry Langan (b. Longford, 1938), interview 04/05/2014, PI/SB/3
Mary Canavan (b. Sligo, 1941), interview 12/02/2013, PI/SB/4
Joseph Rooney (b. Dublin, 1950), interview 25/07/2015, PI/SB/5
Anna Kelly (b. Kerry, 1941), interview 23/07/2015, PI/SB/6
Bridget Mulvey (b. Mayo, 1939), interview 14/05/2014, PI/SB/7
Michael Walsh (b. Clare, 1946), interview 02/09/2010, PI/SB/8
Joan Kernan (b. Roscommon, 1950), interview 07/08/2014, PI/SB/9
Patrick Kernan (b. Roscommon, 1948), interview 07/08/2014, PI/SB/10
Mary McGovern (b. Sligo, 1941), interview 04/03/2014, PI/SB/11
Maeve Maher (b. Leitrim, 1938), interview 07/06/2010, PI/SB/12
Rachel O'Hare (b. Limerick, 1940), interview 09/06/2010, PI/SB/13
Donal Murtagh (b. Kerry, 1946), interview 03/11/2015, PI/SB/14
Patrick O'Dowd (b. Galway, 1941), interview 02/02/2010, PI/SB/15
Patricia Foley (b. Roscommon, 1929), interview 15/10/2009, PI/SB/16

Select bibliography

Archival collections

Ahmed Iqbal Ullah Race Relations Resource Centre, Manchester

Irish in the UK Papers

Archive of the Irish in Britain, London

Birmingham Irish Community Forum
Brent Irish Advisory Service
Greater London Council and Irish Community
Irish Chaplaincy in Britain
Irish County Associations
Irish Studies in Britain Magazine
Leeds Irish Health and Homes
London Irish Centre
London Irish Women's Centre
An Teach Irish Housing Association
Troops Out Movement

Birmingham Archdiocesan Archive

Williams Papers

Birmingham City Archives

Banner Theatre Collection
Irish Community Collection

Select bibliography 231

Breandan MacLua Archive, Liverpool

Irish Post Collection
The Bell Collection

British Cartoon Archive, University of Kent, Canterbury

BCA/MC1019, M. Cummings, 'Begorrah – can't have you fearful English living with us ..', Sunday Express, 16 November 1961
BCA/03673, Joseph Lee, 'Sure an' it's himself ..', Evening News, 26 June 1963
BCA/18222, Stanley Franklin, 'Sure, and I hope you're not tinking o' saying no to us, m'darlin', Daily Mirror, 2 May 1967
BCA/12466, David Langton, 'Sure and the local pubs here'll be bearing the brunt of it, Paddy ..', Sunday Mirror, 10 December 1967
BCA/12530, George Smith, 'That's the first break we've had since the breathanalyser', Evening Standard, 19 December 1967
BCA/1299, Osbert Lancaster, 'Sure, and how could Oi be ann immigrant, me not possessing a British passport', Daily Express, 26 February 1968
BCA/14063, Norman Mansbridge, 'The crooked pillar', Punch, 16 October 1968
BCA/16161, JAK, 'Bloody foreigners', Evening Standard, 26 August 1969
BCA/19885, Paul Rigby, 'Is that the freedom they are fighting us for?', Sun, 12 March 1971
BCA/MW2785, Emmwood, 'Stand up all those in favour of sterner measures', Daily Mail, 10 August 1971
BCA/20971, JAK, 'With our luck this one probably is Jack Lynch!', Evening Standard, 20 August 1971
BCA/21346, Paul Rigby, 'Shure, an' it's time we started showing the British what sort of people we really are!', Sun, 1 November 1971
BCA/21955, Cummings, 'If only the British Army will get out, the IRA will undertake the new political shape of Ireland', Sunday Express, 6 February 1972
BCA/22116, Mac, "S'alright chaps, no more grilling – we're just going to let you de-fuse your own bombs instead', Daily Mail, 4 March 1972
BCA/22866, Paul Rigby, 'I wonder if they knew how many times ...' Sun, 18 July 1972
BCA/ MW2935, Emmwood, 'I'm beginning to get suspicious ...', Daily Mail, 5 December 1972
BCA/24072, B. Cookson (no caption), Evening News, 9 March 1973
BCA/03673, Les Gibbard, 'When Irish eyes are smiling', Guardian, 9 March 1973

Dublin Diocesan Archives

McQuaid Papers

Hull History Centre

Records of the National Council for Civil Liberties

232 Select bibliography

London Metropolitan Archives
London Strategic Policy Unit Collection

Greater Manchester County Record Office, Manchester
Manchester Bomb Collection

National Archives, Kew
Home Office Papers

National Archives of Ireland, Dublin
Department of the Taoiseach

Salford Diocesan Archives, Manchester
Marshall Papers

Autobiographies, diaries and memoirs

Böll, H. *Irish Journal* (Evanston, IL, 1957).
Campbell, P. *Tunnel Tigers* (Jersey City, NJ, 2000).
Foley, D. *Three Villages* (Waterford, 2003).
Healy, J. *The Grass Arena* (London, 1988).
Healy, J. *No One Shouted Stop! The Death of an Irish Town* (Achill, 1968).
Keane, J. B. *Self-Portrait* (Cork, 1969).
Keaney, B. *Don't Hang About* (Oxford, 1985).
Kerrigan, G. *Another Country: Growing Up in '50s Ireland* (Dublin, 1998).
Lally, M. *Memoirs of a Mayo Immigrant* (Aberdeenshire, 2006).
MacAmhlaigh, D. *An Irish Navvy: The Diary of an Exile* (London, 1964).
McGahern, J. *Memoir* (London, 2005).
MacGill, P. *Children of the Dead End* (Edinburgh, 1914, 1999).
Mangan, A. M. *Me and Mine: A Warm-Hearted Memoir of a London Irish Family* (London, 2011).
O'Brian, G. *Out of Our Minds* (Belfast, 1994).
Ó Ciaráin, S. *Farewell to Mayo: An Emigrant's Memoirs of Ireland and Scotland* (Dublin, 1991).
O'Donoghue, J. *In a Strange Land* (London, 1958).
Phelan, J. *We Follow the Roads* (London, 1949).
Power, R. *Apple on the Treetop* (Dublin, 1980).
Roberts, R. *The Classic Slum: Salford Life in the First Quarter of the Century* (London, 1971).

Commemorative and community history projects

Birmingham Irish Association. *We Built this City: In Our Own Words*, No Fuss Productions, 2017.
Chinn, Carl. *Birmingham Irish: Making Our Mark* (Birmingham, 2003).
Coventry Irish Society. *Irish Heart, Coventry Home*, dir. Ciaran Davis, 2018.
Cowley, Ultan. *McAlpine's Men: Irish Stories from the Sites* (Duncormick, Co. Wexford, 2010).
Cowley, Ultan. *The Men Who Built Britain: A History of the Irish Navvy* (Duncormick, Co. Wexford, 2011).
Ethnic Communities Oral History Project. *Caoin na Gael: The Hammersmith Irish Reminiscence Group* (London, 2000).
Garcia, Mike. *Rebuilding London: Irish Migrants in Post-war Britain* (Dublin, 2015).
Harrison, Gerry. *The Scattering: A History of the London Irish Centre, 1954–2004* (London, 2004).
Irish Arts Foundation. *A Place Called Home: The Untold Stories of the Irish in Leeds*, dir. Patricia Doherty, 2017.
Irish Elders Now Project. *I Only Came Over for a Couple of Years*, dir. David Kelly, 2005.
Irish in Britain. *Irish Voices*, dir. Siobhan O'Neill and Carl Stevenson, 2013.
Keegan, Alan. *Irish Manchester* (Stroud, 2004).
Keegan, Alan and Claffey, Danny. *More Irish Manchester* (Stroud, 2006).
Keegan, Alan and Claffey, Danny. *Irish Manchester Revisited* (Stroud, 2013).
Luton Irish Forum. *Catching the Boat*, 2013, https://catchingtheboat.squarespace.com.

Newspapers and periodicals

The Bell
Blackfriars
Christus Rex
Connacht Tribune
Construction News
Daily Express
Daily Mail
Daily Mirror
Donegal News
Dublin Opinion
Evening Herald
Evening News
Evening Standard
Evening Standard Magazine
The Furrow
Guardian

234   Select bibliography

Irish Examiner
Irish Independent
Irish Monthly
Irish Post
Irish Press
Irish Studies in Britain
Irish Times
Manchester Evening News
Middleton and North Manchester Guardian
Moston Express
Munster Express
New Statesman
An Pobal Eirithe
Sligo Champion
Southern Star
Stockport Express
Sun
Sunday Express
Sunday Mirror
Sunday Times
Studies
The Times
Tom Tom
Troops Out of Ireland
Tuam Herald
Warrington Guardian
Wigan Observer

Official publications and reports

Bunreacht na hEireann (The Constitution of Ireland) (Dublin, 1980).
Commission on Emigration and Other Population Problems. *Reports* (Dublin [1955]).
Dáil Éireann Debates, 1945–1965.
Ethnic Minority Groups in Manchester (City Planning Department, 1984).
Hansard, *Parliamentary Debates*, House of Commons, vol. 881, November 1974.
Hickman, M. J. and Walter, B. *Discrimination and the Irish Community in Britain: A Report of Research Undertaken for the Commission for Racial Equality* (London, 1997).
Labour Party. *Towards a United Ireland. Reform and Harmonisation: A Dual Strategy for Irish Unification* (London, 1988).
London Strategic Policy Unit. *Policy Report on the Irish Community* (London, 1984).
Mass Observation. *The Journey Home: A Mass-Observation Report on the Problems of Demobilisation* (London, 1944).

Parliamentary Papers. *Economic Survey for 1947*, Cmd 7046 (London, 1947).
Parliamentary Papers. *Report of the Committee of Inquiry Under Prof. E. H. Phelps-Brown into Certain Matters Concerning Labour in Building and Civil Engineering*, Cmnd 3714-I (London, 1968).

Film, television and documentaries

Arise, You Gallant Sweeneys!, dir. Ian Nesbitt, Outside Films, 2010.
The Comedians, ITV, Granada, 1971–1993.
Fawlty Towers, BBC2, 1975–1979.
I Only Came Over for a Couple of Years, dir. David Kelly, 2005.
In the Name of the Father, dir. Jim Sheridan, 1993, UK, Hell's Kitchen Films.
Irish Heart, Coventry Home, dir. Ciaran Davis, 2018.
Irish Voices, dir. Siobhan O'Neill and Carl Stevenson, 2013.
The Irishmen: An Impression of Exile, dir. Philip Donnellan. BBC, 1965.
Kings, dir. Bill Collins, Newgrange/Irish Film Board, 2007.
The Men of Arlington, dir. Enda Hughes, BBC1 Northern Ireland, 24 October 2011.
Only Fools and Horses, BBC1, 1981–1991.
A Place Called Home: The Untold Stories of the Irish in Leeds, dir. Patricia Doherty, 2017.
Prime Time: Ireland's Forgotten Generation, RTE1, 22 December 2003.
We Built this City: In Our Own Words, No Fuss Productions, 2017.

Mid-twentieth-century social surveys and social commentary

Arensberg, C. *The Irish Countryman* (New York, 1937).
Arensberg, C. and Kimball, S. T. *Family and Community in Ireland* (Cambridge, MA, 1968).
Brody, H. *Inishkillane: Change and Decline in the West of Ireland* (London, 1973).
Colclough, J. R. *The Construction Industry of Great Britain* (London, 1965).
Hickey, J. *The Irish Rural Immigrant and British Urban Society* (London, 1960).
Hickey, J. *Urban Catholics: Urban Catholicism in England and Wales from 1829 to the Present Day* (London, 1967).
Jackson, J. A. *The Irish in Britain* (London, 1963).
O'Brien, J. (ed.), *The Vanishing Irish* (London, 1954).
Rex, J. and Moore, R. *Race, Community and Conflict: A Study of Sparkbrook* (London, 1967).
Rose, E. J. B. et al. *Colour and Citizenship: A Report on British Race Relations* (Oxford, 1969).
Russell, M. 'The Irish Delinquent in England', *Studies: An Irish Quarterly Review* 53:210 (1964), 129–141.
Sykes, A. J. 'Navvies: Their Work Attitudes', *Sociology* 3:1 (1969), 21–35.
Sykes, A. J. 'Navvies: Their Social Relations', *Sociology* 3:2 (1969), 157–172.

Published academic books and articles (post-1970)

Abrams, L. *Oral History Theory* (London, 2010).
Akenson, D. H. *The Irish Diaspora: A Primer* (Belfast, 1993).
Austin, T. 'The Lump in the Construction Industry', in T. Nicholas (ed.), *Capital and Labour: A Marxist Primer* (London, 1980), 76–98.
Ayers, P. 'The Making of Men: Masculinities in Interwar Liverpool', in M. Walsh (ed.), *Working Out Gender: Perspectives from Labour History* (Aldershot, 1999), 66–83.
Ayers, P. 'Work, Culture and Gender: The Making of Masculinities in Post-War Liverpool', *Labour History Review* 69:2 (2004), 153–167.
Bailkin, J. 'Leaving Home: The Politics of Deportation in Postwar Britain', *Journal of British Studies* 47:4 (2008), 852–882.
Beale, J. *Women in Ireland: Voices of Change* (London, 1986).
Beaumont, C. 'Women, Citizenship and Catholicism in the Irish Free State: 1922–48', *Women's History Review* 6:4 (1997), 563–585.
Bhabba, H. K. *The Location of Culture* (London and New York, 1994).
Bourdieu, P. *Distinction: A Social Critique of the Judgement of Taste* (London, 1979).
Bourdieu, P. *The Logic of Practice* (Cambridge, 1990).
Boyce, D. G. *The Irish Question and British Politics 1868–1996* (London, 1996).
Bracken, P. J. and O'Sullivan, P. 'The Invisibility of Irish Migrants in British Health Research', *Irish Studies Review* 9:1 (2001), 41–51.
Breen-Smyth, M. 'Theorising the "Suspect Community": Counterterrorism, Security Practices and the Public Imagination', *Critical Studies on Terrorism* 7:2 (2014), 223–240.
Brown, C. *The Death of Christian Britain: Understanding Secularisation, 1800–2000* (Cambridge, 2001).
Brown, C. 'Secularization, the Growth of Militancy and the Spiritual Revolution: Religious Change and Gender Power in Britain 1901–2001', *Historical Research* 80:209 (2007), 393–418.
Brown, C. 'Sex, Religion and the Single Woman c.1950–1975: The Importance of a 'Short' Sexual Revolution to the English Religious Crisis of the Sixties', *Twentieth Century British History* 22:2 (2011), 189–215.
Brubaker, R. and Cooper, F. 'Beyond "Identity"', *Theory and Society* 29:1 (2000), 1–47.
Buckley, M. 'Sitting on Your Politics: The Irish among the British and the Women among the Irish', in J. MacLaughlin (ed.), *Location and Dislocation in Contemporary Irish Society: Emigration and Irish Identities* (Cork, 1997), 94–133.
Busteed, M. *The Irish in Manchester c. 1750–1921: Resistance, Adaption and Identity* (Manchester, 2016).
Butler, J. *Gender Trouble: Feminism and the Subversion of Identity* (London, 1990).
Canavan, B. 'Story-Tellers and Writers: Irish Identity in Emigrant Labourers' Autobiographies, 1870–1970', in P. O'Sullivan (ed.), *The Irish World Wide: History, Heritage, Identity*, vol. 3: *The Creative Migrant* (London and New York, 1995), 154–169.
Chamberlain, M. 'Gender and the Narratives of Migration', *History Workshop Journal* 43 (1997), 87–108.

Chambers, I. *Migrancy, Culture, Identity* (London, 1994).
Clear, C. 'Too Fond of Going: Female Emigration and Change for Women in Ireland, 1946–1961', in D. Keogh, F. O'Shea and C. Quinlan (eds), *The Lost Decade: Ireland in the 1950s* (Cork, 2004), 142–156.
Collinson, D. and Hearn, J. '"Men" at "Work": Multiple Masculinities in Multiple Workplaces', in M. Mac an Ghaill (ed.), *Understanding Masculinities: Social Relations and Cultural Arenas* (London, 1996), 61–76.
Coogan, T. P. *Wherever Green is Worn: The Story of the Irish Diaspora* (London, 2000).
Corbally, J. 'The Jarring Irish: Post-War Immigration to the Heart of Empire', *Radical History Review* 104 (2009), 103–125.
Curtis, L. *Ireland: The Propaganda War* (London, 1984).
Curtis, L. *Nothing but the Same Old Story: The Roots of Anti-Irish Racism* (London, 1984).
Curtis, L. P. *Anglo-Saxons and Celts: A Study of Anti-Irish Prejudice in Victorian England* (Newton Abbot, 1971).
Curtis, L. P. *Apes and Angels: The Irishman in Victorian Caricature* (Washington, DC, 1997).
Daly, M. *The Slow Failure: Population Decline and Independent Ireland, 1920–73* (Madison, WI, 2006).
Daniels, M. 'Exile or Opportunity? Irish Nurses and Wirral Midwives', *Irish Studies Review* 2:5 (1993), 3–21.
Davies, A. *Leisure, Gender and Poverty: Working-Class Culture in Salford and Manchester, 1900–1939* (Buckingham, 1992).
Davis, G. *The Irish in Britain: 1815–1914* (Dublin, 1991).
Dawson, G. *Soldier Heroes: British Adventure, Empire and the Imagining of Masculinities* (London, 1994).
Delaney, E. 'State, Politics and Demography: The Case of Irish Emigration, 1921–71', *Irish Political Studies* 13:1 (1998), 25–49.
Delaney, E. *Demography, State and Society* (Liverpool, 2000).
Delaney, E. *The Irish in Post-War Britain* (Oxford, 2007).
de Nie, M. *The Eternal Paddy: Irish Identity and the British Press, 1798–1882* (Madison, WI, 2004).
Dixon, P. 'Britain's "Vietnam Syndrome"? Public Opinion and British Military Intervention from Palestine to Yugoslavia', *Review of International Studies* 26:1 (2000), 99–121.
Dixon, P. '"A Real Stirring in the Nation": Military Families, British Public Opinion, and Withdrawal from Northern Ireland', in G. Dawson, J. Dover and S. Hopkins (eds), *The Northern Ireland Troubles in Britain: Impacts, Engagements, Legacies and Memories* (Manchester, 2017), 41–56.
Dunne, C. *An Unconsidered People: The Irish in London* (Dublin, 2003).
Earner-Byrne, L. 'The Boat to England: An Analysis of the Official Reactions to the Emigration of Single Expectant Irishwomen to Britain, 1922–1972', *Irish Economic and Social History* 30 (2003), 52–70.
English, R. *Armed Struggle: The History of the IRA* (London, 2003).
Ewart, H. '"Coventry Irish": Community, Class, Culture and Narrative in the Formation of a Migrant Identity, 1940–1970', *Midland History* 36:2 (2011), 225–244.

Ewart, H. *Caring for Migrants: Policy Responses to Irish Migration to England, 1940–1972* (Liverpool, 2017).
Ferriter, D. *The Transformation of Ireland: 1900–2000* (London, 2004).
Fielding, S. *Class and Ethnicity: Irish Catholics in England, 1880–1939* (Buckingham, 1993).
Finn, T. *Tuarim: Intellectual Debate and Policy Formulation in Ireland, 1954–1975* (Manchester, 2012).
Finnegan, F. E. *Poverty and Prejudice: A Study of Irish Immigrants in York, 1840–1875* (Cork, 1982).
Fitzgerald, P. and Lambkin, B. *Migration in Irish History, 1607–2007* (Basingstoke, 2008).
Fitzpatrick, D. *Irish Emigration 1801–1921* (Dublin, 1984).
Fitzpatrick, D. 'A Curious Middle Place: The Irish in Britain, 1871–1921', in R. Swift and S. Gilley (eds), *The Irish in Britain, 1815–1939* (London, 1989), 10–59.
Foster, R. F. *Modern Ireland: 1600–1972* (London, 1989).
Foster, R. F. *Paddy and Mr Punch: Connections in Irish and English History* (London, 1995).
Foucault, M. 'Nietzsche, Genealogy, History', in P. Rabinow (ed.), *The Foucault Reader* (London, 1991), 76–100.
Foucault, M. *The Will to Knowledge: The History of Sexuality*, vol. 1 (London, 1998).
Francis, M. 'A Flight from Commitment? Domesticity, Adventure and the Masculine Imaginary in Britain after the Second World War', *Gender and History* 19:1 (2007), 163–185.
Fuller, L. *Irish Catholicism since 1950: The Undoing of a Culture* (Dublin, 2002).
Gabriel, Y. 'Narrative Ecologies and the Role of Counter-Narratives: The Case of Nostalgic Stories and Conspiracy', in S. Frandsen, T. Kuhn and M. Lundholt (eds), *Counter-Narratives and Organization* (London, 2016), 208–225.
Garrett, P. M. 'The Abnormal Flight: The Migration and Repatriation of Irish Unmarried Mothers', *Social History* 25:3 (2000), 330–343.
Garvin, T. *Preventing the Future: Why Was Ireland So Poor for So Long?* (London, 2004).
Giles, J. *The Parlour and the Suburb: Domestic Identities, Class, Femininity and Modernity* (Oxford, 2004).
Gilley, S. 'English Attitudes to the Irish Minority in England, 1789–1900', in C. Holmes (ed.), *Immigrants and Minorities in British Society* (London, 1978), 81–110.
Gilroy, P. *There Ain't No Black in the Union Jack: The Cultural Politics of Race and Nation* (London, 1987).
Girvin, B. 'Church, State and Society in Ireland sine 1960', *Eire-Ireland* 43:1 (2008), 74–98.
Girvin, B. 'Contraception, Moral Panic and Social Change in Ireland, 1969–79', *Irish Political Studies* 23:4 (2008), 555–576
Glynn, S. 'Irish Immigration to Britain, 1911–1951: Patterns and Policy', *Irish Economic and Social History* 8 (1981), 50–68.
Goulbourne, H. *Ethnicity and Nationalism in Post-Imperial Britain* (Cambridge, 1991).
Goulbourne, H. *Race Relations in Britain since 1945* (London, 1998).

Gray, B. 'From "Ethnicity" to "Diaspora": 1980s Emigration and "Multicultural" London', in A. Bielenberg (ed.), *The Irish Diaspora* (Harlow, 2000), 65–88.

Gray, B. 'Breaking the Silence: Emigration, Gender and the Making of Irish Cultural Memory', in L. Harte (ed.), *Modern Irish Autobiography* (New York, 2007), 111–131.

Green, A. 'Individual Remembering and "Collective Memory": Theoretical Presuppositions and Contemporary Debates', *Oral History* 32:2 (2004), 35–44.

Green, N. 'The Politics of Exit: Reversing the Immigration Paradigm', *Journal of Modern History* 77 (2005), 263–289.

Green, N. 'Time and the Study of Assimilation', *Rethinking History* 10:2 (2006), 239–258.

Greenslade, L., Pearson, M. and Madden, M. *Generations of an Invisible Minority: The Health and Well-Being of the Irish in Britain* (Liverpool, 1991).

Hall, S. 'Introduction: Who Needs "Identity"?', in S. Hall and P. du Gay (eds), *Questions of Cultural Identity* (London, 1996), 1–17.

Harris, A. *Faith in the Family: A Lived Religious history of English Catholicism 1945–82* (Manchester, 2013)

Harris, C. 'The Family in Post-War Britain', in J. Obelkevich and P. Catterall (eds), *Understanding Post-War British Society* (London, 1994), 45–57.

Harte, L. 'Migrancy, Performativity and Autobiographical Identity', *Irish Studies Review* 14:2 (2006), 225–238.

Harte, L. '"Loss, Return and Restitution": Autobiography and Irish Diasporic Subjectivity', in L. Harte (ed.), *Modern Irish Autobiography* (New York, 2007), 91–110.

Hickman, M. J. *Religion, Class and Identity* (Aldershot, 1995).

Hickman, M.J. 'Incorporating and Denationalising the Irish in England: The Role of the Catholic Church', in P. O'Sullivan (ed.), *The Irish World Wide: History, Heritage, Identity*, vol. 5: *Religion and Identity* (London and New York, 1996), 196–216.

Hickman, M. J. 'Reconstructing and Deconstructing "Race": British Political Discourses about the Irish in Britain', *Ethnic and Racial Studies* 21:2 (1998), 288–307.

Hickman, M. J. 'Alternative Historiographies of the Irish in Britain: A Critique of the Segregation/Assimilation Model', in R. Swift and S. Gilley (eds), *The Irish in Victorian Britain: The Local Dimension* (Dublin, 1999), 236–253.

Hickman, M. J., Thomas, L., Nickels, H. and Silvestri, S. 'De/Constructing "Suspect Communities": A Critical Discourse Analysis of British Newspaper Coverage of Irish Communities and Muslim Communities', *Journalism Studies* 13:3 (2012), 340–355.

Hickman, M. J. and Walter, B. 'Deconstructing Whiteness: Irish Women in Britain', *Feminist Review* 50 (1995), 5–16.

Hillyard, P. *Suspect Community: People's Experience of the Prevention of Terrorism Acts in Britain* (London, 1993).

Hoffman, C. 'Community History', in J. Craig-Norton, C. Hoffman and T. Kushner (eds), *Migrant Britain: Histories and Historiographies. Essays in Honour of Colin Holmes* (London, 2018), 103–105.

Holohan, A. *Working Lives: The Irish in Britain* (Hayes, Middlesex, 1995).

Hornsby-Smith, M. P. *Roman Catholics in England: Studies in Social Structure since the Second World War* (Cambridge, 1987).
Hornsby-Smith, M. P. and Dale, A. 'The Assimilation of Irish Immigrants in England', *British Journal of Sociology* 39:4 (1988), 519–544.
Howard, K. 'Constructing the Irish of Britain: Ethnic Recognition and the 2001 UK Census', *Ethnic and Racial Studies* 29:1 (2006), 104–123.
Hutchinson, J. and O'Day, A. 'The Gaelic Revival in London, 1900–22: The Limits of Ethnic Identity', in R. Swift and S. Gilley (eds), *The Irish in Victorian Britain: The Local Dimension* (Dublin, 1999), 254–276.
Inglis, T. *Moral Monopoly: The Catholic Church in Modern Irish History* (Dublin, 1993).
James, D. *Dona Maria's Story: Life History, Memory and Political Identity* (Durham, NC and London, 2000).
Jenkins, R. *Rethinking Ethnicity: Arguments and Explorations* (London, 1997).
Johnston, R. and McIvor, A. 'Dangerous Work, Hard Men and Broken Bodies: Masculinity in the Clydeside Heavy Industries: c. 1930–1970s', *Labour History Review* 69:2 (2004), 135–151.
Johnstone, R. 'What Is Cultural Studies Anyway?', *Social Text* 16 (Winter 1986–1987), 38–80.
Keating, J. 'Faith and Community Threatened? Roman Catholic Responses to the Welfare State, Materialism, and Social Mobility, 1945–62', *Twentieth Century British History* 9:1 (1998), 86–108.
Kennedy, P. *Welcoming the Stranger: Irish Migrant Welfare in Britain since 1957* (Dublin, 2015).
Kidd, A. *Manchester: A History* (Edinburgh, 2002).
King, L. *Family Men: Fatherhood and Masculinity in Britain, 1914–1960* (Oxford, 2015).
Kirk, J. and Wall, C. *Work and Identity: Historical and Cultural Contexts* (Basingstoke, 2011).
Kushner, T. *The Battle of Britishness: Migrant Journeys, 1685 to the Present* (Manchester, 2012).
Kushner, T. 'Colin Holmes and the Development of Migrant and Anti-Migrant Historiography', in J. Craig-Norton, C. Hoffman and T. Kushner (eds), *Migrant Britain: Histories and Historiographies. Essays in Honour of Colin Holmes* (London, 2018), 22–32.
Lambert, S. *Irish Women in Lancashire, 1922–1960: Their Story* (Lancaster, 2001).
Lambert, S. 'Irish Women's Emigration to England, 1922–60: The Lengthening of Family Ties', in A. Hayes and D. Urquhart (eds), *Irish Women's History* (Dublin, 2004), 153–167.
Langhamer, C. *Women's Leisure in England: 1920–60* (Manchester, 2000).
Langhamer, C. 'The Meaning of Home in Postwar Britain', *Journal of Contemporary History* 40:2 (2005), 341–362.
Langhamer, C. *The English in Love: The Intimate Story of an Emotional Revolution* (Oxford, 2013).
Layton-Henry, Z. *The Politics of Immigration: Immigration, 'Race' and 'Race Relations' in Post-War Britain* (Oxford, 1992).
Lelourec, L. 'Responding to the IRA Bombing Campaign in Mainland Britain: The Case of Warrington', in G. Dawson, J. Dover and S. Hopkins (eds), *The Northern*

Ireland Troubles in Britain: Impacts, Engagements, Legacies and Memories (Manchester, 2017), 263–278.

Lennon, M., McAdam, M. and O'Brien, J. *Across the Water: Irish Women's Lives in Britain* (London, 1988).

Lynch, A. (ed.), *The Irish in Exile: Stories of Emigration* (London, 1988).

Mac an Ghaill, M. 'The Irish in Britain: The Invisibility of Ethnicity and Ethnicity and Anti-Irish Racism', *Journal of Ethnic and Migration Studies* 26:1 (2000), 137–147.

Mac an Ghaill, M. 'British Critical Theorists: The Production of the Conceptual Invisibility of the Irish Diaspora', *Social Identities* 7:2 (2001), 179–201.

MacRaild, D. 'Irish Immigration and the "Condition of England" Question: The Roots of an Historiographical Tradition', *Immigrants and Minorities* 14:1 (1995), 67–85.

MacRaild, D. *The Irish Diaspora in Britain, 1750–1939* (London, 2011), 80–88.

McGladdery, G. *The Provisional IRA in England: The Bombing Campaign 1973–1997* (Dublin, 2006).

McGuire, C., Clarke, L. and Wall, C. 'Battles on the Barbican: The Struggle for Trade Unionism in the British Building Industry, 1965–67', *History Workshop Journal* 75 (2013), 38–39.

McLaughlin, G. and Baker, S. *The Propaganda of Peace: The Role of Media and Culture in the Northern Ireland Peace Process* (Bristol, 2010).

Meaney, G., O'Dowd, M. and Whelan, B. *Reading the Irish Woman: Studies in Cultural Encounter and Exchange, 1714–1960* (Oxford, 2013).

Midgley, M. *The Myths We Live By* (London, 2004).

Miller, D. *Don't Mention the War: Northern Ireland, Propaganda and the Media* (London, 1994).

Miller, K. A. *Emigrants and Exiles: Ireland and the Irish Exodus to North America* (New York, 1985).

Miller, K. A, 'Emigration, Ideology and Identity in Post-Famine Ireland', *Studies: An Irish Quarterly Review* 75:300 (1986), 515–527.

Miller, K. A. *Ireland and Irish America. Culture, Class, and Transatlantic Migration* (Dublin, 2008).

Moran, J. *Irish Birmingham: A History* (Liverpool, 2010).

Morgan, D. *Discovering Men: Critical Studies on Men and Masculinity* (London, 1992).

Mort, F. *Capital Affairs: London and the Making of the Permissive Society* (New Haven, CT, 2010).

Moulton, M. *Ireland and the Irish in Interwar England* (Cambridge, 2014).

Myers, K. 'Historical Practice in the Age of Pluralism: Educating and Celebrating Identities', in K. Burrell and P. Panayi (eds), *Histories and Memories: Migrants and Their History in Britain* (London, 2006), 35–53.

Ni Laoire, C. 'Young Farmers, Masculinities and Change in Rural Ireland', *Irish Geography* 35:1 (2002), 16–27.

Nocon, A. 'A Reluctant Welcome? Poles in Britain in the 1940s', *Oral History* 24:1, 1996, 79–87.

Nora, P. 'Between Memory and History: *Les Lieux de Mémoire*', *Representations* 26 (1989), 7–24.

O'Carroll, I. *Models for Movers: Irish Women's Emigration to America* (Dublin, 1991).
Offer, A. 'British Manual Workers: From Producers to Consumers, c. 1950–2000'. *Contemporary British History* 22:4 (2008), 537–571.
Ó Gráda, C. *A Rocky Road: The Irish Economy since the 1920s* (Manchester, 1997).
O'Grady, A. *Irish Migration to London in the 1940s and 1950s* (London, 1988).
O'Hare, L. (ed.), *Thousands are Sailing: A Collection of Memories* (London, 2000).
O'Shea, K. *The Irish Emigrant Chaplaincy Scheme in Britain, 1957–82* (Naas, 1985).
O'Toole, F. 'The Ex-Isle of Erin: Emigration and Irish Culture', in J. Mac Laughlin (ed.), *Location and Dislocation in Contemporary Irish Society: Emigration and Irish Identities* (Cork, 1997), 158–178.
Ó Tuathaigh, M. A. G. 'The Irish in Nineteenth Century Britain: Problems of Integration', *Transactions of the Royal Historical Society* 31 (1981), 149–173.
Paul, K. 'A Case of Mistaken Identity: The Irish in Postwar Britain', *International Labour and Working-Class History* 49 (1996), 116–142.
Paul, K. *Whitewashing Britain: Race and Citizenship in the Postwar Era* (New York, 1997).
Popular Memory Group. 'Popular Memory: Theory, Politics, Method', in Richard Johnston (ed.), *Making Histories: Studies in History-Writing and Politics* (London, 1982), 205–252.
Portelli, A. *The Death of Luigi Trastulli and Other Stories: Form and Meaning in Oral History* (New York, 1991).
Portelli, A. *The Battle of Valle Giulia: Oral History and the Art of Dialogue* (Madison, WI, 1997).
Portelli, A. 'What Makes Oral History Different?', in R. Perks and A. Thomson (eds), *The Oral History Reader*, 2nd edn (London, 2006), 32–42.
Rex, J. 'Immigrants and British Labour: The Sociological Context', in K. Lunn (ed.), *Hosts, Immigrants and Minorities* (London, 1980), 122–142.
Roberts, E. *A Woman's Place: An Oral History of Working-Class Women 1890–1940* (Oxford, 1984).
Roper, M. 'Slipping Out of View: Subjectivity and Emotion in Gender History', *History Workshop Journal* 59 (2005), 57–72.
Roper, M. *The Secret Battle: Emotional Survival in the Great War* (Manchester, 2009).
Royle, E. *Modern Britain: A Social History 1750–1985* (London, 1989).
Ryan, L. 'Aliens, Migrants and Maids: Public Discourses on Irish Immigration to Britain in 1937', *Immigrants and Minorities* 20:3 (2001), 25–42.
Ryan, L. 'Sexualising Emigration: Discourses of Irish Female Emigration in the 1930s', *Women's Studies International Forum* 35:1 (2001), 51–65.
Ryan, L. 'Moving Spaces and Changing Places: Irish Women's Memories of Emigration to Britain in the 1930s', *Journal of Ethnic and Migration Studies* 29:1 (2003), 67–82.
Ryan, L. '"I Had a Sister in England": Family-Led Migration, Social Networks and Irish Nurses', *Journal of Ethnic and Migration Studies* 34:3 (2008), 453–470.
Rycroft, C. *Critical Dictionary of Psychoanalysis* (London, 1995).
Samuel, R. and Thompson, P. (eds), *The Myths We Live By* (London, 1990).

Savage, M. 'Affluence and Social Change in the Making of Technocratic Middle-Class Identities: Britain, 1939–55', *Contemporary British History* 22:4 (2008), 457–476.
Schaffer, G. and Nasar, S. 'The White Essential Subject: Race, Ethnicity, and the Irish in Post-War Britain', *Contemporary British History* 32:2 (2018), 209–230.
Schwarz, B. '"The Only White Man in There": The Re-Racialisation of England, 1956–1968', *Race & Class* 38:1 (1996), 65–78.
Scott, J. 'Gender: A Useful Category of Historical Analysis', *American Historical Review* 91:5 (1986), 1053–1073.
Scott, J. 'The Evidence of Experience', *Critical Inquiry* 17 (1991), 773–797.
Scully, M. '"Emigrants in the Traditional Sense"? Irishness in England, Contemporary Migration and Collective Memory of the 1950s', *Irish Journal of Sociology* 23:2 (2015), 133–148.
Segal, H. *Introduction to the Work of Melanie Klein* (London, 2008).
Short, J. R. *Housing in Britain: The Postwar Experience* (London, 1982).
Smith, G. 'Beyond Individual/Collective Memory: Women's Transactive Memories of Food, Family and Conflict', *Oral History* 35:2 (2007), 77–90.
Smith, M. L. R. *Fighting for Ireland? The Military Strategy of the Irish Republican Movement* (London and New York, 1995).
Somers, M. R. 'The Narrative Constitution of Identity: A Relational and Network Approach', *Theory and Society* 23:5 (1994), 605–649.
Sorohan, S. *Irish London during the Troubles* (Dublin, 2012).
Stoler, A. L. and Strassler, K. 'Memory Work in Java: A Cautionary Tale', in R. Perks and A. Thomson (eds), *The Oral History Reader*, 2nd edn (London, 2006), 283–309.
Summerfield, P. 'Women in Britain since 1945: Companionate Marriage and the Double Burden', in J. Obelkevich and P. Catterall (eds), *Understanding Post-War British Society* (London, 1994), 58–72.
Summerfield, P. *Reconstructing Women's Wartime Lives* (Manchester, 1998).
Sutherland, E. 'Modes of Exploitation and Safety in the British Construction Industry', *Radical Statistics* 69 (1998), 34–52.
Swift, R. 'The Historiography of the Irish in Nineteenth-Century Britain', in P. O'Sullivan (ed.), *The Irish World Wide: History, Heritage, Identity*, vol. 2: *The Irish in the New Communities* (London and New York, 1996), 52–81.
Swift, R. and Gilley, S. (eds), *The Irish in the Victorian City* (London, 1985).
Swift, R. and Gilley, S. (eds), *The Irish in Britain, 1815–1939* (London, 1989).
Thompson, P. *The Voice of the Past: Oral History* (Oxford, 1978).
Thomson, A. *Anzac Memories: Living with the Legend* (Oxford, 1994).
Thomson, A. '"Unreliable Memories?" The Use and Abuse of Oral History', in W. Lamont (ed.), *Historical Controversies and Historians* (London, 1998), 23–34.
Thomson, A. 'Moving Stories: Oral History and Migration Studies', *Oral History* 27:1 (1999), 24–37.
Thomson, A. '"Tied to the Kitchen Sink"? Women's Lives and Women's History in Mid-Twentieth Century Britain and Australia', *Women's History Review* 22:1 (2013), 126–147.
Tosh, J. *Why History Matters* (Basingstoke, 2008).

Travers, P. '"There Was Nothing for Me There": Irish Female Emigration, 1922–71', in P. O'Sullivan (ed.), *The Irish World Wide: History, Heritage, Identity*, vol. 4: *Irish Women and Irish Migration* (London and New York, 1995), 146–167.

Ugolini, W. *Experiencing War as the 'Enemy Other': Italian Scottish Experience in World War Two* (Manchester, 2011).

Ugolini, W. 'Weaving the Italian Experience into the British Immigration Narrative', in J. Craig-Norton, C. Hoffman and T. Kushner (eds), *Migrant Britain: Histories and Historiographies. Essays in Honour of Colin Holmes* (London, 2018), 117–127.

Walter, B. *Outsiders Inside: Whiteness, Place and Irish Women* (London, 2001).

Walter, B. 'Whiteness and Diasporic Irishness: Nation, Gender and Class', *Journal of Ethnic and Migration Studies* 37:9 (2011), 1295–1312.

Walvin, J. *Passage to Britain: Immigration in British History and Politics* (Harmondsworth, 1984).

Waters, C. '"Dark Strangers" in Our Midst: Discourses of Race and Nation in Britain, 1947–1963', *Journal of British Studies* 36:2 (1997), 207–238.

Webster, W. '"There'll Always be an England": Representations of Colonial Wars and Immigration, 1948–1968', *Journal of British Studies* 40:4 (2001), 557–584.

Weight, R. *Patriots: National Identity in Britain 1940–2000* (London, 2002).

Werly, J. M., 'The Irish in Manchester, 1832–49', *Irish Historical Studies* 18:71 (1973), 345–358.

Whyte, J. H. *Church and State in Modern Ireland, 1923–1979*, 2nd edn (Dublin, 1980).

Whyte, J. H. 'How Much Discrimination Was There under the Unionist Regime, 1921–68?', in T. Gallagher and J. O'Connell (eds), *Contemporary Irish Studies* (Manchester, 1983), 1–36.

Wildman, C. 'Religious Selfhoods and the City in Interwar Manchester', *Urban History* 38 (May 2011), 103–123.

Wills, A. 'Delinquency, Masculinity and Citizenship in England 1950–1970', *Past and Present* 187 (2005), 157–185.

Wills, C. 'Women, Domesticity and the Family: Recent Feminist Work in Irish Cultural Studies', *Cultural Studies* 15:1 (2001), 33–57.

Wills, C. *That Neutral Island: A History of Ireland during the Second World War* (London, 2008).

Wills, C. *The Best Are Leaving: Emigration and Post-War Irish Culture* (Cambridge, 2015).

Wills, C. *Lovers and Strangers: An Immigrant History of Post-War Britain* (London, 2018).

Winter, J. 'The Generation of Memory: Reflections on the "Memory Boom" in Contemporary Historical Studies', *Archives and Social Studies: A Journal of Interdisciplinary Research* 1:0 (2007), 363–397.

Wood, L. W. *A Union to Build: The Story of UCATT* (London, 1979).

Unpublished thesis

Hall, Reginald Richard, 'Irish Music and Dance in London, 1870–1970: A Socio-Cultural History (DPhil thesis, University of Sussex, 1994).

Index

Note: page numbers in *italic* refer to figures.

abandonment 61–62, 91, 107
accommodation 8
activist groups 10, 12–13
Adams, Gerry 211
adjustment, difficulty of 157
administrative procedures 41, 42
advice manuals 85, 159, 166–167
affluent society, the 121–122
agency 15, 18, 38, 97, 151
Akenson, D. H. 5
alienation 96, 138
Aliens Act, 1905 221
ambitious emigrant, the 50–55, *51*, 60
Anglo-Irish conflict 8, 116
Anglo-Irish Treaty 7, 189
Anglo-Irish war, cultural legacies 7
anti-Irish hostility 136, 141
anti-Irish racism 10
assimilation 24, 5–6, 10, 18, 27
audience 25–26
autobiographical remembering 20, 28
autobiographical truth 197

Bell, The 49, 50
belonging 121, 130, 139, 144, 198, 206, 212
  communities of 162
  discursive Catholicism and 152–168
Birmingham 99–100, 133, 136, 154, 156
Birmingham Six, the 197
Birtill, Angie 10–11, 12
Bishop Casey scandal 172
Boland, Fr A. P. 94
Böll, Heinrich 38–39, 40
Bolton 163
Bourdieu, P. 111
Brady, Rory 201–202
Brexit vote 220–221
British identity 4, 6–7
British–Irish antagonism 15
British–Irish relations 1, 6–7, 15, 26–27, 223
British markets, Irish dependence on 39
British misrule 35
Britishness 7, 8–9, 197, 203, 205, 221–222
Butler, Bernard 56

Camden Irish Centre 118
case histories 29
categorical designations 9–10

Catholic Church 85, 118
  agency 151
  as agent of patriarchal control 178
  authority 62–63, 171–173
  autonomy 183
  control 170–171
  falling away from 149, 153
  importance of 149–150, 166
  influence 179
  lapsation problem 153
  liberationist critique of 172–173, 179
  model of virtuous settlement 167–168
  opposition to departure 57–58
  power 151–152, 155, 173, 179, 181–182
  regulatory imperatives 182
  restraining influence 150
  roles of 170, 171
  sanctification of poverty 173–174
  scandals 172–173, 180
  stigmatisation of poverty 170–171
  turning against 177–181
Catholic culture 83–84
Catholic family, the 40
Catholic journals 85
Catholic-nationalist cultural hegemony 38
Catholic organisations 57
Catholic Truth Society 85
Catholic Welfare Bureau 94
Catholic welfare networks 9, 94–95, 100
census, 1951 106
chain migration 41
Chamberlain, Mary 78
Chambers, Iain 77
Chorlton Irish Club 119
Christian Brothers 172
Christian Workers 56
Christus Rex 83
citizenship rights, dual 3
city life, representations of 48–49
clerical abuse 152, 180
collective remembering 18–19
Collinson, D. 107
'coloured immigrants' 3, 188, 189
Commission for Racial Equality 17
Commission on Emigration 51–52
Commission to Inquire into Child Abuse 172
Commonwealth, the 15
Commonwealth Immigrants Act, 1962 188, 190, 221
community activism 14
composure 20, 23, 28, 124, 168, 204, 224
Concannon, Helena 49
Conservative Party 113
construction industry 53–54, 112–113, 120–121, 122
  Irish firms 122–123
  Irish success in 124–125
  Manchester 126–128, 128–133
Construction News 123
construction workers 105–144
  absence of Englishmen 121
  anxieties 135–136
  aspirations 123–124, 133–134
  casualism 111, 120–121
  collective mythology 142–144
  conditions 133–138, 164
  discourse function 106–107
  economic advancement 126–128
  homelessness 107
  idealised 121–128
  injuries 138, 139
  Irish infiltration 105–106
  labour crisis 105–106, 109, 110
  masculinity and 115–121, 129
  motivation 109
  piece-work 113, 122
  progression 126–128, 128–133
  reputation 117–118
  self-made man, the 125–128, 128–133, 147n.62
  social networks 127–128
  transient lifestyle 111–112
  wages 112, 122, 134
  work process 113–114
consumerism 88, 153
contextual details 41
Coogan, Tim Pat 70, 71

Cork 62, 89, 93, 176
Cork Examiner 176–177
courtship 88, 90–91, 92, 163, 174–175
crime 94
Culhane, Fr Robert 149
Cullen, Clare 89–92, 174–181, 183
cultural accommodation 223
cultural awkwardness 70
cultural bias 7
cultural circuit, the 20–21, 23, 27, 36–37
cultural degeneration 37
cultural forgetting 190
cultural legacies 7
cultural myth, production of 20–21
cultural transfer 37
culture, and emotion 24
cultures of adjustment 83, 150

Dáil, the 37
Daly, Kate 208–212, 213
dancing and dance venues 82–85, 90
Dawson, Graham 23, 24, 137
defensive splitting 135–136, 137
degradation 57
deindustrialisation 221
Delaney, Enda 70, 83
demographic Ireland 39
denationalisation 5
departure
  Catholic Church opposition to 57–58
  emotional impact 39, 40, 62, 69
  justification 65–70
  meanings of 70–72
depersonalisation 44
deprivation 65
de Valera, Eamon 56–57
deviant migrant, the 155–156
discrimination 5, 10, 11, 153, 197, 204, 214, 215
Discrimination and the Irish Community in Britain 11, 197
discursive Catholicism 149–168
disidentification 131
Doherty, Joe 133–138, 138–141, 201–202, 204–209, 213

domestic service 79–81
Donnellan, Phillip 107
dowry 43
drinking 84, 169
Dublin 44
Dublin Opinion 49, *51*
Duffy, Bill 50–55, 55–56, 59, 60, 125–128, 128–133, 134, 138–139, 168–171, 180, 183
Dun Laoghaire 70
Durig, Rev. Dr 57

Ealing 112
economic betterment 50–56, *51*, 126–128
economic compulsion 59–60, 61–62, 163, 165–166
Economic Survey for 1947 105
education 5, 129–130, 170
embarkation regulations 44
emigrant numbers 36
emigrant subjectivities 70–71
emigration problem, the 37
emotional adaption 150, 224
emotional bonds, rupturing of 44
emotional conflict 68–69, 71–72
emotional loss 48
emotion, and culture 24
employment opportunities 48, 50–55
  women 48, 78, 80–81, 176–177
Englishness 27, 132–133
English people, early encounters with 80
ethnicity and ethnic mobilisation 10–14, 17, 144
ethnic turn 4–6, 220
exclusion 136–137, 140
exile 44–45, 70, 71, 107
exile myths 56
exit myths 35–38
experience, reconstruction of 214–215
experiences, continuities in 3
exploitation 107, 136–137, 138, 205–206
exportation 40

faith, preserving 149
family 42, 85–86, 91–92, 182
  religious selfhoods and 152–168
family-centred settlement 156
Federation of Irish Societies 13, 141
feminine independence, fantasy of 100
feminine opportunity 87–92, 99–100
feminine virtue 63–64
femininity 45, 76–101, 178, 179
  assertive 88, 92
  Catholic 86, 174
  competing models of 93–99
  'Fields of Athenry, The' (ballad) 44–45
  sexual knowledges and 88–89
fighting 115, *115*
financial prudence 92
Fitzgerald , P. 78, 108
Fletcher, Paul 123
Foley, Donal 106, 137
folk music revival 117
Forde, Michael 200–201
forgetting 107, 207
freedom 88, 100, 109, 154
Furrow, The 149

Gaelic Ireland, idealised 39
Garrigan, Olive Mary 83, 84
general public, the 34n.65
Gibbons, Ivan 11–12
Giles, Patrick 37, 57
Gilroy, Paul 11, 27
Glasgow 26
God, betrayal of 58
Good Friday Agreement 17, 192
'good girl emigrant', the 85
Gorton 158–159, 160
Grady, Brenda 40–45, 46, 48, 55, 78–87, 92
Great Britain
  Catholic population 149
  economic growth 121–122
  economic recovery 105, 109–110, 142
  reconstruction 99

Green, Nancy 38
Guildford Four, the 197
guilt 55–56, 69, 71–72

habitus 111, 121
Hagan, Sean 163–168, 171, 181–182, 183, 195–196, 197–199, 201, 203, 207, 209, 212–213
Hall, Richard 117
Hall, Stuart 16
Harris, Alana 160
Harte, Liam 108
Healy, John 52
Heaney, Denis 109–112, 119–120, 121, 123–124, 126, 127, 128, 130, 132
Hearn, J. 107
Hickey, John 152
Hickman, Mary J. 4, 5, 6, 12
historical knowledge, status of 19
historiography 1, 3, 4, 26, 108
homeland, the 70, 138–141
homelessness 10–11, 107, 138
homemaking 159
home-ownership 122
homesickness 91, 175
Hornsby-Smith, M. P. 5
house-building 112, 113, 122
housing 2, 81, 110, 153–154, 158–159, 164
Hughes, Enda 107
hunger strikes 13
hypermasculinity 116–118

identity 26, 48, 221–222, 225
  British 4, 6–7
  Catholic 4
  collective 27
  conflict 201, 214
  cultural 16
  emigrant 37
  ethnic turn 4–6
  Irish 4–6, 14, 16, 27, 204, 212–215, 223–224
  minority 223
  national 71
  performances of 214

public narratives of 224
racialised categories of 14
identity construction 14, 100–101, 222, 224–225
identity history 222
immigration 8
immorality 94
impoverishment 62–70
individualism 112
industrial mobilisation 52
industrial modernisation 36
Industrial Schools 172
insecurity 129
integration 4, 14
inter-marriage 3, 97–98
interpretative reconstruction 23
interviews 25–26, 29–30
intrafamilial relations 40–48
invisibility 5–6, 6–17, 215, 222
Ireland
   British colonialism 6
   disidentification with 131
   idealisation of 138–141
   national crisis discourses 71
Irish associations 154
Irish clubs 9
Irish Commission on Emigration 87
Irish Community Care 141
Irish ethnicity, boundaries of 9
Irish identity 14, 16, 27, 223–224
   ethnic turn 4–6
   militant narrative 204
   rethinking 212–215
Irish in Britain Representation Group 10, 13, 203–204, 206
Irish muscle, myth of 121, 124, 130, 132, 140
Irish music 117
Irish nationalist ideology 39–40
Irishness 7–8, 189, 193, 201, 209, 213, 215
Irish Post 10, 13, 118, 155–156, 171
Irish Question, the 7, 188, 189
Irish suffering, myth of 13
Irish Times 49, 106
isolation 96, 100, 107, 157–158
itinerancy 111–112

Jackson, J. A. 105
Jenkins, Richard 16–17
Jenkins, Roy 199

Keane, John B., *The Contractors* 88–89, 124–125
Kidd, Alan 82–83
Kushner, Tom 221

labour crisis 105–106, 109, 110
labour market 105–106, 111, 110, 142
labour movement 80
Labour Party 113
labour recruitment scheme 79–80
Lally, Margaret, *Memoirs of a Mayo Immigrant* 151
Lambert, Sharon 6
Lambkin, B. 78, 108
landing controls 110
learning 128–133
leave-taking 38–48, 53–55, 59–61, 65–70
   emotional impact 68–69
   internal struggle 60
   justification 65–70
   narrative inconsistencies 67–68
   significant others and 71
Leese, Richard 205
Legion of Mary 84, 94–95
liberation 55
liquid modernity 22
lodging-houses 153–154
London 10–11, 67, 89–92, 99–100
   West End 93–98
London Irish Counties Association 9
London Irish Women's Centre 10, 10–11
London Rest Centre 83
loneliness 83, 86, 100
Long, Rosie 62–70, 93–99
Loss, sense of 69, 86–87, 100
Lymm 79–81

MacAmhlaigh, Donall 116, 122, 150
McGahern, John, *The Barracks* 76–77
McGreevy, Ronan 172
Mac Lau, Brendan 10

McMahon, Bryan 99, 100
Magdalene Asylums 172
Manchester 53–54, 59, 81–83, 86, 99–100, 133, 136, 140, 158, 168–169
  bombing, 1996 192–212, 212–214
  Catholic culture 83–84
  construction industry 126–128, 128–133
  Irish Heritage Centre, Cheetham Hill 194
Manchester Evening News 200
Manchester Evening Times 192
Manchester Guardian 189
Mangan, Anna May, *Me and Mine* 181, 184
marriage and married life 47–48, 85, 156, 182
  attitudes to 85–86
  bad 97
  Catholic understandings of 159–160
  dissatisfaction with 174–177, 178–179
  as a redemptive moment 87
  religious selfhoods and 158–161, 163–168
  threat to 57
marriage guidance literature 160
Marshall, Bishop Henry 88
masculine self-fashioning 142
masculinity 40, 59, 60, 167, 169, 204, 205
  Catholic 160
  construction workers and 115–121, 129
  domestication of 106
  employment and 107, 114, 129
  Irish 115–121, *115*
  machismo virtues 129, 135
  self-made man, the 125–128, 128–133
  stereotypes 136
  work on the land and 111
materialism 122, 174, 179–180
Maze Prison, hunger strikes 13

memory 42, 223–224
  autobiographical remembering 20, 28
  collective 21, 28, 141–144
  collective remembering 18–19
  communal 28, 215
  composite 196–197
  evolution of 143
  function of 214
  interpretative reconstruction 20
  Kleinian account 23–25
  production 19–22, 25, 27, 92, 167, 180, 223
  public 20–21
  religious selfhoods and 181–184
  reshaping 209–210
  selfhood and 20
  subaltern 18
  theory of 19–23
  uchronic 179
  unreliability 23
Men of Arlington House, The (documentary) 138
Middleton pub attack 200
Midgely, Mary 220
migrant numbers 3, 72n.2, 72n.6
migrant reception, politics of 188–190, *191*
Miller, Kerby 35, 56
Ministry of Labour 110
minority history 222–223
minority status 5
modern sensibility, crystallisation of 37
modern work, devaluation of 59
moral dangers 83–84, 154–155, 166
moral debasement 57
moral regulation 84
moral restraint 166–167
Mort, Frank 94
motherhood 174, 182
motivation 15, 42–43, 46, 50–55, 56, 59–60, 70, 79, 87, 89–90, 163, 165, 169
Moulton, Mo 7, 189
mourning 87
multiculturalism 10, 13–14, 215

multicultural racism 6
myths 27–28, 28, 220
    exile 56
    exit 35–38
    importance of 181
    meaning of 142–144

narration
    relational mode 41–42
    stream of consciousness 44
narrative reconciliation 24–25
national belonging 11
national crisis discourse, Ireland 71
national imaginaries 35
National Insurance numbers 67
nationalist mythology 13–14
NHS 118
'no Irish' signs 11, 136, 137, 148n.95
Northampton 148n.95, 150
Northern Ireland, exit myths 35–38
Norton, William 36
nostalgia 89, 107, 138–141, 183–184
nurses 118

obligation, and self-determination 38–55
occupation, mobility 3–4
O'Donoghue, John 113–114
O'Dowd, John 119
O'Faolain, Sean 38, 79
Oldham 98–99
'Open Letter to Irish Girls about to Emigrate, An' (Garrigan) 83
oppression history 14
oral history 17–26, 28, 29, 101
    contribution 18–19
    discursive mediation 19
    interviews 25–26
    memory and 19–25
    narrative ecology 21
    narrative inter-subjectivity 19–20
    narrative production 23
    recovery approaches 18–19
othering 215
O'Toole, Fintan 39
outcast status 2, 4
overcrowding 42

patriarchy 78
patriotism 56–57
Pearse, Patrick 35, 56
personal commemoration 160
personal development 64–65, 91, 92
piece-work 113, 122
Pioneers 168–169
popular culture 8, 48
Popular Memory Group 20
Popular Memory Theory 1, 223, 224–225
population, Irish-born male 106
Portelli, Alessandro 29, 179
post-colonial immigrants 8
post-war crisis 36–37
post-war discourse 4–5
poverty 62–70, 170
Power, Richard 154
powerlessness 45
pre-marital sex 84
pre-marriage experiences 89–92
Prevention of Terrorism Act, 1974 13, 197, 203–204
priests 152, 156, 172–173, 180
producerist discourse 110
prostitution 95–96
Provisional Irish Republican Army 11
    bombing campaign *194*, 196–197
    Manchester bomb, 1996 192–212, 212–214
public housing 153
public memory 20–21
purity 97

Quinn, Paul 58–62

race relations 5
racial purity 8, 10
racial tensions 98
racism 5, 197, 220, 221
recovery history 18
recruitment schemes 41
redemption, women 78–87
regret 165
regulatory discourse 84, 86
Reilly, Michael 200
religiosity 152

religious authority figures 62–63
religious authority, renunciation of 152
religious leakage 97–98
religious selfhoods 149–184
  belonging and 152–168
  communities of belonging 162
  contestation 168–171
  discursive Catholicism and 149–168
  economic circumstances and 166
  family and 152–168
  marriage and 158–161, 163–168
  memory and 181–184
  preserving faith 149
  privatisation of 183
  reworking 168–181, 183
  turning against the Church 177–181
Report on Irish Workers in London 85
Report on the State of the Irish Poor 142
reputation 117–118
respectability 13, 118–119, 150
responsibility, sense of 65
returnees 52, 99
return migration 175–177
revisionist perspective 2–3, 4
Roberts, Robert 2
Rose, Leonard 192
Rugby 116
rural belonging 58–60
rural life 40–41, 45–47, 58–60
  limitations of 45–47, 50–53, 55
  rejection of 40–41, 49–50, 55–56, 57, 79, 85–86, 126, 156, 165–166
Ryan, Louise 6, 77

Salford 2
sameness 188–189
Samuel, Raphael 220
Scotland 106
Scott, Joan 19
seasonal migrants 52
secularisation 97
segregation 2, 5
self, the 25, 28, 37

  Catholic models of 182
  loss of 44
  opposing images of 62–70
self-authorship 55
self-construction 101, 108
self-determination, and obligation 38–55
self-development 88, 173
self-expression 91
self-fulfilment 65
selfhood 4, 15, 16–17, 20
  ethnic turn 223–224
  gendered 152
self-made man, the 125–128, 128–133, 140, 147n.62
self-reconstruction 168
sex industry 94, 95
sexual crimes 94
sexual danger 95
sexual knowledges 88–89
shame 62–70, 71–72, 96, 171
Shaw, Derek 192
Sheil, Fr Leonard 97–98
significant others, roles of 165
sin 88, 97
Smellie, Jim 10–11
social cohesion 221
social differentiation 131–132
social expectations 169–170
socialisation 155
social life 47, 82
social mobility 2, 3–4, 88, 121–122, 130, 152–153
social networks 127–128, 150
social problematisation 155
social workers, Catholic 83, 149
societal transformation 15
Society of St Vincent de Paul 62
Somers, Margaret 19
Sorohan, Sean 6
spectatorship 95
standards of living 142, 153
state, the 4–5
status 2
stereotypes 9, 106, 136, 142
Stevenson, Fr R. L. 57–58
stigma, of desertion 55–72

Stoler, Ann Laura 17, 18
subaltern memory 18
subject-formation 24
subjective change 143–144
Summerfield, Penny 25, 101
suspicion 184, 206–207, 209, 212, 213, 215
Sykes, A. J. M. 114–115, 117

terrorism 192–212, *194*
Thompson, Paul 220
Thomson, Alistair 17, 18, 34n.65, 77–78, 101
Tosh, John 222
Towcester 114
transition, narrative of 49–50
transnational communication 22
transnational networks 15, 48–49
travel restrictions 41
Troubles, the 6, 11, 12–13, 22, 190
   anti-Irish hostility 136
   British discourse 199–200, 214–215
   identity conflict and 202, 214
   Manchester bomb, 1996 192–212, 212–214
   Middleton pub attack 200
   official representations of 193
   political murders 198
   rethinking 212–215
   Whitehall bomb, 1973 *194*
Tuam Herald 49

Ugolini, Wendy 221
unfairness 81
United States of America 123–124
urban reconstruction 112

values 55
venture capitalists 126–127
victimhood 45
victimisation 197, 201, 210

virtuous settlement, Catholic model of 167–168

wages 81, 88, 112, 122, 134, 164–165
Wales 79–81
Walsh, Aileen 45–48, 55, 156–163, 168, 171, 177, 178, 181–182, 183
Welfare State 188
welfarism 153, 155
West, Henry 200
white homogeneity 18
whiteness 6, 16, 215
whitewashing 8–9
wideboys 93–94
Wills, Clair 71
women
   aspirations 42–43
   dangers facing 93–98
   employment opportunities 48, 78, 80–81, 176–177
   empowerment 77
   experience of leave-taking 38–48
   freedom 79, 81, 100
   historiographical representations 77
   liminality 76–101
   maternal obligations 160
   opportunities 87–92, 99–100
   potential pitfalls 83
   redemption 78–87
   rejection of rural life 40–41, 49
   social mobility 88
   status of 40, 46–47, 48, 78
   wages 81
work ethic 118–119
working class, affluent 106

xenophobia 221

Young Christian Workers 84

EU authorised representative for GPSR:
Easy Access System Europe, Mustamäe tee 50,
10621 Tallinn, Estonia
gpsr.requests@easproject.com